SHOOTING
for
TIGER

SHOOTING
for
TIGER

How Golf's Obsessed
New Generation Is Transforming
A Country Club Sport

WILLIAM ECHIKSON

PublicAffairs
NEW YORK

Designed by TK
Text set in TK
Library of Congress Cataloging-in-Publication Data
ISBN: 978-1-58648-578-8
First Edition

10 9 8 7 6 5 4 3 2 1

For My Eldest Son Samuel, Who Inspired This Adventure

CONTENTS

My Son ... the Golfer

Sam Echikson, age 15, and already a 1.8 handicap.

When my son Samuel picked up a tiny tennis racket at the tender age of three, he swung it with grace. Later, he was good enough to earn a spot on a top-ranked Belgian club soccer team. On a trip to America, he hit a home run in one of his first baseball games at camp.

Yet one by one his athletic passions dropped away. At tennis tournaments, parents screamed on the sidelines. Samuel tensed, and all too often he came off the court in tears. He dropped off the elite soccer team after a year, finding the sport too stressful, and proceeded to turn in what seemed a strange direction—toward golf.

I couldn't understand why a graceful, athletic child would embrace an old person's sport. When I was growing up, my dad's country club blocked me from venturing onto its course. Manufacturers didn't make clubs small or light enough for kids under ten. The game seemed slow and boring. You didn't work up a sweat. You walked. A round took up most of the day.

What kid, I wondered, would emulate a pudgy forty-something duffer?

But as Samuel began playing my apprehensions fell away. Golf no longer resembled the game I remembered from my own childhood. It has become a kid's passion as well as an old man's pastime. It has changed from a cloistered sport into a family activity—the greens are often filled with parents and kids playing together. Golf shops are now well stocked with irons and woods small enough for toddlers.

Samuel's grandparents bought him his first set of clubs. He whacked wiffle balls around their garden. During the summer those same grandparents treated him to lessons. Soon Samuel was out on the adult courses swinging away with scaled-down clubs. Within a matter of weeks, we joined a country club and he began teeing up on weekends.

Despite a preference for grunge skateboard outfits, Samuel dresses in conservative polo shirts and slacks for the golf course. Although he remains shy around most adults, he agrees to play in tournaments with mature golfers because he believes competition is the only way to improve.

Golf appeals to Samuel's individualistic nature. As he tells me, on the course, he's playing against himself. He's in control. He avoids being subsumed by a team. In soccer, if he missed a pass teammates often screamed at him. In golf he discovered a refuge. His playing partners, whether kids or adults, are polite. "I like the idea of challenging myself, not competing against anybody else," he says. "I like the calmness of the game. It's just you and the ball out there."

Although solitary, golf also offers unrivaled opportunities to me as a parent. The golf course has proven the best place to spend time with my son. Few activities bring a father and a teenager together. In the hours we spend walking fairways, Samuel expresses his feelings, his hopes, and his fears. The other day, when we were out on the course with our friend Marc and his fifteen-year old son Sasha, I asked the boys why they liked golf above other sports.

"It's something I can do with my dad," Sasha responded.

Children often take up a sport at least in part to please a parent, usually the father. When Sam played soccer and scored a goal, I cheered more than any other spectator. In golf tournaments, where stress boils like a pressure cooker, I try my best to leave him alone. On the soccer field, where Sam participated as one of many players, few of his mistakes resulted in crushing defeat. On the golf course, when I see my son standing over a short putt I often turn away, unable to watch. If he misses, I feel a jolt of anguish drill into my gut.

My own history with the game had a much more ambivalent beginning. When I was a child in New Jersey, I dreamed of playing professional tennis. My dad played golf with his friends or with my mother, but the game was never a passion of mine. I occasionally managed eighteen holes with my own friends and took a few lessons. After I graduated from college I began to enjoy the game more, joining my father and mother when I returned home. But I became serious only when Sam became passionate about it.

Golf now provides a glue between my family's generations. Some of our happiest moments occur when Sam, my dad, and I walk together on the fairways. A few years ago, when Sam was eleven, he, my father, then seventy-two, and I, forty-five, played the famous Ballybunion and Lahinch links courses in Ireland. For my dad, the experience was bittersweet. At Ballybunion's third hole, five-foot-tall Sam smashed his drive close to 100 yards beyond my father's.

On a later trip to Scotland, it was my turn to experience the same sting. With the wind to my back, I whacked a 250-yard drive that brought a delighted smile to my face. Sam, then five foot, eight inches tall, teed up. He drew back the club, bringing it above his head further than I could, and whipped it down.

Crack!

The ball shot off at a lower trajectory than mine, climbed a bit, and kept accelerating. My child had hit his drive 300 yards, as far as an experienced, talented adult. Although I was delighted to see Sam succeed, his thunderous drive killed my confidence in my own golf game. For months after the trip to Scotland I could not hit a ball straight. Every shot seemed short. I began to recover only after I accepted that I needed to approach the game in a different fashion than my son did. I required longer-hitting irons to reach the greens on par fives in three shots. Samuel comes close to getting there in two.

As I watched Samuel participate in golf tournaments, I became more sensitive to the feelings of other golf parents. Like other ambitious players, Samuel rises at 4:30 a.m. for his qualifying rounds and trudges around fairways dripping in 75 percent humidity and 101 degree heat. During one event, he hit a ball onto a cart path and it bounced out of bounds. Another ball dug a hole in the fairway and could not be found. I winced. His hopes of entering the main draw vanished. It took my son three holes—and another lost ball in a water hazard—to regain his composure. He began hitting the ball better. On the eighteenth and final hole, Samuel walked off with a giant smile.

In one tournament in Petersburg, Virginia, Samuel started with a more than acceptable 76, only four shots over par. The leader, professional and Ryder Cup veteran Lanny Wadkins's son Tucker, clocked in at a far superior 67. On the final day Samuel was two under par after nine holes when he lost his concentration. On the second to last hole, his second shot smashed into the back of the green and bounced over into the rough. He ended up recording a disastrous triple bogey, finishing with a disappointing double bogey for an 80. His playing partners struggled. One cherubic boy from Florida consistently chose the wrong club, leaving himself short of the flag. Off on the side, his father criticized his son's mistakes. "I'm watching, praying, begging," he lamented.

Although ambitious parents have always existed (what would Mozart have been without his possessive father, Leopold?), modern American culture seems to have transformed an exceptional attitude into a common rule, with parents pushing their children into specialized extracurricular pursuits at ever-younger ages. Young dancers and musicians must shoot to be the next Baryshnikov and Barenboim. By the age of six, kids participate in organized baseball, basketball, and football leagues. Gymnasts, figure skaters, and tennis players become professional stars by the time they reach their teens. Children are enrolled in sports academies and thrust into the limelight as they traverse puberty.

If an infant with a musical ear never benefits from an opportunity to play a piano or attend music class, there's little chance of a world-class musician emerging. Similarly, a coordinated child who never walks out onto a golf course has no hope of becoming a successful adult professional. A child aiming for excellence must have a passion for the pursuit. The drama being played out on the fairway, perhaps in an extreme fashion, echoes the issues facing all modern parents and children.

For every impossible, overbearing parent I encountered on my journey through the world of junior golf, I met many constructive and encouraging fathers and mothers who leveraged golf as a vehicle to encourage the best from their children. My son's passion propelled me to undertake this project in an attempt to better understand him and become a better father. Samuel's talent whetted my appetite, not for a father son memoir, but for a wider exploration of the emergence of elite junior golf. I soon discovered that many parents who share my hopes and worries pose similar tough questions, and not just about golf. How should they encourage their kids? How hard should they push? As I set out to follow the teenagers hoping to become the next Tiger Woods, I hoped to discover answers.

CHAPTER 1

Clock Nazis

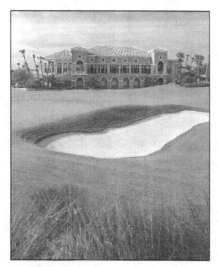

Mirasol Country Club's Disney-esque clubhouse and 18th green.

W ELL BEFORE THE SUN RISES, golfers begin arriving at the Country Club at Mirasol, a luxury gated development in Florida's exclusive Palm Beach Gardens. Players loosen their wrists by tapping balls on the putting green. They move onto the practice range, pulling open-faced clubs called wedges out of their bags and taking half swings to strike short shots that rise helicopter-fashion, almost vertically, and fall back to the ground a few yards away. Like pianists exercising their fingers, they move down the scale of irons—nine, eight, seven, six, five, and four—lengthening their swings and making the ball fly a few extra yards with each respective club. They take bulb-shaped, steel, or titanium-headed "woods" and lengthen their swings into wide, graceful arcs that propel balls far off into the horizon. Although play begins at 7:30 a.m., these serious golfers practice for two hours before teeing off.

Palm trees surround the Mirasol's 50,000-square-foot clubhouse. Painted in gold and ochre, the inside of the club is decorated with mirrors, heavy rugs, and mahogany furniture. Rather than a genuine ornate European villa, the gaudy combination reflects "a Disney version of Spain or Italy," according to a retired physician from New Jersey, who, like many of the club's members, is a wealthy refugee from the North. If Mirasol's clubhouse verges on luxury kitsch, the development's two eighteen-hole golf courses exude class, their undulating, manicured fairways situated in the savage beauty of raw Everglades and surrounded by a nature reserve. The courses have long served as a stern test for the world's top pros at the annual Professional Golf Association's (PGA) Honda Classic. Both measure more than 7,000 yards long, are defended by narrow fairways, and, outside this small, safe landing area, ferocious, jungle-high wild grass and deep sand traps,

This particular week Mirasol is opening its exclusive greens not to adult pros but to eighty-four of the world's top-ranked golfers between the ages of twelve and eighteen. For the next three days the teens will battle the dog-day humid heat of a Florida summer in the Birks & Mayors Junior Championship. The event launches the American Junior Golf Association (AJGA) summer season, a pressure-packed few months in which fairway dreams are stirred and fuelled. Some young golfers hope to shoot well enough to be named an AJGA All-American. Others are eager to finish high enough in the top events to score a golf scholarship to college. Many aim to become professional golfers, maybe even reaching the highest heights and winning the Masters or the United States Open. But few boys jump from the junior to the men's professional tour, and only one or two girls succeed in doing so each year.

Together, the prodigies and their parents will crisscross the United States, traveling thousands of miles to compete in a series of elite tournaments. Day after day, week after week, competitors and parents will rise each day before dawn and return to motels at nightfall after strenuous days of practice and competition. Most often, they'll take their meals in a McDonald's or Burger King. A gourmet meal might be a T-bone and cheesecake at Ponderosa Steakhouse.

Adult professionals who play four weeks of competitive golf in a row complain about the mental and physical toll of travel and tournaments. Yet many top-ranked juniors will compete for seven straight weeks in June and July because the vast majority of the elite golf tournaments are packed into the summer vacation. Once school restarts, the schedule slows, but only slightly. In October the golf equipment manufacturer Ping hosts a major event in Oklahoma, and at Thanksgiving the season closes with the Polo Junior Classic in Orlando, where the AJGA anoints ten young men and women as All-Americans.

At Polo, the AJGA chooses one boy and one girl as Players of the Year. A number of past Players of the Year have gone on to make lasting marks in the sport, starting with two-time winner Tiger Woods, three-time champion Phil Mickelson, and on the woman's tour, professional superstars Paula Creamer and Morgan Pressel. More than 160 AJGA alumni compete on the PGA tour, while dozens of recent graduates star on the Ladies Professional Golf Association (LPGA) tour. As Ivan Lendl, the father of three teenagers who are avid junior golfers, and a former professional tennis player with eight Grand Slam (major tennis championship) titles and millions of dollars in prize money, describes it, "The AJGA runs the Rolls-Royce of junior golf tournaments."

In the AJGA universe, aspiring twelve- to fifteen-year-olds start at the bottom in Junior All-Star events. If they flourish, they move up to regular tournaments open to all AJGA members. (Mirasol is a "regular" tournament, though a high-quality one because it takes place in golf-crazy Florida.) If players excel at these regular tournaments, the AJGA invites them to its elite "invitational" events, the junior equivalents of the grown-up majors such as the Masters and U.S. Open. In addition to the AJGA's packed summer schedule, the separate United

States Golf Association (USGA) organizes two eighteen-and-under national championship, the United States Junior Amateur for boys and the United States Girls Junior.

Both the number of elite teen golf tournaments and the number of contestants have increased at a steady clip over the past two decades. The 2007 summer schedule included eighty-one events in twenty-one states, and, on average, three tournaments were hosted each week. About 5,200 top teenagers participated. Three-quarters of them were boys, one-quarter girls. They hailed from all over the world. Even after paying the $205 annual membership fee, they struggled to gain entrance into tournaments that accept no more than one hundred players. After numerous complaints about favoritism, the AJGA stopped subjective analysis of applicants' golf resumes in 2003 and adopted an elaborate "performance-based entry system." Players now earn stars by scoring well in regional and local golf tournaments. When they accumulate four stars, they are accepted into AJGA events. At Mirasol, entry requires a minimum of two stars. An alternate route of entry into tournaments is available in single-round, eighteen-hole qualifying contests held the day before official tournaments. For the 2007 Mirasol event, eighty-two young players from as far away as Troy, Michigan; Albuquerque, New Mexico; and Hausen, Switzerland competed. Only the top half dozen boys and three girls are admitted into the main draw.

Throughout the summer, college coaches, professional agents, and sports equipment representatives watch and grade. Huge sums of money await the lucky few on the top of the pyramid. By her mid-teens, the teenage phenomenon Michelle Wie had secured endorsement deals from Nike, Omega, and Sony that *FORTUNE Magazine* estimated earned her $19.5 million in 2007. By his twenty-first birthday, Tiger Woods had acquired millions from prize money and endorsements.

Most golf prodigies have played the game since they were toddlers. By the time they become teens, almost all have quit other organized athletic activities. Many are homeschooled, working on their computers early in the morning so they are free for a full afternoon of practice. Others enroll at full-time golf academies, where they attend classes in the morning and hit the fairways after lunch. But for all of these young players, golf is the lens through which they view the world. Ambitious junior golfers do not spend hours cruising malls, hanging out at parties, or going to movies. Their passion allows little room for traditional rites of teenage passage. To succeed they must display rare intensity, discipline, drive, and confidence. They must wake up early each morning pondering their potential future in the bright lights.

Since the start of competitive junior golf, the entrance age has continued to drop. The AJGA, founded in1979, originally catered to sixteen- through eighteen-year-olds. A few years into its existence it began accepting fifteen-year-olds, then fourteen-year-olds, then thirteen-year-olds, and after a long battle, twelve-year-olds. When Michelle Wie's parents insisted that she be able to play as an eleven-year-old in 2000, executive director Stephen Hamblin drew the line. Wie went on to skip junior competitions altogether, playing adult tournaments only. By the time she was eighteen, she was damaged physically and mentally. Her experience convinced Hamblin of the necessity of age limits. "You just can't skip the stages of development," he explains.

For every future golf star who emerges, hundreds of talented children flame out. All hit a golf ball with authority. All are able to make a ball curve right or left and can strike it high or low. Yet each year, only one or two junior golf standouts, most often female, jump right from the juniors to the pros. A huge mental gap separates adults from juniors in golf. "There are many players who are physically as good as anybody out here," says thirty-year-old Geoff Ogilvy, an Australian who won the 2006 U.S. Open. "But it takes much more than four rounds of golf to be a success." Many talented twenty-year-olds arrive each year, and almost none succeed before they are at least twenty-five. The crowds and stress are just too much. "The kids hit the ball just as far and well, no question about it," Stewart Cink, the AJGA alumnus and present-day PGA tour professional star, says of today's juniors. "But everybody out here can hit the ball. Everybody can chip and putt. You have to find a new frontier to get an edge."

Those teens who stumble in the summer events will see their dreams shattered. If they fail to do well, they will not receive an offer for a college scholarship. Any hopes of becoming the next Tiger Woods will vanish. Unlike football or basketball players who court physical disaster every time they go out on the field or court, the main dangers for golfers are mental. Golf demands a combination of practiced repetition and patience. If the body bends at the wrong moment, the ball veers off in the wrong direction. If the hands shake, putts roll beyond their targets.

Much of the tension felt by ambitious teen golfers stems not just from tough competition, but from the sheer conflicts posed by growing up. For the most part, teen golfers are a close-cropped, clean-cut group. Like adults at an upscale golf resort, they dress in bright polo shirts and well-pressed khaki pants or shorts. Some listen to their iPods before they play to calm their nerves. Most spend their free time discussing the world they know—how they played that day or their hopes for the next round—but keep their feelings bottled up. As these prodigies perfect their games, they must avoid the traditional teenage temptations. The freedom of a driver's license, flirtations with members of the opposite sex, and the desire for new experiences all threaten to interfere with a teenage golfer's game. One mom calls it the "sixteen-year-old hump—girls, grades and golf." Another adds a fourth G: physical growth, a factor that threatens to easily unhinge a golf swing.

Parents of young golfers also confront an inordinate amount of pressure. They pour enormous amounts of time, money, and psychic energy into raising exceptional children. Although most sports provide opportunities for parent–child bonding, golf raises the bar of expectation. Kids pick up football, baseball, and soccer on their own by playing with neighbors in the back yard. With golf, someone must guide them, drive them to the course, and accompany them to tournaments.

Every player requires a different degree of parental pushing and encouragement. Many of the most controlling fathers and mothers believe they must exert pressure on their kids to see desired results, even though psychologists warn that their children often turn their hobbies into anxiety-producing obsessions. "You have to challenge them," insists Petr Korda, a former Czech tennis star whose fourteen-year-old daughter Jessica is competing at the Mirasol tournament. "Kids get quickly satisfied. You have to show them that it's necessary to be hungry, not to give up."

Many solicitous parents devote themselves full time to developing their children's golf talent. On the practice range and on the course, fathers and mothers offer children comments about their performance, often as though they were part of a team.

"We're hitting it left," they might say. "We're missing those putts. We're scoring badly."

Many golfers who manage to avoid teenage pitfalls still end up rebelling against overbearing parents. "I can think of cases where parents drove them away from the game," established professional Stewart Cink admits. "After college, the kids have had enough. There are even kids who get out here on the pro tour with their parents and eventually somebody has to step in and say, 'Dad, you are over here and the kid is over here.' This happens at a different age for everybody. One thing is common: It's always an outside party, a swing coach, a trainer, a caddie, who sees what is going on and steps in and says, 'I know he is your son, but this isn't working out'."

———

AJGA tournaments mimic the protocol of big-time pro events and treat teenage players like budding stars. When juniors register for the Birks

& Mayors at Mirasol, they receive pink Ralph Lauren Polo shorts and caps and a dozen Titleist Pro V balls. Contestants wear AJGA towels and caps with pride. As tournament director Gus Montano points out, "If they wear an Association cap, other kids there know, 'he's been there'." When a player tees off on the first hole, a staff member announces his or her name and hometown over a loudspeaker. During the rounds, a team of officials is on hand to resolve any disputes and make sure the game's long list of rules is respected. Standard bearers posting scores follow the leaders hole by hole. On the final day, after the winner is announced, trophies are handed out and thank-you speeches are given. For Mirasol's tournament director Montano, the sole significant difference between one of his junior events and an adult pro tournament is that he and his coworkers do not have to build spectator stands and install portable toilets.

Despite the professionalism, the junior golfer organization stresses its differences from the professional tour, emphasizing that it is a non-profit association for amateurs. Mention the word "tour" and executive director Hamblin quickly corrects it. Both the men's and women's pro tours are organized by and for the benefit of players in a closed club, he points out. In contrast, Hamblin says his association's events are open to newcomers who have the results necessary to participate. To many, this emphatic distinction seems semantic. Pro tours accept successful newcomers while demoting or refusing entry to poor performers. Just as the pro tournaments bring together the world's best golfers, Hamblin's organization allows the world's top juniors to face off.

For players and parents, this contest comes at a high price. Teenagers are allowed to accept free equipment and clothing from sponsors, but their expenses are nevertheless significant. AJGA membership costs $205 each year. All-star or regular AJGA tournaments cost $250 a pop, and the entry fee for elite invitational events is $300. And that's only the beginning. The average price per tournament, including travel, hotels, and entry fees, is about $1,000. Some parents spend upward of $30,000 on travel and lodging for the ten- to twelve-week summer season.

Summer expenses represent only a small portion of the overall financial and emotional burden of nurturing a potential pro golfer. Many young golfers attend golf academies during the school year. Even for those who don't, swing coaches, physical trainers, and even sports psychologists are required. This, in addition to the cost of equipment and green fees, or as is more common, country club memberships, adds up. Most often, the total bill swells beyond $100,000 a year, according to Dave Peterson, a Houston investment advisor and parent of seventeen-year-old player John. He recalls with horror "blowing $5,000" on one tournament in San Diego because the only hotel available cost $400 a night. Although many parents justify the investment as necessary to obtain college scholarships for their children, most end up spending more on teenage golf than they would on education. "You have to be a multimillionaire to play this sport," Peterson concludes, exaggerating only a little.

In response to the financial burden imposed by its game, the AJGA has instituted a scholarship program. Each year it grants more than $200,000 to less-privileged golfers to guarantee their participation. The AJGA negotiates special hotel room prices and arranges for members of the host country club to accommodate players. It attempts to convince host country clubs to provide free meals for the competitors. For its part, the USGA provides additional funds to minority groups. Yet to date, most elite junior golfers hail from high-education and high-income families. In 1976, twelve African Americans played on the professional tour. A decade after Tiger Woods turned professional, he remains the only African American player on the PGA tour. Not a single African American woman competes on the LPGA.

As high as the stakes are, junior golfers receive few sun-kissed moments of teenage athletic glory. No cheerleaders root for them. No fans whisper at the mall, "There he is. There's the next Tiger." Junior golfers do not become the big man on high school campuses. Instead, they train and play in near anonymity. Only a few spectators, mostly family members, attend even the most prestigious junior tournaments, where there are few television cameras, few electronic scoreboards, and no souvenir tents or ticket boxes. Entry is free. No gallery ropes or concession stands are necessary. At the end of each day, players, families, and friends gather round the large manual scoreboard on the eighteenth green and watch the scores trickle in. The *Palm Beach Post* buries its brief mention of the Mirasol tournament on a back page of the sports section.

Elite junior golf is an extreme version of an already isolating sport, one that demands stamina, self-confidence, and sacrifice with little promise of immediate recognition. Pros benefit from caddies who carry their clubs, but teenagers lug their own heavy bags for up to ten miles, even in the sweltering summer heat. The AJGA prohibits carts and caddies in an attempt to hold down costs and prevent wealthier players from hiring expensive first-rate help. At competitions, parents must stay on the sidelines, where they are allowed to dole out umbrellas, sweaters, and refreshments and cheer a smooth shot. They are forbidden from offering any other guidance on what club to hit with or what strategy to follow. If a parent interferes, the child is penalized two strokes. "The parents are told to stay a shot ahead of their kids," Montano explains. The ban produces an elaborate, kabuki-style shadow dance. During play, many middle-aged figures can be seen popping in an out of the palm trees that surround the fairways, trying to see how their children are progressing.

At all AJGA events, alarm bells ring early. Tournament organizers schedule dawn start times to free up the course for country club members in the afternoons and often to avoid extreme summer heat. Staff members wake up at 4:30 a.m. to prepare. Fifty summer interns, mostly college students, supplement fifty-five full-time employees. Seven interns and six full-timers are working Mirasol, drilling holes at each green, placing coolers of cold drinks next to the tee boxes, building scoring tents, and putting garbage bags in bins.

Within minutes of opening at 6 a.m., Mirasol's practice range is filled. Tim Lovelady, a court stenographer from Alabama who is accompanying his son Tom for a 7:30 tee time, worries about the seriousness of the entire junior golf process. During these tournaments, the kids don't stroll carefree along the fairways, and few smile. "They don't laugh and they don't chit chat," Lovelady observes. "They just play." The seriousness extends to the tournament officials, who monitor progress along the golf course, making sure they keep up with the quick pace required by play policy. The AJGA has declared war on six-hour rounds of golf. It believes four and a half hours suffice to complete eighteen holes.

"You know the joke from the *Seinfeld* show about the Soup Nazis?" Lovelady asks me, a smile spreading across his face. "Well, these guys are the Clock Nazis!"

CHAPTER 2

Beginnings of a Beloved Pastime

AJGA events are run along professional lines. Here, a young volunteer carries a scorecard for a group of players.

JUNIOR GOLFERS TEEING UP on frantic Florida fairways have come a long way from the European links where the sport was born. During the Middle Ages, stick and ball games were played all along the coast of Holland, Belgium, France, and Scotland. Dutch historian Steven van Hengel traces documents mentioning a Dutch hobby of "kolf" (meaning club) and "spel metten colve" (or game with clubs) back to 1297. In "kolf," players used a stick to hit a leather ball at a target several hundred meters away; the winner was the player who reached the target with the fewest number of hits. Images of the game appear in Dutch paintings and on pottery and tiles. In the clubhouse at Kennemer Golf Club, near the Dutch city of Harlem, a seventeenth-century painting by Wybrand Simonsz de Geest shows a smiling boy and girl holding what look like golf clubs. "We always have enjoyed commercial contacts with the Scots just across the North Sea, so it's not surprising we shared habits of ball games," says Pieter Aalders, Kennemer's managing director.

Modern golf, with its codification of fairways, greens, roughs, and eighteen holes, is derived from fifteenth-century Scotland. King James II of Scotland, in an Act of Parliament dated March 6, 1457, banned the sport because it interfered too much with archery practice. Scots played on the dunelike terrain along the coast "linking" the sea and the land. Greenkeeping was left to nature. Rabbits munched on the grass, creating carpetlike fairways and putting areas. Courses followed the natural, undulating topography and originally contained more or fewer than the now standard eighteen holes. During the fifteenth century St. Andrews's layout featured eleven holes, which ran in a line from the town to the far end of the property. In the eighteenth century two holes were combined, reducing the total to nine, and the accepted practice became to begin with nine holes out, turn around, and finish with nine holes back. In these early days the putting greens around the hole were not manicured areas of finely cut grass, but simply part of the playing area. They were called *fair Greens*.

The Honourable Company of Edinburgh Golfers drafted the first official rules of golf on March 7, 1744, for a local tournament. The ball should be "teed" up at the beginning of a hole and should be used until it was sunk in the hole. A penalty stroke was imposed on balls hit out of bounds. "If the Ball comes among Watter, or any Wattery Filth, you are at liberty to take out your Ball & bringing it behind the hazard and Teeing it you may play it with any Club and allow your Adversary a Stroke for so getting out your Ball," the rules stated. Players were expected to play wherever the ball landed. "Neither Trench, Ditch or Dyke, made for the preservation of the Links, nor the Scholar's Holes or the Soldier's lines, shall be accounted a Hazard."

In the centuries since then, golf's basic rules have been amplified, scrutinized, and debated, but its founding principles remain the same.

Players tee the ball off a wooden peg, the tee, which is drilled into a small, manicured elevation of earth called the tee box. Once the ball comes to rest in the smooth fairway or the surrounding rough, they hit it again. Close to the target, players take small swings with lofted clubs and chip the ball. On the green, they putt, tapping the ball along the smooth velvet grass into the hole using as few strokes as possible. Flags placed in the hole allow players to aim with accuracy.

Golfers compete in two types of competitions, stroke and match play. In *match play*, each hole represents a separate contest, which is won, lost, or tied. The winner is the player who captures the most holes. If one player takes an insurmountable lead, he or she wins the match. A 6&5 score means one player is ahead by six holes, with five left. When the number of remaining holes equals the lead and the worst a player can do is tie, the match is said to be "dormie," derived from the French verb *dormir*, meaning to sleep. Matches tied after eighteen holes are declared a tie or continued with a playoff. *Stroke play* is simpler than match play. Players count the number of shots taken for the entire round or tournament, and the lowest score wins. Penalty points are added to the score for various violations of rules. With rare exceptions, junior golfers compete on strokes. Each player often acts as scorer for another member of the group.

On a well-designed golf course, a round of golf resembles a symphony, with each layout enjoying its own rhythm and melody. Courses average six to seven miles in length and are composed of par threes, par fours, and par fives, with pars representing the number of strokes required to complete a hole. Most eighteen-hole courses consist of four par-three, ten par-four, and four par-five holes, for a total par 72. Par-five holes run between 475 and 690 yards long, requiring a skilled golfer to choose between trying to reach the green in two shots or play safe in the regulation three. Par fours range 250 to 475 yards, demanding two strokes, the drive from the tee and the approach from the fairway, to land on the green. Although a 490-yard monster may be classified as a par four if it slopes downhill allowing drives to roll a long way on the fairway, a 300-yard minnow may play as a par four, if the hole veers left and right in a dogleg, forcing two shots to the green. Par threes are reached in a single shot. On all holes, par includes two putts.

A *bogey* (a term derived from the "Bogey Man" character in a late nineteenth-century British song who lived in the shadows and sang, "I'm the Bogey Man, catch me if you can") occurs when a player is one shot over par. A double bogey is two shots over par, and a triple is three shots over par. In the other direction, a *birdie* represents one stroke under par, an *eagle* two strokes under par, and an *albatross* three strokes under par. (These terms derive from nineteenth-century American slang, when "bird" denoted cool.) In practice, few golfers ever attain the regulation 72 on a par-72 golf course. Even pros need to play nearly error-free to post a score in the mid-60s.

Handicaps level the playing field and allow weaker players to compete against stronger ones. The term comes from horseracing, in which jockeys put their "hands in a cap" to draw odds. At first, handicapping was subjective; clubs passed judgment on players' abilities. By the mid-nineteenth century a more objective system had been established, calculating the average of a player's best three scores in the current season compared to the course's par. After fierce debate, American golf authorities implemented a new system in 1967, counting the best ten of the last twenty rounds. More recently, to ensure increased uniformity, a slope rating measuring how difficult a course plays for average golfers has been added into the handicap formula. A high handicap, say twenty-five, portrays a player who, on most days, scores twenty-five over par. In compensation, he receives twenty-five strokes. Handicaps run like golf scores—the lower the better. Pros, and most juniors competing in the AJGA, do not have handicaps; they are considered "scratch."

At Mirasol's par-72 Sunset Course, opened in 2002, architect Arthur Hills composed a beautiful example of melodic modern golf course design. The opening dogleg par four plays at 395 yards from the back tees, neither too long nor too intimidating, allowing the hole to serve as a gentle prelude for the main movements to come. Thick, wild underbrush line the fairway's left side and a long, snake-shaped sand bunker is strung across the right. But the fairway is wide, allowing a significant margin for error. Good golfers can drive with a three wood and face only a short iron shot to the green.

Although the second hole is another par four, about the same length, 395 yards from the back tees, it steps up the danger. An alligator-infested swamp running along the right side of the fairway and three bite-sized sand traps strung across the fairway threaten to gobble up errant tee shots. The second shot must land a small green well defended by a deep sand bunker on its right, water behind, and brush to the left.

Players trudge along a path that traverses a wetland to reach the third tee. This hole, a 415-yard par four demands a dramatic, intimidating drive over a wide lake and a second shot to a small green perched on the edge of water. In order to augment the challenges and the visual pleasure, architect Hills has moved tons of earth to sculpt rolling, undulating fairways. Golfers enjoy few flat lies and must hit most of their balls on either an uphill or downhill slope. Similarly, the greens offer few flat putts; most times, players must navigate uphill and downhill putts that often break sharply to the left or the right.

By the time the golfer reaches the fourth hole, another demanding 417-yard par four, the course's melody has been well established. Once again, the drive must carry over water, with the second shot aiming at a green tucked between water on the right and two deep sand bunkers on the left.

The rhythm varies starting with the next hole, the fifth, a monster 626-yard par five. Even the best golfers need three shots to reach the green. They must drive over a large patch of water and keep away from deep sand bunkers on the right and water on the left. Three trees in the middle of the fairway attempt to block their progress. The green is tucked to the left behind a deep bunker and the water's edge. The sixth hole is a long 219-yard par three that requires carrying another tee shot over water to a flag hidden behind a raised bunker. The seventh is the longest par four yet, 427 yards. It is squeezed between two bodies of water and demands two tough shots: a drive over the first lake followed by an intimidating, long second shot over the second lake to a long, narrow green surrounded on three sides by yet more water.

At first glance, the short 159-yard par three eight hole looks like a breather. Surprisingly, many junior competitors at Mirasol find their concentration flagging at the appetizing prospect of a green reachable with a short iron and proceed to plop their balls in the turquoise water running along the fairway's right edge. The ninth hole, a 544-yard par five, offers a tantalizing choice between risk and reward. Many strapping young golfers can reach the green in two shots. But they also risk hitting out of bounds on the narrow landing zone to a two-tiered green surrounded by wild underbrush.

The back nine resembles the front nine, with two par threes, five par fours, and two par fives. Holes ten through fourteen are par fours of varying lengths, starting with water, sand, and underbrush dangers and followed by a long 218-yard par three, a long par 572-yard par five with dangerous swamps coming into play on both the first and second shots, a short 187-yard par three, a reachable-in-two 515-yard par five, and a strenuous, uphill 476-yard par four finish.

Like most courses, Mirasol plays at different lengths for different levels of golfers: shorter for women than men and shorter for poor players than for more accomplished ones. The men's championship tees run 7,192 yards. At Mirasol, the boys will compete over 6,873 yards and the girls 6,048 yards. In 2006 Mirasol's boy champion, Richard Lee of Arizona, shot rounds of 72–65–71 for a total of eight under par. The girls' winner, Vicky Hurst, turned in scores of 74–68–69 for five under par. Both were close to the scores of an accomplished professional.

King James IV of Scotland commissioned a set of his own golf clubs in 1502. His original club heads were constructed out of tough woods like beech, holly, pear, and apple. Shafts were made from ash or hazel and connected to the head with a splint and bound tightly with leather straps. The clubs were handcrafted and well beyond the means of the average consumer.

Forged iron heads appeared in the 1700s, and after the end of World War II synthetic and composite materials were developed, making for ever-lighter and faster tools. Graphite shafts, introduced in 1973, offer greater rigidity, lightness, and strength than steel. More recently, metal heads have replaced wood ones, and a high-tech arms race among manufacturers has erupted, producing clubs of various shapes and sizes— round, square, and bulblike—and a wide choice of shafts of varying degrees of stiffness. Despite the space age innovations, three major types of clubs continue to prevail: woods, irons, and putters. Woods, even if topped with a metal head, drive long shots from the tee or fairway, while irons angle precision shots to greens. . Wedges, irons for short shots, are played from sand or the rough and for approach shots to the green. Putters, with their flat heads, roll the ball along the green.

Ball technology has undergone similarly dramatic modernization. Originally, handcrafted balls were made with goose feathers tightly packed into a horsehide or cowhide sphere called the "Featherie." During the nineteenth century, scientists developed the inexpensive and durable gutta-percha ball or "Guttie," fashioned from the rubber sap of the Gutta tree. Modern golf balls have a two-, three-, or four-layer design constructed from various synthetic materials. The surface pattern of 300– 450 dimples affects the ball's aerodynamics, and its materials determine distance, trajectory, spin, and feel. Some balls are made of hard plastics to gain distance, while others constructed from softer materials stop fast.

In Scotland, virtually every social class traditionally played golf. "Golf is a game of the people," Robert Harris, a leading English golfer, declared in 1953. "It is played by the Common Man as a sport and a relaxation from the worries of life." When golf crossed the Atlantic Ocean in the late nineteenth century, the common person's hobby took on an aristocratic aura, becoming an elite country club sport, largely in the Northeast. Delegates from five of the country's leading golf clubs gathered in 1895 to form the United States Golf Association (USGA). Charter members included the Newport Golf Club, Shinnecock Hills Golf Club, the Country Club in Brookline, St. Andrews Golf Club in Yonkers, and the Chicago Golf Club. That same year, William G. Lawrence won a "national amateur championship" at Newport Golf Club in Rhode Island. Runner-up C. B. Macdonald called for the formation of a governing body to run a universally recognized national championship.

The USGA now operates out of a spacious, old-fashioned manor house in New Jersey horse country. It runs thirteen national championships, including perhaps the world's most famous golf event, the United States Open, which brings together the world's best professional golfers. Along with its British counterpart, the Royal & Ancient in St. Andrews, Scotland, the USGA is responsible for determining equipment and setting the game's rules. Delegates from both organizations meet every four years to consider rule changes. In the interim, each organization publishes an annual list of regulations, which is sent to all members participating in professional and American Junior Golf Association (AJGA) tournaments.

The annual USGA rule book constitutes a complicated contract between the player and the game. In what often reads like a legal treatise, the USGA details how to handle almost every circumstance of play. Consider the unlikely scenario of a practical joker who removes the flagstick from the hole and sticks it in another hole. Players are unaware of the action and hit at the flagstick rather than the hole. Despite having been led astray, no replays are allowed. Instead, players must "accept the resultant advantage or disadvantage," according to the USGA rule book. In another ruling, the USGA permits moving a ball from what it describes as a "dangerous situation." But what constitutes a "dangerous situation?" A rattlesnake or bee's nest would qualify, but poison ivy does not.

An ingrained sense of etiquette governs golf alongside these strict rules. Unlike many sports, players compete, for the most part, without the supervision of a referee or umpire. They are expected to call penalties on themselves. For many parents, golf teaches important lessons of honesty because it requires players to keep their own scores and because it has little history of steroid abuse, though both the men's and women's professional tours have begun drug testing. "The game relies on the integrity of the individual to show consideration for other players and to abide by the rules," the USGA says in its primer. "All players should conduct themselves in a disciplined manner, demonstrating courtesy and sportsmanship at all times, irrespective of how competitive they may be. This is the spirit of the game of golf."

Despite its difficulty, or perhaps because of it, golf has managed to achieve wide popularity. In 2005 *Golf Digest* counted some 32,000 golf courses in the world, with about half of them in the United States. From the 1950s through the turn of the twenty-first century, the number of golfers in the United States tripled, increasing at about 3.9 percent a year. The game spread to other English-speaking countries such as Australia, and more recently to places as far removed as Sweden and Spain, and China and South Korea. Today it's a global passion, with professionals from all over the world. Although Americans dominate junior tournaments, Europeans and Asians are increasingly visible at AJGA events.

As golf cast a spell over millions, it has spawned a serious backlash. One criticism is environmental. Like Mirasol, most courses are built alongside huge concrete housing developments. Developers offer golf as an enticement to home buyers and make their real money on the housing. Even without real estate projects, many criticize the sport for defacing some of the world's most beautiful spots. "Golf eats land, drinks water, displaces wildlife, fosters sprawl," argues novelist Jonathan

Franzen. Other criticisms range from the game's stuffy politeness to its difficulty. Franzen dislikes "the self-congratulation of its etiquette, the self-important hush of its television analysts," and comments that "the point of the game seems to be methodical euthanizing of workday-sized chunks of time by well-off white men." Comedian Robin Williams, in one of his best-known stand-up routines, riffs this criticism by imitating a drunken Scotsman who invented a sport that requires knocking a ball into "a gopher hole." In a serious vein, observers note that this Scottish pursuit is steeped in Calvinist notions of sin and salvation. Many of the most famous places in golf lore have monikers such as Hell Bunker on St. Andrew's Old Course's fourteenth hole or the perilous three-hole stretch at Augusta National, home of the annual Masters, dubbed Amen Corner.

In recent years, this backlash has caused golf's growth to stagnate. The total number of golfers fell by 2 percent in 2006 to 28.7 million, according to the National Golf Foundation, based in Jupiter, Florida. Amid this decline, junior golf represents a ray of hope. The number of golfers between the ages of six and seventeen increased to 4.8 million in 2005, up from 4.4 million in 2000.

Junior golf's growth mirrors the rise of Tiger Woods. More than anyone else, Woods updated the sport's old fogy image. He broke into the big time at the age of twenty in 1996, when he turned professional and won two out of his first seven professional events. He made golf appear youthful, cheerful, and athletic. Half Thai and half African American, Woods offered a new face and a new style to a sport traditionally the territory of white men and women. Junior wannabes emulate Tiger, spending days out on the range hitting practice balls and hours in the weight room. "For many 16-year-old boys, Tiger made it cool to play golf," says Hamblin, the AJGA executive director. "This fit-looking guy swept away the image of the overweight man."

Before Tiger Woods redefined the sport, Jack Nicklaus earned the title "Golden Bear." Nicklaus captured eighteen major championships in a career that stretched from 1962 to 1986. He was only twenty-two years old when he won his first U.S. Open in 1962. His main rivals at the Open were thirty-three-year-old Arnold Palmer and forty-nine-year-old Sam Snead.

In the 1950s in Columbus, Ohio, when Nicklaus was a teenager, he put his clubs away during the winter. In junior high school, he starred as quarterback, punter, and placekicker on the football team; center on the basketball team; and catcher on the baseball team. He spent little time in the weight room, and his physique reflected this reluctance to train. Nicklaus was chubby; his various nicknames were "Ohio Fats," "Blob-O," and "Whaleman." At the age of ten, Nicklaus took up golf at his local Scioto Country Club. In the summer he joined the Friday morning class for junior members held by the Scioto professional Jack Grout. Every two or three weeks he received a private lesson from Grout. The Scioto pro, unlike modern gurus who adopt complex scientific equations to teach golf swings, reduced golf to three main principles: keeping the head still throughout the swing, keeping the body balance centered, and gaining distance by keeping the arc of the swing as wide as possible. Throughout his career, Grout was Nicklaus's only teacher.

As a child, Nicklaus avoided dreams of future professional stardom, and to this day he preaches the virtues of his stable childhood. His youthful passion for several sports helped him avoid allowing golf "to beat me down to one thing," and, he believes, accounted for his long career at the pinnacle of the game. During a visit to the World Golf Hall of Fame in autumn 2007, Nicklaus decreed the single-minded specialization on golf alone as idiotic. His advice to young golfers conflicts with present-day wisdom. "I think kids should be playing everything, doing everything," he said. "Eventually, if you want to specialize in something, that's fine. But go out and enjoy."

The Nicklaus several-sport, kids-should-be-kids childhood endured throughout the 1960s and 1970s. Tom Watson graduated in 1967 from a Kansas City high school, where writer David Owen remembered him as "the quarterback (and leading rusher) on the varsity football team, which won the conference championship when he was a senior, and as a shooting guard in basketball." Like Nicklaus, Watson stashed his golf clubs from August until April. At Stanford, Watson walked onto the golf team, and he didn't make his decision to try the Professional Golf Association (PGA) tour until the end of his senior year. Today, talented young athletes specialize in a single sport in early childhood, and as Owen explains, "no genuine golf prospect would risk a career-ending injury by running quarterback keepers on half-frozen Midwestern football fields."

Today's all-consuming, precocious golfing intensity dates from the 1970s, scripted in large part by a bespectacled, portly, aw-shucks-style sportswriter for a local weekly from a suburb of Atlanta, Georgia, named Mike Bentley. As a sportswriter, Bentley covered high school golf, only to run out of stories during the summer because no formal junior golf events took place in Dekalb County, or anywhere else in Georgia. At the time, the country's best juniors experienced most of their summer competitive golf in volunteer-run local tournaments and state amateur events. They left their home state only for a few events, often only for the USGA's national Junior Amateur. High school golf offered slim chances for exposure. Scores went unpublished, and coaches had no place to turn for information on prospective recruits. Bentley was irked that Georgia Tech had gone seasons with unclaimed scholarships. "Scholarship money was available and it was going unused because kids had no place to showcase their talents," recalls Bentley in his best good ol' boy drawl. "There was nothing for these kids, nothing."

During the summer of 1974, when he was twenty-seven, Bentley launched the Dekalb County Junior Golf Association. The inaugural season consisted of a half-dozen events. Ninety-nine boys and girls signed up. Each paid a $2 entry fee. Other funding came from the local Coca-Cola distributor, and a little later, the local Commercial Union. All officials volunteered. Players' mothers contributed sandwich lunches, and Bentley engraved the trophies.

The summer climaxed with a season-ending championship, modeled on the supreme Georgia golf tournament. "From the get go, I wanted to do stuff like the Masters, the calling out of the name and home city on the first tee, the whole pomp and circumstance," Bentley recalls. "I wanted to do it better than anybody else did it, so that the kids came away from first tournament, thinking, 'damn, I have hit the big time.'" At his tournaments, he insisted that parents keep their distance. "I didn't let the parents on the golf course," he says. "I didn't want a Little League situation."

Bentley ran his fledging organization out of his house and his 1975 silver Dodge Colt station wagon. He soon expanded out of Georgia to include the entire southeast. His 1976 season-ending championship took place at Pinehurst's famed Number Two course. Davis Love III, a future pro star, won the boys' division. The next year Bentley went national. He printed up a one-page promotional brochure, stating his new American Junior Golf Organization's goals: "to serve as a clearinghouse and information center for junior golfers" and to sponsor and conduct national junior golf tournaments. An advisory board was assembled. Tom Watson, who that year had won the Masters and British Open and was named PGA Tour Player of the Year, agreed to become the organization's first honorary chairman. "Watson was a real gentleman, a smart guy, an academic, and he saw the need," Bentley recalls. Professional Golf Association Tour commissioner Deane Beman and Don Padgett, president of the Professional Golf Association of America, also agreed to serve. Padgett gave Bentley a list of addresses for every junior who attempted to qualify for that year's Junior Professional Golf Association Championship. Bentley used it for his initial mailing. He asked $10 for a first-year membership. More than 3,000 joined.

The aristocratic USGA, based in the genteel horse country of Far Hills, New Jersey, opposed Bentley's initiative. It stuck to its role setting the games' rules and running national championships and saw no need for a junior circuit. "Our mission is not creating the next great players on this country," says Steve Czarnecki, the USGA's assistant director of grants and fellowships. "We are an association of member clubs and we are there to serve them."

In Bentley's mind, "the USGA folks were snooty." He aggravated traditionalists first by challenging traditional rules for junior eligibility, insisting that all high school students play through the age of eighteen. The USGA included only those aged seventeen and younger in its annual junior championship. "When Mike first raised the idea of creating a nationwide junior golf tour to showcase the best players, people in the business thought he was crazy," recalls Chris Haack, who played in the early events, worked in the organization for sixteen years, and now is the golf coach at the University of Georgia. "Who in the heck would send kids around the country to play in golf tournaments? At the time, most junior golf was mom and pop, run out of somebody's garage and out of a backroom of a country club."

The AJGA held its first Tournament of Champions in August 1978 at the Inverrary Country Club in Lauderhill, Florida, longtime site of the pro tour's Jackie Gleason Classic. Contestants came from across the country. The field included future pro standout Mark Calcavecchia. Eventual champion Willie Wood shot a final-round 69 for a four-shot victory. At a later tournament that year, held at the Tampa-based Innisbrook Resort, Bentley named an All-American team and organized a banquet. "A lot of the kids never had been to a banquet or dressed up," he recalls. "We thought this would be special." Haack received the association's first-ever sportsmanship award, and Willie Wood, who later became a solid tour pro, was named the first Rolex Junior Player of the Year.

Bentley's fledging organization grew fast. An Atlanta oil geologist named Digger Smith put up a $200,000 matching fund contribution in

1981 to build and furnish its first offices, a 4,000-square-foot brick colonial at Horseshoe Bend Country Club in Roswell, Georgia. The original three-tournament season morphed into a thirteen-event schedule, and parents around the country clamored for events to be held near their homes. "There were no national tournaments in New England during the 1980s—my son and I had to travel all the way to Florida to find competition," recalls Barbara Lander, chairwoman of the Mirasol tournament.

Growth brought the organization to a turning point. Bentley was going through a midlife divorce. Even though, like many entrepreneurs, he recognized that he was "good at the visionary thing, less good at the managing thing," he wanted to stay on. Digger Smith believed the association required professional management, and the board asked the founder to resign. Bentley moved to Blanco, Texas, outside of Austin, where he joined the Texas Restaurant Association and started running an antiques business on eBay. Today he has little contact with the organization, only occasionally attending tournaments. While he understands and supports the reasons for his departure, he harbors some regrets that he let go of "his baby."

Bentley's successor, Stephen Hamblin, brought much-needed discipline to the organization. His father, Robert Allen Hamblin, was an officer in the U.S. Air Force. As a child, Hamblin answered the phone, "Capt. Hamblin's residence, Stephen speaking." Today in his fifties, with his hair thinning, Hamblin continues to sport a trim, youthful figure and carries himself like a disciplined military officer. He has a chiseled face and serious mien, with a hard jawline and intense, deeply set eyes.

Hamblin's grandfather taught him how to play golf when he was twelve years old. He competed in high school and one college golf event as a fifth-year senior at Michigan State. "I just wasn't good enough to be a touring pro," he acknowledges. He now plays to a 2.6 handicap. During college summers, Hamblin worked at Pinehurst with then-head professional and taskmaster Jay Overton. It proved a good fit. Overton liked to call 4:00 a.m. staff meetings. Hamblin enjoyed them and later passed on his early-morning preferences to the running of junior golf tournaments. During the pro tour's Colgate Hall of Fame Classic at the resort, Hamblin slept overnight in a temporary merchandise trailer that guarded the cash registers. "I have always worked with people who were passionate, whether in the golf industry or with my dad in the military," he says. "There's a right and a wrong way to do things. You do things with a passion—and you try to do them right."

When Overton left Pinehurst for Innisbrook in Florida, he hired Hamblin as an assistant golf professional. Hamblin soon became head professional at Innisbrook's Copperhead Course, which was then home to the AJGA's end-of-the-year gala. The tournament's sixteen- and seventeen-year-olds, and the event's professionalism, surprised him. By accepting the position as executive director, Hamblin gave up a comfortable life for a much more uncertain challenge. His first child was on the way. His new employer's finances looked shaky. Local sponsors, the Coca-Cola distributorship and the Commercial Union, were withdrawing support. Hamblin filled the gap. At professional tournaments, pros play a round with sponsors before the regular event. Hamblin paired juniors and local businessmen on the day before the tournament, encouraging the businessmen to sponsor the events. Many within the organization were skeptical that grown-ups would pay to play with kids. "We figured that adults would love to meet with future Tigers," he says.

In his relentless pursuit of sponsors, Hamblin encountered continuing criticism that junior golf had moved too far and too fast to commercialize youth sports. When Buick signed on to sponsor an event in Flint, Michigan. Buick executives asked if they could give the winners the use of a car for a year. But many of the contestants did not yet have driver's licenses. Instead of allowing Buicks at the golf courses, Hamblin put the Buick name on a bag tag, a shirt, a towel, and a hat. "The goal is to avoid too overt sponsorship," Hamblin explains. "We want low-key, background support."

Rolex, Polo, and Titleist, among others, have agreed to Hamblin's terms, all attracted by the ASJA's elite demographics. Titleist began with a three-year, seven-figure deal two decades ago and replaced it in 2006 with a ten-year, eight-figure commitment. In September 2000 the financially stable AJGA moved into a new colonial-style, three-floor, 14,000-square-foot building in Braselton, about forty-five minutes north of Atlanta. The headquarters is situated on the Chateau Elan Winery and Resort, a real estate development complete with real vines, a real winery in a faux chateau, a spa, several golf courses, and million-dollar homes for wealthy urban refugees. The AJGA's annual budget now surpasses $8 million. About two-thirds of its funding comes from sponsors, and the junior golfers contribute the rest in membership and tournament fees.

Within the golf industry, Hamblin's organization has become a training ground. Experience working at the AJGA carries the prestige of a Harvard MBA, according to Mark Brazil, director of the pro tour's Wyndham Championship in Greensboro, North Carolina. Most AJGA employees are right out of college, and many are former interns. There is still competition just to become an intern; only about 50 are accepted out of 550 applicants.

As the upstart golf organization gained ground, juniors no longer found it possible to play a different sport each season and remain competitive. To play with the best, they needed to train consistently throughout the year, not halting to play an interim sport during the colder months.

More than any other individual, Phil Mickelson symbolized the emergence of this new style of junior golfer. Mickelson was born in June 1970. Other than golf, he enjoyed football and baseball, playing them from the age of four or five. He became a quarterback on the football team, only to break his arm. It proved harder for him to give up baseball. "I really, *really,* loved baseball," he recalls in his autobiography. "I was a pitcher (I threw right handed) and actually pitched a no-hitter."

When he was eleven, he felt he had to make a choice. "It was going to be baseball or golf," Mickelson remembers. "I had made the local all-star baseball team but that required a lot of practice and dedication during the summer months—the very time that all my junior tournaments started."

Mickelson went to talk to his dad.

"If you wanted to play baseball or golf professionally, in which would you have a better chance of making it?" his father asked.

"I don't know," the young Mickelson acknowledged.

"In baseball, you're going to be a number on somebody's team," his dad said. "In golf, however, you can play when and where you want to—because you are your own boss."

Once he had made the decision, Mickelson quit the baseball team and began playing junior golf tournaments. He became a player representative on the AJGA's board and the only boy ever to win the Rolex Player of the Year award three times, in 1986, 1987, and 1988. In each of these years, he captured the Rolex Tournament of Champions, and he established the record, which holds today, for most career wins: twelve. Instead of participating in adult amateur events in his senior year, he continued to compete in the junior events as a way to share his final junior days with teammates and friends.

———

While Bentley's organization established junior golf as a bona fide sport, Tiger Woods accelerated and advanced the early learning curve required to be a serious golfer in a competitive field. So many stories have been told about his childhood that even Tiger admits it is sometimes difficult to distinguish fact from fiction.

When his father practiced his golf swing, Tiger purportedly mimicked his motion in his crib. One day when Tiger was nine months old, his father recalled, he sat down to rest, only to see his son climb down from his high chair, grab a club cut down for him, and put a ball in place. "Little Tiger waggled his club once, looked at his target, waggled the club again, then executed a carbon copy in miniature of Earl's swing, striking the ball squarely into the net," writes biographer John Strege. At the age of two, he entered a competition for boys aged ten and under and won. At three, he broke fifty for nine holes for the first time, shooting a 48. At five years of age, he appeared on the television show *That's Incredible*. He received his first autograph request when he was still too young to have a signature. When other kids drew racing cars, Tiger drew trajectories of irons.

Earl Woods, a retired Army Green Beret and lieutenant colonel, quit his executive job at McDonnell Douglas to accompany his son full time. Tiger first beat his father, a good golfer, by a single stroke when he was eleven years old. He shot 71. That same summer he entered thirty-three junior tournaments and won them all.

As a teenager, Tiger remained a terror. He captured Player of the Year in 1991 and 1992 and failed to match Mickelson only because he played adult amateur events in his final year of eligibility. He became the youngest ever Player of the Year, still rail thin and just shy of sixteen years old. AJGA leaders recall many examples of Tiger's almost supernatural concentration. During a Thanksgiving tournament in Tucson, Tiger needed to hit a 250-yard wood second shot to a par-five green. A television reporter in a golf cart drove up to him. Tiger backed off his shot. "Just tell me when you are ready," he told the broadcaster. "I was sitting there and saying, 'nobody that young can be that cool'," Hamblin recalls.

Along with mental toughness, Tiger exhibited an incredible ability to will the ball where he wanted, even in the most difficult situations. On the eighteenth hole in the final group of a tournament, Tiger hit his ball into a bunker. He had a downhill lie and only about a few feet of green to roll his ball before the flag. "No way he can do anything with this," Mark Brazil, the former junior golf tournament director, recalls a fellow spectator whispering to him. Tiger whacked the ball out of the sand and rolled it to within a foot of the hole. He putted out for a par—and victory.

Earl Woods was often described as a sporting father with dollar signs in his eyes—a man who pushed his son too hard, too soon. He referred to his son as "The Chosen One" and compared him at various times with Mahatma Gandhi, Muhammad Ali, and Nelson Mandela. But Woods insisted he was misquoted on each occasion. "The greatest misconception the public seems to have of me is that I am a dominating, possessive, dictatorial stage father," he said in an interview with *Golf Digest*. "That is exactly 180 degrees from the truth." His purpose in raising Tiger was not to raise a good golfer, he insisted. "I wanted to raise a good person."

Young Tiger, according to his late father, showed prodigious talent and passion for the game and set his own agenda. By his account, he tried to convince Tiger to play baseball or another sport, only to be rebuffed by his son, who said it would distract him from golf. This was no overbearing stage father who orchestrated the prodigy's life à la Mozart. On the contrary, Earl claimed that he had to rein in Tiger and take him off the golf course to finish his homework. Most parents at junior tournaments trudge alongside their children, watching every shot from the sidelines. Earl Woods never followed Tiger for eighteen holes. Instead, he found the best piece of shade on the course, where he would set up camp and listen to classical music.

Since Tiger's time, no one has displayed the same ability to dominate junior golf. At Mirasol the nearest thing to a new Tiger Woods is not a boy. It is a seventeen-year-old girl named Vicky Hurst.

CHAPTER 3

A Female Tiger

Vicky Hurst shows her power off the tee.

Vicky hurst steps up to Mirasol Sunset Course's first tee at 8:33 a.m. She plants her feet, addresses the ball, and takes a measured breath. Majestically, she pulls the large steel-headed Cleveland driver backward. It rises in a slow, steady arc, stopping at a perfect angle just above the head. Then the club cracks down, accelerating to whiplash speed.

Whack!

The ball gives off a sharp hiss and rises like a bullet shot from a rifle, carving a gentle right-to-left arc before smashing into the ground and rolling along the grass. It finally stops close to the 280-yard marker, 60 or more yards farther than most junior girls are able to drive their balls and 30 or so yards beyond that of the average adult on the ladies' professional tour. While her rivals are hitting long four- or five-irons into the greens, Hurst often only needs a nine-iron or pitching wedge. This gives her a huge advantage. The higher number club, the more lofted its face, and the easier it is to control the ball, striking shots high that plop softly and stop sharply near the flag.

At seventeen, Hurst is the defending Mirasol champion, a 2006 Junior All-American, number two on the Polo girl rankings of all American junior girl golfers, and a genuine Player of the Year candidate. She represents a new breed of strong female athletes who are turning pro in their teens and transforming the once sleepy women's game into a high-powered spectacle.

Hurst's performance in the summer of 2007 would determine whether she would attend college or attempt to jump to the Ladies Professional Golf rout. Although very few boys make the leap direct from high school to the pros, girls mature faster, physically and emotionally. During the past few years the best female prospects, such as Paula Craemer and Morgan Pressel, have gone straight to the pro tour. Even though they have won millions of dollars, Craemer and Pressel appear to be giggly teenagers rather than mature superstar athletes. Both have struggled to win the most prestigious championships. In contrast, the two dominant women golfers of the past two decades, Swede Annika Sorenstam and Mexican Lorena Ochoa, opted to attend college before turning pro, and they encourage teenagers like Hurst to stay in school. "The best recommendation is to go in college, stay in college," Ochoa says. "College is only once in your life. The tour is always there afterward."

Hurst lives in Melbourne, Florida, about an hour and a half drive north of Mirasol on the state's Atlantic coast. Her presence helps transform a "regular" American Junior Golf Association (AJGA) event into an elite one. Like all junior tournaments, at Mirasol, junior players are separated by sex, with groups of three girls teeing off from the first tee starting at 7:30 a.m. in nine-minute intervals, and groups of three boys following at 8:42 a.m. Both boys and girls play on the same golf course, but the boys' tees are set a total of 800 yards back from the girls'.

For most of the competitors, their performance this week will help determine whether they are invited to more prestigious invitational AJGA tournaments later in the season. Many of the highest-ranking girls, such as Ivan Lendl's daughters Isabelle and Marika, are skipping this event. Their strong performances in the previous year already have earned them entry into the season's invitationals. Hurst's high ranking also guarantees that she will be invited no matter how she fares; she is playing in the early season event because it takes place near her home and because she believes it will help hone her skills and sharpen her competitive edge.

Hurst inspires a combination of awe and fear among her rivals. She not only hits the ball longer than anyone competing, she also makes her fluid, jaw-crunching drives seem like effortless arias. Other girls tense and sweat under the pressure. Even in the hottest weather, it is difficult to spot a wrinkle in Hurst's outfit or a hint of fear in her face. Hurst oozes power and athleticism and never seems to break her stride. She does not just walk down the fairway; she struts, each movement forward resembling a purposeful, almost militaristic marching step. Her shoulder-length hair is pulled back into a neat braid, and her taut body is poised.

While no one doubts Hurst's enormous talent, many find her inscrutable. Whether she hits a perfect shot or a rare poor one, her placid face shows little emotion. Around other teenage girls, Vicky often giggles. When she smiles, she reveals glorious pearly white teeth and budding feminine charm. Around adults, however, the muscles of the same face tighten, the insouciant swagger of an aspiring golf course tigress vanishes, and she answers in a shy monotone. Some of her onlookers question whether she has the mental toughness to become a true champion. She has never won an AJGA Invitational, finishing second several times and earning the unpleasant sobriquet "Ms. Second."

Hurst's family is reminiscent of Tiger Woods's. Earl Woods was a Green Beret and lieutenant colonel. Hurst's father, Joe Hurst, was an Air Force colonel, who retired from service after twenty-six years. Woods's mother, Kultida, is Thai. Hurst's mother, Koko, is Korean. Earl Woods met Kultida when he was stationed in Southeast Asia. Joe Hurst met Koko when he was stationed in Korea.

Both Hurst and Woods know what it's like to lose their biggest fan. Earl Woods died of cancer in June 2006 when his son was an established superstar and an expectant father. In April 2006 Hurst's father died after a stroke. His daughter was only fifteen. When her mother called her with the news, she was waiting out a thunderstorm during a qualifying event for an adult Ladies Professional Golf Association (LPGA) tournament in Orlando. It was the only time she withdrew from a golf event.

For both Tiger and Vicky, mothers have played crucial disciplinary roles in their lives. Kultida Woods is often presented as a loving figure who packed her prodigy into the car and drove him hours to play in tournaments, then retreated from the picture to allow Earl Woods to step forward and take center stage as the driving, encouraging, watchful father. Insiders like Tiger's junior golf rival Ted Purdy say Kultida was a driving, determined mother who rivaled her husband's involvement in her son's golf career. "This idea that Kutilda was the reserved, nurturing mother is inaccurate," Purdy says. "She was always present and made her opinion known."

Behind her calm appearance, Koko Hurst displays the same side of Asian parenting, an uncompromising demand for a strong work ethic and unfailing obedience. A short, compact woman who serves as her daughter's main coach, she follows Vicky along the sidelines, watching and monitoring, offering few words of encouragement. Hurst's father Joe seems to have been the nurturing parent, an easygoing, sweet-natured personality. "My dad loved golf," Vicky recalls. "Every chance he got, he would go off to the golf course. He wasn't my coach or anything; he didn't know that much about the fundamentals of the game. He just always encouraged me."

Hurst knows her ultimate goal: to play on the professional tour. It is what she has dreamed about since she was a little girl, when she and her parents realized her undeniable talent. She would prefer to spend more time on the fairways than inside a classroom. Yet she often wonders whether she is ready for the leap into the high-powered world of adult professionals. Two months before Mirasol, she competed again against Swedish superstar Sorenstam, Mexican challenger Ochoa, and the two rising American teen stars Craemer and Pressel at the LPGA Ginn Open in Reunion, Florida. Hurst shot a 73 and 75 and failed to make the cut for the final two rounds. "I wasn't nervous," she insisted to a local journalist afterward. "I just played badly."

For all her self-assurance, the seventeen-year-old Hurst remains susceptible to interior doubt, and on the golf course, periods of poor decision making. In introspective moments, she acknowledges the prospect of failure. If anything, she feels more pressure playing junior tournaments than with the pros. At adult tournaments, the young amateur plays almost incognito. If she scores poorly, almost no one notices. At junior events, she must learn to live with the reputation of being the favorite. "When I play with the adults, I learn a lot," she says. "Here everyone expects me to succeed."

Vicky is the younger of the two Hurst daughters. Kelly, two and a half years older, is more intellectual and less driven as a competitor. Although a good golfer, recruited by the University of Florida, Kelly failed to make the varsity team in her freshman year and says she will only play junior varsity in the upcoming season. At the Mirasol event, when her sister is practicing, Kelly plunges herself into books, reading on a lawn near the main scoreboard. She plans to attend summer school and has her eye on Yale for law.

While Kelly exudes emotion, Vicky appears quiet and meditative "It's tough, even for me, to understand sometimes how she's always so calm," Kelly admits. "She never thinks negative stuff. If you ask her what went well, what was the worst hole, she won't be able to tell you. She's forgotten. She just moves on to the next shot."

Off the golf course, Vicky Hurst lives in T-shirts and jeans and almost never wears makeup. A fan of *America's Next Top Model*, however, she pays close attention to her appearance on the course. At

Mirasol she sports white shorts and a blue polo shirt. Her long black hair flies out under a distinctive golfer's beret, the tam-o'-shanter. She started wearing caps at age ten, originally a Ben Hogan beret, switching to the tam-o'-shanter in honor of her favorite golfer, Payne Stewart, a longtime professional star who lost his life in an air crash. "I love the caps because of Payne Stewart—he had a great demeanor on the course, a quality person and player," she explains. Like Hurst, Stewart owned a smooth, silky long swing. He also translated his fashion sense into an impressive marketing tool, and Hurst seems to have the same idea. She owns multiple berets and matches them to her different outfits.

Golf runs in the Hurst genes. Vicky's grandfather Al was ninety-three years old when he went out and played nine holes, set up a tee time for the next day, and died quietly in his sleep. Koko Hurst was about thirty-nine weeks pregnant in June 1990 when she, her husband, and two other men played golf at Andrews Air Force Base in Maryland. She was on the sixteenth hole when her water broke. Joe Hurst had just hit one of his best shots of the day, setting up for a five-foot birdie. Joe never took his putt. He left the ball on the green and darted for a nearby hospital. "Vicky was born in two hours," Koko recalls. "I was beating all three guys when we left, too."

When Vicky was seven years old, her parents took her to the Samsung woman's tournament at the World Golf Village in northeastern Florida just north of St. Augustine. Even as a little girl she was enthralled. The World Golf Village includes the World Golf Hall of Fame and its exhibits on the world's greatest players. "For the first time, I saw golf professionals playing in real life surrounded by adoring fans, cameramen and media all over the place and I knew then that I wanted to be like those players," she says.

From the first swing, her talent impressed even hardened, skeptical pros. "As a ten-year-old, she was still small like her mom but she already had a great flow and rhythm," recalls her swing coach, Mike Bender of Timacuan Country Club near Orlando, Florida. "You could see that she was a solid athlete." Voted one of America's Top Ten teachers by *Golf Digest*, Bender knows how to judge talent. He also coaches such pros as Masters' champion Zach Johnson and female pro standout Seon Hwa Lee. The tomboy Hurst played midfield in soccer and guard in basketball and competed in junior tennis tournaments. She even tried out competitive swimming and tae kwon do.

Her inaugural victory in a golf tournament came at the age of eleven. Soon afterward Vicky was emptying the pockets of adults at the Suntree Country Club in Melbourne. "I would pay her a dollar for each hole she beat me, plus a dollar for each par, two dollars for a birdie and five for an eagle," recalls Dennis Dahlman, the Suntree president. "I never saw a swing so smooth, with such a wonderful tempo." In 2005 Hurst shot a ten-under-par 62—with a few missed birdie putts—to win a high school district title. Afterward she left Cocoa Beach High School for Holy Trinity, a local Catholic school. Since Trinity has no girls' golf team, Hurst joined the boys' team. She played number one in all three high-school years. As a sophomore she shot back-to-back rounds of 67 in the Class 1A state finals, matching Morgan Pressel stroke for stroke, until Pressel birdied the second extra hole to win the playoff.

Hurst qualified for the 2006 women's United States Open. At the tournament, held that year in Newport, Rhode Island, she suffered through rounds of 78 and 82 and missed the cut by ten strokes. Hurst could smash the ball as far as or farther than most of the pros, but she struggled to manage the course like an adult. Where mature women played a par five in three safe shots, Hurst often tried to reach the hole with two bombs. The pros teed off with a safe three wood, a forgiving club used on the fairway that sacrifices distance for accuracy. Hurst continued to blast away with her large titanium-headed driver, even though her ball risked running out of the fairway.

A few weeks after the women's Open debacle, Hurst cracked again at the United States Junior Open in Charlotte, North Carolina, at Carmel Country Club. Match-play finals are a marathon, contested over two eighteen-hole rounds, one played in the morning and the second right after lunch. Hurst faced wisplike, thirteen-year-old Jenny Shin from Torrance, California. She outdrove Shin by 40 to 50 yards, a key advantage on the long 6,396-yard course. After the first eighteen holes, the match remained tied. Hurst burst ahead in the afternoon round, winning the twenty-second, twenty-third, and twenty-fourth holes. Shin thought the match was over. "I was pretty numb," she acknowledged.

Instead of coasting and conserving her lead, however, Hurst continued to fire full-barrel drives down the fairway. She went for the green on a 295-yard par four and drove instead into the deep rough. It took her two chips to reach the green, and she still faced a nine-foot par putt. She left the ball short. On the thirty-third hole, Hurst only needed to tap in a two-foot putt. But her ball hit the edge and stayed out. On the thirty-fourth hole, she had a fifteen-foot birdie putt to win. But she left it inches short. "I just didn't play the correct break on that one," she later conceded. The thirty-sixth and final regulation hole was a long, uphill par five. Hurst pulled her second shot into the left rough, and her third shot stopped twenty-five feet above the flag. Although she still had two putts to win, she knocked her ball ten feet by and missed the comeback.

The match was tied.

In sudden death, Hurst sent her approach shot flying into a left-side water hazard. After she hit her next shot thin into a greenside bunker, she walked over to the rules official and conceded. "It was tough," she told a press conference, particularly the nightmare of "that shot in the water."

After the dramatic defeat, Hurst returned to her first formal golf teacher, Bender, who spotted immediate flaws in her swing. Hurst took her clubs back in too upright a fashion and then came back down at the ball with too steep a trajectory. This sharp movement limited her control over the ball and sent balls flying left and right of target. Bender flattened her hands and slowed her backswing. As usual, Hurst proved a quick study.

Hurst's progress over the past months is visible right from her first shots at the Mirasol tournament. She birdies six of the first nine holes. Her drives blast off straight and long and allow her to reach the par fives in two shots. Her irons brake close to the flag. "Watching her is watching a young Annika," says an awed Barbara Lander, the tournament chairwoman. Hurst herself seems a little surprised at her prowess.

"Everything on the front nine was working well for me today," she admits.

Right after she finishes the ninth hole, however, the sky turns dark. BB gun–sized raindrops are popping all about. A warning trumpet blares. Play is suspended, and competitors scurry to wait out the delay in the clubhouse banquet room. When the golfers return to the course two hours later, Hurst seems a bit sluggish. "I just wasn't in my aggressive mood anymore," she admits. She scores an even-par 36 on the back nine.

Although by the end of the round Vicky has managed a stunning 66, or six under par, Koko Hurst seems dissatisfied. She believes her daughter should be ten under par. "You should kill this course," she tells Vicky afterward.

From its beginning, golf has appealed to women. Mary Queen of Scots played in the mid-1500s and is credited with introducing the concept of "caddie" to the sport. (She brought sons of French noblemen to Scotland to serve as pages in the court and regularly took such "cadets" with her on the course.)

Slowly but surely, more and more women took up the game. The United Kingdom's Royal and Ancient instituted a Ladies Open in 1893. Women's red tees, which shortened the distance between most holes and made them more appropriate to female shot making, were developed. But the playing field was hardly level. Many country clubs continued to ban "women and dogs" from their courses. When twelve pioneers founded the Ladies Professional Golf Association in the 1950s, they were greeted with indifference. Prize money was inconsequential. Only a few participants shot under-par rounds. Nancy Lopez, a pro star during the 1970s and 1980s, remembers how she needed to fight to pursue her passion. All-male school teams had to be opened up. Country club restrictions needed to be lifted.

Traditionally, female golfers wore an intimidating array of clothing that covered them head to toe and were hobbled by high-buttoned shoes. Long skirts prevailed through the 1930s. Early women pros sported dull, drag khaki shorts and bland, short-sleeved navy shirts. It took a bubbly blond named Laura Baugh in the 1970s, who sported miniskirts and lightweight, flowing designer T-shirts, to inject an exciting dash of color and style into the sport. In recent years stars such as Paula Craemer and Nathalie Gulbis have continued the trend, reveling in miniskirts and revealing tops, which have been adopted by most of the junior golfers.

Girls remain the minority at junior tournaments, accounting for only a fifth of the total AJGA membership, though their percentage is rising and their quality improving. Two decades ago, female juniors often stumbled in with scores in the 80s on par 72 courses. Today, top-rated junior female hopefuls shoot in the 70s. These are, for the most part, children of Title IX, the 1972 law that required colleges to give equal money to women's sports as they did to men's. Before Title IX, many derided female sports as a freak show. Later, when women's sports became a priority, female players enjoyed an advantage over boys for college scholarships. Because so many boys are recruited for football and basketball—two sports that draw large numbers of spectators and make money—Division I schools can award as many as 6 golf scholarships to girls but only 4.5 golf scholarships to boys. Division II schools allow 5.4 scholarships for girls but only 3.6 for boys. (Two or more athletes share most golf scholarships.) Golf coaches struggle to recruit women to play college golf. Recruits have more choices, and many of the most talented junior girls consider turning pro before or during school.

Many girls, tempted by opportunities for college scholarships and professional stardom, struggle to cope with the pressure involved in shooting for their dreams. Kristen Hill, a pert, brunette seventeen-year-old from Weston, Florida, tees off in Mirasol's final threesome, at 9:27 a.m. She rose well before dawn to make it to the course, more than an hour's drive from her home. Hill, who is less polished than Hurst, exhibits a magnetic, winning smile and immediate warmth. Her father, David Hill, who works at home as an investment advisor and drives his daughter to her golf events, suffers from multiple sclerosis. Each round with his daughter represents a personal triumph of will.

Hill starts out strong, sinking a thirty-foot putt for par on the second hole. At the par-three sixth, she sticks her shot within tap-in distance and goes one under par. But golf is a precision game that penalizes the slightest error. On the eighth hole, Hill suffers what her father describes as a "Waterloo." The short, 125-yard par three plays over a pond. The safe shot heads left and long. Hill hits right and short. Her ball plops into the water, for a stroke penalty. If Hill had teed up left of the water and miss hit, her shot would have crossed into the hazard near the green, offering an easy recovery chip. Instead, she had teed up on the right and must return to her point of departure and hit another ball the full distance of the hole. Her second tee shot lands left of the green. She proceeds to flub her chip, leaving it far short of the target, and ends with a triple bogey.

The seventeen-year-old Hill has been playing serious, competitive golf for a full decade. When she was only seven years old, her father took her to a driving range and put a club in her hands. "Right away, her swing was better than mine," he recalls. Hill soon gave up tennis and volleyball to concentrate on golf. By age eleven she was shooting in the mid-70s, competitive enough to gain a full college scholarship. She is good friends with the Pressel family, whose oldest daughter Morgan

played in the adult U.S. Women's Open as a seventh grader and already
stars on the LPGA tour. She often practices with Morgan's younger sister, Madison. Even as David Hill recognized the long odds against his
daughter becoming a famous golf pro, her progress hooked him. He
took sustenance from his daughter's golf dreams. "I became like a
drunk at a party, addicted to my daughter's success," he admits.

His addiction clashed with his daughter's doubts. Kristen Hill played
a few tournaments with Cheyenne Woods, Tiger's niece, who was being
filmed for television. "The cameras in my face freaked me," she admits.
As she began competing, she discovered that dozens of other teenage
girls were as good as or better than she was. Most of the Mirasol's par-
five holes are about 500 yards long, reachable in two shots for the
stronger girls. Hill hits her drive an average of only about 230 yards, requiring her to take three shots. When her father considered hiring a
trainer to increase the length of her drives, his daughter resisted.
Coaches insisted on changing the mechanics of her swing, and she felt it
was too difficult to follow their instructions. "I'm a feel player," she says.
"I want to have fun out there." At fourteen, Hill gave up her early
dream to become a professional. She would aim only to play college golf.
Her decision shocked David Hill, who pushed her to reconsider.

"You are acting like an idiot," Kristen chastised her father. When
she saw a loud parent pushing a junior golfer, Kristen pointed him out.

"You are just like that, Dad," she said.

When David Hill caught himself "talking loud "to his daughter, he
realized she was right.

"I said, 'is this me?'" he recalls. "If I used to be a drunk at a party, I
am now a recovering alcoholic."

For the rest of his daughter's round, David Hill keeps his voice
down and fights to keep his face from contorting when his daughter
makes an error. Kristen Hill finishes her round with a three-over-par
75. Most golfers would be thrilled with such a performance on a course
like Mirasol, with its tough bunkers, vast expanses of water hazards,

and slick greens. At this level of golf, however, Hill knows her performance is insufficient. Instead of being over par, she needs to be under the regulation score to have a legitimate chance of winning.

Another Mirasol player, Alexis Thompson, nicknamed Lexi, represents the type of prodigy that so frightens Kristen. She started playing at age five and entered her first golf tournament when she was seven. Now just twelve years old and in seventh grade, she already plays golf full time. Each morning Thompson rises around 6:00 a.m., and after an early breakfast, studies online for two hours. By 10:00 a.m. she is out on the course where, except for a lunch break and an additional hour of online study at home, she practices for seven to eight hours a day. "School was just getting in the way of my golf," she explains.

The Thompsons run a homemade golf academy out of their house in Coral Springs, Florida. Thompson's twenty-five-year-old brother Nick played top junior events, graduated from Georgia Tech, and competes in the adult golf minor leagues, the Nationwide Tour. Her fourteen-year-old brother Curtis is competing in the boys' tournament at Mirasol. "I would just watch my brothers hit balls and they got me into it," Thompson says. According to her father Scott, Alexis benefits from the examples in her family. "She sees her brothers' success and knows it can be done." Almost every day, the brothers play matches against their sister. Alex describes the family competition as fun, but her father, who admits to having to referee his competitive children, sees them as more brutal.

Lexi, who has grown a solid three inches over the past few months, into a sturdy five foot, six inches, just might, her father predicts, become as tall and powerful as Vicky Hurst. On the golf course, Thompson displays youthful exuberance. The previous December, she became the youngest winner in the history of the Doral Publix Junior Championship, an international event drawing players from around the world. In April she became the second-youngest winner of an AJGA event, claiming the Aldila Junior Classic in Durham, North Carolina.

She carded consecutive rounds of two-over-par 74 for a tournament total of four-over-par 148, despite missing a series of short putts.

Most amazing, Thompson advanced through the U.S. Women's Open sectional, qualifying at Heathrow Country Club outside Orlando, and distinguishing herself as youngest player ever to qualify for the most important championship in women's golf. For the summer, Scott Thompson has mapped out a five-week itinerary spanning 21,620 miles, thirteen events, and ten states. To accompany his daughter, he has quit his job at an electronics firm and spends his days at home in front of a computer investing his savings and charting his children's golf careers. He describes himself as a "recreational" golfer and says his children's tight schedule leaves him little time left to play more than a dozen rounds each year. "Some parents may say I am pushing, but Lexi wants to do this," he insists.

Few doubt Alexis Thompson's talent or desire to compete, but many of her playing partners at Mirasol question her maturity. Golf requires constant concentration, and even the best players suffer lapses. When she three-putts the fifteenth hole at Mirasol, she screams, "I hate this mother-fucking game." After a rules official is called, Thompson apologizes and is allowed to continue with only a warning. But she proceeds to bogey the final three holes and finishes with a five-over-par 77. "She was whining, she was cussing, she was slamming everything," Andrea Watts, another competitor, observes. "If she had brushed it off, gotten over it, said, 'I made a mistake, that was dumb, but there is nothing I can do to change it. Let me focus on the next shot.' If she had done that, she probably could have birdied one of the three final holes."

While Thompson struggles to mature, other promising, pedigreed young competitors grapple with the physical process of growing up. Fourteen-year-old Jessica Korda is the lithe, blond-haired daughter of former Czech tennis star Petr Korda, who won the 1999 Australian Open. After being fined for using anabolic steroids, Korda retired to Florida with his wife, fellow Czechoslovak tennis pro Regina Rajchrtova. Like Ivan Lendl, the Kordas encouraged their daughter to pursue a more genteel sport. "In tennis, people would set the goals for her, even before she picks up the racket," Korda says. "Plus, compared to tennis, you last longer in golf."

Except for her braces, Jessica Korda looks like a budding model. A golf swing is a well-oiled motion of repetition, requiring its practitioner to move the club along the same, precise angle each time. Jessica's burgeoning height has thrown off the correct vector and the rhythm of her previously long and fluid swing. She suffers through a 75 in her first round at Mirasol. In her second round, she continues to battle with her body, spraying shots around the course. Even so, she manages to keep even par through seventeen holes.

But Korda's second shot on the par-four eighteenth hole flies into the left trap in front of the green. In golf speak, she "short-sides" herself, giving almost no space to get the ball out of the bunker and roll it on the green. "What a stupid shot," her father says. "If you want to miss, you have to hit it right because the flag is in the back left of the green." Korda compounds her problems by taking two shots to get out of the trap. She sinks her first putt but takes a bogey and finishes with a 73.

After the round, Korda heads to the practice range's sand trap. She spends an hour practicing, under the approving scrutiny of her famous father. Petr Korda understands. When he was growing up, his father told him that he needed to lose of lot of matches in order to become a champion, and he has carried the message forward to his daughter.

———

Golf is a ridiculously difficult sport to conquer. Although it doesn't require as much athleticism as basketball, the muscular power of football, or the lightning-quick hand-eye coordination of baseball, it demands good timing and superb touch. It demands that a player hit a small ball into a target several hundred yards away before rolling it into another small hole at the end of a giant green, as well as hitting a variety of further shots of varying length and difficulty over a range of terrain. Many young golfers make it through fifteen or sixteen holes, only to falter, lose focus, and end up with a disastrous fairway to hell. Girls, even fast-growing Jessica Korda or Rambo Vicky Hurst, remain unable to power the ball as far as teenage boys. Overall, though, the girls mature more quickly and lose their temper less often than the boys. Put simply, they seem to make fewer stupid mistakes and their scores are more consistent.

Vicky Hurst's first round 66 at Mirasol is a stroke ahead of the leading boy, and after two days the last place girl is nine strokes ahead of the last place boy. During the second round Hurst fails to "eat up" the course as her mother has ordered and records a one-under-par 71. She puts balls above flags when she should leave them below. She smacks drivers when a three wood would suffice. "Everything was just a little off," she says afterward.

Hurst's lapse round allows Andrea Watts, a powerfully built seventeen-year-old Korean American, to pass her on the leader board. In the first round, Watts shot an impressive 69. In the second round she did even better, firing a five-under-par 67. This gives her a total of 135, one shot better than Hurst's 136. Third-place Elizabeth Alger trails by three shots.

A native of Colorado, Watts has played few tournaments in Florida and has marked few finishes of note. Compared with Hurst, many at Mirasol have never heard of her. But Andrea Watts is determined to become a serious competitor. She recently left her Colorado home, where she could play golf only half a year, for Florida. She now trains at the ultimate junior golfer facility—a full-time golf academy.

CHAPTER 4

Living, Breathing, and Sleeping Sport

Andrea Watts won several tournaments in
Colorado before moving to Florida.

WHEN ANDREA WATTS WAS fifteen years old, her mom drove her to New Mexico to play in an American Junior Golf Association (AJGA) Junior All-Stars event. After the first round, Andrea found herself in last place. On each of the following days she improved, and she ended up fifth.

"Mom, I want to be part of this," she said. "I need to play all year-round."

Sunee Watts's life—her friends and her profitable business importing beauty products from Asia—were all in Colorado.

Andrea was a star student at a top Denver prep school and seemed destined to attend an Ivy League college. She knew her goal to become a pro golfer was unreachable if she stayed in snowbound Colorado and attended university in New England. During the thirteen-hour ride back from New Mexico, Andrea pressed to move to Florida. Her mom resisted. She hoped her daughter would become a doctor or lawyer, not a professional golfer.

"If you have any money saved up for college, let's use it now and I'll get a scholarship," Andrea argued.

"Andrea's tongue is like a three-inch sword—it is dangerous to resist, and she used every word in her large vocabulary," her mother recalls.

Andrea feels American first, Korean second, with only the straight, dark-brown hair and slight angle to her eyelids to suggest her Asian parentage. Her father, a colonel in the Air Force, died a week before she was born. Watts's father had met Sunee in Korea, and they moved together to Colorado, buying a house on a golf course. After her first round in the Rockies, where Sunee spotted deer, fox, and other types of wildlife, she decided that golf "was the game for the Gods."

Sunee Watts became a four handicapper who often brought her toddler out onto the course. "I was in diapers in the sand trap," Andrea jokes. Andrea entered pee wee junior tournaments starting at age nine. Her mom pushed her to excel, giving her a training regime and making sure she lived up to it.

Sports never came naturally to Andrea. In volleyball and basketball, she shied away from the ball, and to this day she avoids the weight room. At five foot ten and 160 pounds, she is a big-boned, wide-shouldered girl. She struggles to squeeze into a tight golf skirt and polo shirt. It's not that she dislikes fashion; she just doesn't feel ready to act like a woman. She hates the acne on her otherwise attractive face, and she's not interested in boys. But golf allows Watts to prove herself out on a course, where competition is key.

Though Sunee Watts didn't want to leave what she fondly refers to as "snow country," she lived for her daughter and was eager to please her. By the time the Wattses reached Denver on their way back from the tournament, Sunee had relented. "It broke her heart, but she was willing to do whatever it took to make me happy," Andrea remembers.

In August 2006 Sunee rented out their Colorado house and decamped with her daughter to Bradenton, just south of Tampa.

Their destination was the David Leadbetter Golf Academy, located on Highway 41, wedged between an all-you-can-eat oyster bar and a Florida strip mall. A big sign out front reads "The Home of Junior Golf." Andrea joined Petr Korda's daughter and Ivan Lendl's daughters as academy full-timers.

Along with the AJGA, the Leadbetter Academy has led the way in revolutionizing junior golf, producing an impressive host of professional golfers. Over the past few decades, sports academies capable of attracting the world's best athletes have been cropping up on American soil. This ultra-capitalist institution can, however improbably, trace its roots back to communism. Soviet bloc countries placed talented children in special sports schools, where they were transformed into Olympic champion swimmers, gymnasts, and runners. The state paid the tuition and benefited from the medals its students took home. With the collapse of the Soviet Union, communist sports academies fell by the wayside. But the advantages of providing athletes with intense training at ever-younger ages were undeniable. In Europe and Asia, where most regular schools offer no competitive athletics, national federations in sports ranging from soccer to swimming continue to place promising prospects in special schools for exclusive training.

In America, private entrepreneurs offer intense, early athletic studies to budding athletic champions. Legendary coach Nick Bollettieri launched a tennis academy three decades ago at what was then a parking lot in Bradenton. It began as a small, somewhat ramshackle, family-run operation. But Bollettieri's hard-driving style—up at 4:00 a.m. and ready for six hours of tennis a day—soon produced champions like Andre Agassi, Jim Courier, and Monica Seles. Each Bollettieri player shared similar mechanical two-hand backhands and ferocious determination to grind down opponents.

After the International Management Group, a mammoth agency that represents athletes and runs athletic events, bought Bollieteri's operation, it put in place an expansion plan, purchasing the youth division of David Leadbetter's golf academy. When the Leadbetter Academy opened in1994 in Bradenton, it attracted six students, four of whom hailed from abroad. Today, about half of the 200 golf students are Americans. Leadbetter believes the most important element of the academy is the kids' competiveness. "It is like Yale and Harvard—all the kids are striving for the same goal, building an environment of excellence," he says. Though the institution is named after its founder, Leadbetter continues to live and teach trainers at his adult academy in Orlando. Gary Gilchrist, an assistant under Leadbetter, became the junior golf academy's first director. "When I traveled to Bradenton and walked out on the tennis courts, I became really excited by what Bollettieri was doing with those young players," Gilchrist recalls. "If golf went the same way, the kids would become better and better when they were younger and younger."

During Gilchrist's childhood, he says, the consensus was that male golfers peaked around the age of thirty, and women slightly earlier. Gilchrist, a standout on the South African national team who grew up with future pro superstars Ernie Els and Retief Goosen, was convinced that kids needed psychological training, high-stakes competition, and regular monitoring to become great. "You have to deal with the kids' goals, their lively character, their fears, their dreams and their aspirations," Gilchrist says. "We prepare them to win, teach them course management, give them a mental game plan, and show them how to deal with a bad bounce."

In recent years Leadbetter Academy has expanded beyond golf and tennis to include hockey, baseball, soccer, and basketball. What was a 22-acre complex with a small group of tennis wannabes in Bollettieri's time has grown to a sprawling 300-acre, multisport center with ambitious plans for further enlargement. Teachers and visitors use golf carts to make their way around campus. There are a 30,000-square-foot, climate-controlled training dome with multiple National Basketball Association (NBA) regulation basketball courts, seventy-two Har-Tru clay tennis courts, seven Bermuda grass soccer fields, three major league–sized baseball diamonds, two swimming pools, and an ice hockey rink. An indoor International Performance Institute provides weights, resistance machines, and fitness cycles. Sports psychologists are available to all students. In every direction among the palm trees, packs of tanned teens tote golf clubs, soccer shoes, and football equipment. Golf facilities include a double-ended driving range, including four target greens; sand bunkers; putting and chipping greens; and an on-scene administrative building with state-of-the-art video rooms, a pro shop, and a room specially designed to fit golf clubs. As part of their tuition, students have access to the nearby Legacy Golf Club or El Conquistador Country Club. Twenty-four coaches cater to the golf students.

Such dedicated training comes at a high price. For room, board, and sports training, aspiring golfers pay $33,800 a year. Because they don't incur expensive country club and tournament fees, annual tuition for baseball, basketball, ice hockey, and soccer is around $25,000. Tuition at the Pendleton School adds another $11,500, and extra sessions with the coaches can bring the total cost of a year of golf training at the academy close to $70,000. School officials say their motivation is not to churn out assembly-line-style professional golfers, but to help their students win scholarships. More than 90 percent of the Leadbetter graduates go on to college, and over the years they have received millions of dollars in athletic grants. Leadbetter has kids from forty countries around the globe and more than forty American states, and its teachers boast that while there, students learn respect for other cultures and develop valuable discipline skills.

For every Paula Creamer or Maria Sharapova, however, dozens of less-talented prospects enroll with no hope of a professional athletic career. Almost anyone who can pay the steep tuition is accepted. This policy leads to grumbling among some students and parents. Some see the academy as a place where rich parents park their adolescent children. ""Here you pay and they take care of you—a little like qualified babysitting," complains Ivan Lendl, the tennis star. Lendl grew up in communist Czechoslovakia, where athletes trained in special state-run sports schools. He finds the capitalist equivalent far different. The communists chose students on athletic ability. The capitalists require parents to write a check and are less interested in talent. A number of parents and students complain that the academy's attention is focused only on the top prospects, many of whom receive scholarships, while dozens of less-talented students muddle through. "Many of the kids were sent just because their parents thought it was important for them to learn how to play for their future business career," marvels Karen Creamer, Paula's mother.

The Creamers initially enrolled Paula for a single year at the Leadbetter Academy. She loved the program, and Golf Academy director David Wheelan liked her potential. When Leadbetter offered Paula a scholarship to stay on, she accepted with pleasure. Paul Creamer was able to keep his job as an American Airlines pilot and moved his family to Florida from California. Karen and Paul believe that their daughter could not have succeeded on the tour without the academy experience.

Despite the undeniable success of several of its graduates, critics complain that a male golf phenomenon has yet to emerge from the Leadbetter Academy. The only academy graduate on the men's pro golf tour is little-known Dave Gossett. Noted sports psychologist Bob Rotella maintains that professional sports academies are a sham. "For the most part, I think it's nuts," he says. "The Academies are mass producers of mediocrity, because everybody is taught the same thing. If you want to be great, you have to find your own way." Many pro golfers agree, insisting that golfers continue to bloom later than athletes in other sports. Critics complain that academy golf training suffers from a mechanical, cookie-cutter approach. All students display a similar warm-up motion. They place themselves before the ball; adjust their bodies into the correct upright posture; and then move the club backward and forward in a short, ankle-high warm-up movement. Their swings, constantly videotaped and played back on computer screens, are dissected with laboratory precision into a nine-part equation. They share a similar wrist cock at the top and a similar follow-through. In tennis, this computer precision approach produces legions of two-fisted, backhand, backcourt grinders. In golf, this new science of the swing succeeds in producing mechanical, robotlike players, each mimicking the same swing motions.

Teachers at the academy defend themselves by arguing that they adapt the Leadbetter "system" to individual needs and allow unorthodox techniques if they prove effective. They say the academy is a democratic institution—one that allows for the emergence of talent but doesn't reserve acceptance to the very few. The idea is not to nurture pro stars, but to nurture the best possible results from every student. "It's a matter of helping the kids grow up and get ready for college," insists David Wheelan, who runs the golf program. "I may have the talent, but my teachers don't want to think about becoming the next Paula Creamer," says Andrea Watts. Because ten years or more after graduation are required for a male golfer to reach his prime, officials insist that it remains too early to make a definitive judgment on the success or failure of the Leadbetter approach. "We're just beginning to see how this works out," says Wheelan, pointing out that the academy has been open for a little more than a decade and the number of graduates reaching the pro tour is accelerating.

David Wheelan, a native of Yorkshire, England, learned golf in the traditional way, heading down to the local club after school, watching, imitating, and playing. He caddied to earn cash and played in local tournaments. During high school he also played for the local soccer club. As an adult he was good enough to give the European

Professional Golf Tour a shot. He stayed there fifteen years before accepting Leadbetter's invitation to move to Florida, where he became convinced that traditional methods of producing professional golfers were outdated. Leadbetter himself is amazed at the progress of many of his pupils. "We get these kids at the age of 13 or 14 and many are very average," he says. "Two or three years later, these guys and girls are real good players."

It's difficult to argue with Wheelan's logic when measured by the rate of imitation. Academies are multiplying. The most prominent copycat is the International Junior Golf Academy (IJGA), based in Hilton Head, South Carolina, and owned by former high school golf star and New York foreign currency trader Ray Traviglione. The IJGA attracted little attention until original Leadbetter Academy director Gary Gilchrist arrived in 2004 and injected new rigor into the golf curriculum.

At Hilton Head, Traviglione owns and operates not just the Junior Golf Academy, but also the Heritage Academy, which offers a regular high school education in convenient half-day chunks. In addition to golfers, Heritage caters to tennis students, aspiring horse riders, ballet dancers, and musicians. The South Carolina– and Florida-based golf academies charge roughly the same for tuition, room, and board: almost $70,000 a year. The Hilton Head organization doesn't have any contacts with the International Management Group. Instead, it feeds its most promising pupils to a rival agency called Octagon.

By launching his own set of junior golf tournaments called the International Junior Golf Tour, Traviglione has in a sense surpassed Leadbetter. Unlike in the AJGA, there's no reluctance here about employing the word *tour*. "I want the students to learn to juggle studies and athletics, just like at college," says Traviglione. His tournaments are open to both academy and non-academy students. There was a dearth of tournaments during the school year in which kids could hone their competitive edge. "Before us, everything was in the summer," explains Mark Plevyak, who runs the tournaments. Competition is weaker than at the premier summer junior events but allows players to obtain performance points and gain entry into the elite AJGA tournaments.

The Hilton Head Academy enrolls150 full-time students and 650 summer campers. Traviglione sold the operation to a private-equity group in spring 2007 for "north of $10 million," though he continues to run it. Gilchrist, who left to form his own academy in Florida, still coaches some of Hilton Head's star pupils. Traviglione has hired Tiger Woods's coach, Hank Haney, to take over the golf teaching side of his business. With financing from his private equity partners, Traviglione hopes to expand the academy model elsewhere in America, notably to California, where he hopes to attract more Asian players. Hilton Head already has many South American students, while Leadbetter's operation in Bradenton has succeeded in wooing more Asian clientele. Asia is on everybody's mind. "The growth possibility for training Chinese and Koreans is immense," Traviglione says. Future academies could be established abroad, in South Africa, Western Europe, or Latin American. "I think we could have five or six locations worldwide without any cannibalization," Traviglione says.

The academy's influence is pervasive in junior golf. At Mirasol, thirteen students in the draw are from Leadbetter Academy and two from the IJGA, making up about a sixth of the total field. Over the past decade the Leadbetter Academy has produced ninety-seven junior All-Americans and seven Players of the Year.

When the Wattses arrived in Florida, Sunee bought a house off campus in Bradenton. She drives Andrea to the academy for her golf lessons in the morning, picks her up for lunch, and takes her to school in the afternoon. "My life consists of carpooling and going to the gym or library to wait for my daughter to finish her lessons," she complains. Bradenton's nearby beaches and suburban strip-mall sprawl offer little solace or culture to a woman accustomed to living in a city surrounded by attractive alpine nature. Florida's aging population shocked her. "My youngest friend there is maybe 60, 70," she admits.

Andrea faced a different sort of challenge. Academics at the academy proved much easier than they were in her Colorado prep school. "In Denver, I'd come home from school at 5:00 p.m. and would have four hours of homework," Andrea recalls. Golf, on the other hand, turned out to be much more difficult than she expected. Like many academy newcomers, she was confronted for the first time with ambitious athletes who practiced harder than she did. At the academy, athletics are not just about fun—they're hard work. After students arrive, they enter a two-week evaluation period wherein they vie to gain entry into the classes with the best players. Classes are divided by ability, and girls and boys are mixed in groups of about a dozen to a teacher. Andrea was placed in the group with the highest-ranking players, including Ivan Lendl's two oldest daughters, seventeen-year-old Marika and fifteen-year-old Isabelle. During the school year, she and other academy students followed a rigorous schedule. Each weekday Sunee woke her at 6:00 a.m. Within three quarters of an hour, mother and daughter were on the road. Around 8:15 a.m., depending on traffic, they rolled through the Leadbetter back gate.

Morning lessons start at 7:45 a.m., but many of the most determined students warm up on the practice green before then, chipping and putting. To Andrea Watts's amazement, Isabelle Lendl arrives before 7:00 a.m. Even though the Lendls live on campus in an I.M.G. townhouse, and Isabelle is only a ten-minute walk from the practice area, Watts is in awe of her work ethic. Andrea and her mom just manage to make the 7:45 a.m. start time. Off the green, the Lendls spend long hours in the gymnasium. For her part, Andrea gets bored lifting weights and working out.

Academy "school" days follow a strict sequence, which is choreographed, videotaped, and analyzed. On Mondays the teachers set up a video camera and record their students hitting balls with a five-iron. Students also hit a ball in front of a launch monitor that clocks the speed at which their club impacts the ball. After filming, teachers and students repair to a screening room to review technique. Using an electronic stylus, the teachers point out swing flaws. With a split screen, they compare the student in question with a famous pro in the same pose, examining posture and downswing planes. Afterward they return to the driving range for a series of exercises. Sometimes students are armed with batonlike devices that have round magnets attached to the shaft, designed to click smoothly on properly executed backswings. In other instances, students are equipped with a baton under their arms designed to reinforce upright posture and a steady swing. On some days students are drilled on chipping, bunker shots, and putting techniques.

By 11:45 a.m., when many students have already hit hundreds of balls, the morning lesson is completed. Students and teachers pile into the academy cafeteria for a buffet-style, protein-rich meal. After lunch they head to Pendleton School, where classroom time is intentionally condensed—no breaks, no study halls, no electives, and no gym.

When courses finish at 3:00 p.m., students return to Leadbetter or to the El Conquistador golf course to practice further, or to lift weights and work out until dinnertime. Once a week, instead of working out or playing golf, students visit a sports psychologist, where they learn to focus on process (making each swing good) rather than results (whether they will birdie or bogey a hole).

Students who board at Leadbetter bunk with seven others in 1,100-square-foot rooms divided into two fluorescent-lit bedrooms. In an adjacent living room there are study carrels and private laptops. Many golfers room with aspiring football, basketball, tennis, soccer, or baseball players. Strict rules prevail. No chewing gum is allowed. No student can leave the campus premises. Pizza can only be ordered with permission. Lights must be shut off at 10:30 p.m. Anyone caught drinking alcohol on or off campus is suspended. Above all, boys and girls can't frequent each others' dorms. Overall, academy life is somewhat monastic. At the IJGA on Hilton Head, most of the older students live on Daufauskie Island and commute by boat to school. Life outside the daily rigors consists of little more than occasional field trips to the Hilton Head mall for IJGA students and the DeSoto Square Mall for the Leadbetter students. Occasional parties are held at a campus swimming pool, and there is a prom in May. "You don't have much of a social life," Andrea admits.

Over the winter, Andrea adapted to the Leadbetter swing motion and the tough academy rhythm. She began hitting the ball long and straight and gained confidence in her game. "My coach doesn't tell me that I can be the next Paula Creamer, only that I have a lot of potential," she says. Her sports psychologist has helped her reestablish her self-confidence and move away from a negative tendency to label. "She teaches me the process to believe in myself," Andrea explains. "I would say this tournament is a difficult tournament because it has this field or this tournament is easy because only certain players are competing," she recalls. "That's bad. You don't want to label a tournament. If you say a tournament is easy, it takes the pressure off and if you say it's hard, it leads you to choke." Alexis Thompson's three-putt temper tantrum during Mirasol's first round is the type of pitfall Andrea hopes to avoid. Her mother is impressed. "Andrea is a different golfer and a different girl since joining the Academy," says Sunee. "She's ready to compete with the best."

Among hardened junior golfers who are consumed by their passion and struggle to explain it to others, Andrea exhibits a rare sense of introspection. Most teenage phenoms respond to questions in shy, monotone fragments. Andrea answers in reflective, thoughtful sentences. Her intelligence and sensitivity are impressive qualities and bode well for a future in many fields. But they may represent a risk in golf.

Whereas others just go out and hit the ball, Andrea thinks long and hard about her shots, a quality that her teachers fear may cause her difficulty. "She can over-intellectualize the game," worries her academy teacher, Tim Sheredy.

During the winter academy students compete against one another. On the weekends many academy students play local golf tournaments, facing off against other juniors and proficient local amateurs to keep up a steady flow of competition. Most of the winter events do not count in the national rankings, nor do the fields count in the country's top non-academy prospects. It's only after school lets out at the end of May that the serious stuff begins. Mirasol is Andrea's first AJGA event of the season, and she sees it as a test of her progress over the winter.

The first two rounds, in which she has demonstrated true prowess, have raised Andrea's expectations and hope. Each day, throughout the eighteen holes, Andrea has been focused and determined. Now, in the third and final round, playing face to face in the final group with Vicky Hurst, her emotional strength will be tested.

Thundershowers are forecast for the Mirasol's final day of competition, and tournament director Gus Montano wakes up early to check his computer screen. According to the weather report, showers will stay away until the afternoon. Montano decides he can avoid bringing start times forward and hopes play will finish before any rain starts. Players are grouped according to their scores in the previous rounds, with the last-place players teeing off first. Andrea Watts and Vicky Hurst, together in the final group along with third-place Elizabeth Alger, tee off on schedule at 8:33 a.m.

Almost no spectators follow the three girls. Mirasol is a stroke event, with each player counting her total shots and the lowest number triumphing. But since Hurst and Watts are several shots in front of other competitors and are playing together in the last group to tee off, the final day of competition turns into a two-person duel resembling match play. Watts starts out steady, parring the first four holes. She bogeys the par-five sixth hole, but recovers to birdie the par-four seventh, and remains a shot ahead of Hurst. Then, on the water-filled, short par-three eighth hole, she hooks her tee shot into the front trap.

Hurst, wearing lime-green shorts and a pink polo shirt, topped by a matching pink tam-o'-shanter, pounces. She strikes an iron straight at the flag. It ends up seven feet to the right of the hole. As ever, Hurst's face shows little emotion. When she reaches the green on the eighth hole, she examines her putt efficiently and knocks it straight in the hole for a birdie. Watts, who has blasted out from the sand, recovers to make a par.

The two girls are tied.

Hurst keeps up the pressure. On the next hole she plugs her drive into the rough, leaving her ball with a difficult, downhill lie. She still needs only a hybrid, a newfangled cross between a fairway wood and a long iron, to reach the fringes of the 455-yard par five's green. "What an athlete," murmurs Larry Alger, the father of the group's third player, Elizabeth Alger. "This is the moment where Vicky stands apart."

Andrea Watts's second shot finds the sand trap in front of the green. Her body, looking relaxed until this moment, stiffens and then sinks into a picture of desperation, her shoulders sagging in distress.

Hurst chips near the hole, leaving herself with an easy uphill putt for a birdie. "That's the sign of a real pro, knowing to keep it below the hole and come back instead of above the hole with a tough downhill putt," says an impressed Alger.

A shaken Watts takes too much sand, her bunker shot is short, and she's left herself with a long putt. She ends with a par. Hurst rolls in her birdie and takes the lead.

On the fifteenth hole, around 1:00 p.m., with a tied score, the sky erupts. Interns mount an impressive tactical retreat, driving players back to the clubhouse, where they eat lunch and bide their time playing cards.

Two-and-a-half hours later Montano spots a clearing in the clouds and orders his platoon of interns back into action. They ferry players back to the exact spots on the course that they left. No practice is allowed. Once everyone arrives, Montano orders play to resume.

Hurst and Watts are on the tee of the sixteenth hole, a 159-yard par three. Both girls are cold and three-putt for bogeys, leaving Hurst a shot ahead, with two to go. As long hitters, Hurst and Watts are each capable of reaching the next hole, a 461-yard par five, in two shots. Hurst tees off straight down the middle of the fairway. But Watts pushes her drive into the right rough, well behind her rival. The player who is farthest from the hole hits first. Watts pulls an iron from her bag, suggesting she will hit a safe shot into the middle of the fairway and go for the green on her third shot. Instead, she suddenly walks away from the ball, returns to her golf bag, and replaces the iron with a fearsome-looking, bulb-headed wood. She aims to reach the green. "Uh oh, she's thinking too much," her mother worries from the sidelines. Almost on cue, Watts pushes her ball right and out of bounds into a protected wetland swamp.

Hurst spots her chance and rockets her second shot onto the green.

After her penalty, Watts hits right of the green and takes two putts for a double bogey seven. Hurst makes an easy birdie and only needs a simple par on the final hole to secure her victory. Watts finishes with another additional bogey, leaving her with a three-over-par 75 total, five strokes behind Hurst.

As the champion walks off the eighteenth green, she displays almost no emotion. Hurst's final-round score of three-under-par 69 gives her an impressive four-under-par 66–71–69: 206 total. When she dueled down the stretch with Watts, she raised the level of her game. "It was kind of weird since we weren't really playing the course, we were playing each other," Hurst says. "I played real steady. I played safe and let the birdies drop."

She admits that she avoided an attack of nerves.

"I get nervous only when I need to give the victory speech," she explains.

Before the awards ceremony, Montano hands Hurst a form with all the names of the people she must thank. A few minutes later, in front of the assembled competitors and parents, he hands her a solid piece of Waterford crystal and tells the audience that it is "a tradition" for the champion to say a few words. Hurst takes the microphone, and, on cue, launches into a series of thank-yous.

Andrea Watts, sitting in the audience with her second-place trophy, looks close to tears. When she regains her composure, she is asked what happened on the course. "I choked," she answers without hesitation. "It was the epitome of choking. I had the choking attitude. I kept saying 'Andrea, you can beat this girl,' but I don't think I really believed it."

A little later, Watts manages to put her defeat in perspective. A year ago she never could have managed to be in the last group of the final round of an AJGA tournament. Thanks to her second-place finish, she now stands number eighty-four on the AJGA's official list of rankings of players, determined by their results in all its tournaments and other major junior events. Within a few weeks, if her momentum continues, she believes she can reach the top ten. After all, she has given a fright to Vicky Hurst, the nation's second-ranked player.

Her year at the Academy has improved her golf game—and raised her expectations. Before moving to Florida, she felt like an outsider among the elite AJGA golfers. She lacked confidence in her swing and her game. She would look around at the other players competing against her in a tournament and say to herself, "I don't belong." Now, after a year at the academy, she hits the ball better than ever and feels much more comfortable in her surroundings. Her improvement has increased both her confidence and the stress she feels. Golf no longer is just a passion. It has become her life.

The following week, Watts will fly back to familiar Colorado surroundings for another AJGA event for girls in the mountains west of Denver. She will continue on to Ohio and Pennsylvania before flying to Tacoma, Washington, for the United States Golf Association's Girls' Junior Open. If she plays well, she hopes to be picked to play for the East team in the Canon Cup, the competition for its All-Stars, and perhaps head to Sweden as a member of the American team for the Junior Solheim Cup.

As the girls embark on their cross-country journey, the best young teenage male golfers will step up to tee. Their destination is Greensboro, North Carolina, for one of the biggest AJGA tournaments of the year, the FootJoy Invitational. FootJoy is one of the half dozen AJGA Invitationals. Unlike a regular AJGA event like Mirasol, no qualifier is held the day before. Players must be invited, and invitations are only given to ninety-nine standouts. Regular AJGA tournaments last three days. Invitationals stretch into a fourth day. Regular AJGA tournaments attract most of their fields from the region. Invitationals lure players from all over the world. If a player aims to catch the eye of a college coach or have a shot at being named Player of the Year, she or he must do well at these elite events.

At the FootJoy, the favorite is a Leadbetter Academy standout named Peter Uihlein.

CHAPTER 5

A Quintuple Bogey

Peter Uihlein displays a confident pose at the
FootJoy Invitation.

SOME KIDS FIGHT their way onto the fairways, and others are es-
corted out onto the smooth, velvet-green golf carpet. The fighters
must battle their way up the elite golf ladder. Their devoted parents
are often willing to do almost anything to help them achieve their goals.
The privileged, in contrast, grow up frequenting the best country clubs
and learning from top-ranked golf teachers. Their parents prepare the
way for stardom. Their path assured, the questions linger whether their
talent will prove sufficient, and above all, whether they will develop
the inner drive and determination to surpass the stage of spoiled brat
and climb to the top.

Ever since early childhood, Peter Uihlein, this year's seventeen-year-
old front-runner to become the boys' Player of the Year, has been
groomed for golf greatness. His mother, Tina, is the daughter of a suburban Washington, D.C., golf pro. His father, Wally, is the CEO of Titleist, the company that sponsors the American Junior Golf Association

(AJGA) and makes the world's most popular golf balls and shoes. In 2005, at sixteen years and three months, he became the third-youngest player ever to capture the Player of the Year award. The next year he stumbled, and a Californian named Philip Francis dominated him. To date, Uihlein has only won second-tier events, never a top-ranked invitational.

Among junior golf connoisseurs, Uihlein's history of cracking under pressure has generated whispers that he is a so-called choke, a player who freezes up on the course. Tim Sheredy, his teacher at the Leadbetter Academy, acknowledges that his star pupil has "an anger issue." A bad shot often causes him to lose concentration or have a temper tantrum that detracts from play. Uihlein admits that he often breaks down under the pressure of being the favorite. "I still don't think I'm the best player out here," he says.

Since Tiger Woods, no boy has equaled his dominance of junior golf. Charles Howell III, now a top Professional Golf Association (PGA) tour player, earned Player of the Year in 1996 and won eight AJGA tournaments, the same number as Woods. But Howell competed for two more years than Tiger. Brian Harmon took Player of the Year in both 2003 and 2004, but he's not even in the top twenty of-all-time AJGA tournament winners and failed to become the number one player at the University of Georgia. After California teenager Francis played a cut above the rest of the field in 2006, he decided to devote his summer to adult amateur and pro tournaments in preparation for his college career at UCLA. Another precocious talent, Rickie Fowler, who has been accepted by Oklahoma State, is doing the same. Their absence leaves Uihlein alone, attempting to prove that he has matured into one of the best-ever junior golfers. "I want to repeat as player of the year," Uihlein tells journalists. "Woods has done it twice, Mickelson three times. My goal is to get in that record book."

Uihlein looks perfect to be cast in the part of the sun-kissed, budding golf star. He sports angelic, all-American features. Wavy blond hair hangs loosely outside his Titleist-labeled caps. At six foot, one inch, his body is filling out into linebacker shape. The Uihleins don't drive to tournaments. They fly. During events, Uihlein and his mother opt for hotels rather than motels. In Florida they live off the Leadbetter campus in a condo that overlooks Sarasota Bay, and Peter drives a sports car to the academy. His motivation to make a name as a golfer is openly Oedipal. "I want to get out of my dad's shadow," he admits.

Even though Wally Uihlein stands several inches shorter than his son, he does cast a long shadow. A small, squat, intense-looking man, the elder Uihlein exudes authority and gravitas. He was not born into money and speaks with a crackly, working-class, stones-in-the-throat Massachusetts accent. He joined Titleist in 1976 as a regional sales representative. Within a year he was named national sales rep; within six years he rose to become the vice president of sales and distribution; and in 2000 he became chairman and chief executive. As the CEO of the AJGA's principal sponsor, he is arguably the most powerful man in junior golf.

Titleist was founded in 1932, when Acushnet Rubber Company's president, Phil Young, missed what he considered a well-stroked putt. Until then, Acushnet had concentrated on supplying rubber to heavy industries. Young was a Massachusetts Institute of Technology graduate and developed a new way to reconstitute rubber waste and scraps into a workable material. After his missed putt, Young took the ball for an X-ray at his dentist's office. The pictures showed him that the ball's core was off-center. He and an MIT friend spent the next three years creating a machine that could wind rubber string around a rubber core in a uniform manner, which led to the development of a "dead center" golf ball that he named Titleist.

Wally Uihlein's loyalty to Titleist was born in a bet. As a teenager, Uihlein worked behind the counter of the Crystal Springs Country Club in his hometown of Haverhill, Massachusetts. A Titleist rep who was always better dressed than the competition entranced him; once Uihlein caught the rep in a small statistical error and corrected him.

"He looked around and said, 'Who said that?'" Uihlein later told *Golf Digest*. "Because challenging Titleist was borderline heresy."

"You wouldn't wanna bet a dozen Titleist balls on that, would you?" the rep asked.

Uihlein accepted the wager and produced the proof. When the Titleist rep asked him what he wanted to do for a living, Uihlein replied without hesitating. "I want your job," he said. Three decades later, under his leadership, Titleist stands at the top of the golf industry, with $1 billion plus in annual sales, making not only Titleist balls, but also FootJoy shoes and Cobra clubs. Its CEO wears monogrammed shirts and gray suits, though headquarters remain in gritty Fairhaven, Massachusetts, a small, smokestack-dotted, quintessential New England hamlet near where Herman Melville set *Moby Dick* and where, Uihlein likes to joke, "We keep Captain Ahab's leg in a freezer."

Peter Uihlein grew up in North Dartmouth, Massachusetts. According to his mother, before he began walking, Peter picked up a Fischer-Price plastic golf club and whacked balls from his stroller. When he was twelve he signed up for his first AJGA tournament. The organization turned him down. Its minimum age at the time was thirteen, though pressure from Uihlein and others soon forced it to be lowered. Uihlein played his first association tournament after his thirteenth birthday and enrolled in the Leadbetter Academy during the same year, so that he could play competitively year-round.

Among other teenagers, Peter projects a fun-loving, slap-me-five persona. Among adults, he often turns shy. He speaks in a high-pitched voice, which elevates in tone when he's asked questions that annoy him. He hesitates to talk about himself. When pressed about his upbringing, he acknowledges something of a mixed bag of privilege and pain. The perks of being the Titleist CEO's son include playing practice rounds with professional golfers and flying in private jets. But when competing in AJGA tournaments, he insists that he receives no favors and plays with the same Titleist clubs available to other junior golfers.

Tina Uihlein, a tall, rail-thin, attractive blonde, follows her son's game closely. During Peter's rounds, she walks ahead of him to spot stray balls in the case of errant shots, and keeps a careful eye on his every move. Wally Uihlein, who has remained in Massachusetts, sees his wife and son about once a month. "Splitting the family is not easy because my husband is in Massachusetts," Tina admits. "But it's something that Peter wanted to do."

Ten times more men than women are fighting to gain entry to the professional tour. Peter Uihlein has played a single men's pro event, the 2006 Traveler's Championship in Hartford, Connecticut, and he failed to come close to making the cut.

Only a few teen boys have tried to jump straight to the pros, and their example offers little comfort. Ty Tryon reached the elite PGA tour at the 2001 national qualifier at the age of seventeen, and Sean O'Hair quit high school at the same age to play mini-tours. As a professional, Tryon missed a combined thirty-three of forty-four cuts in 2002 to 2004 and now surfaces only at mini-tour events. O'Hair spent seven years in oblivion on various mini-tours before reaching the PGA Tour. In 2006 sixteen-year-old Tadd Fujikawa became the youngest player to make a PGA tournament cut in five decades. He turned pro and failed to make the cut for his first two years as a professional. In light of these failures, *Golfweek* editor-in-chief Eric Soderstrom thinks that the pro tour shouldn't accept anyone under the age of eighteen. "No sponsor exemptions, no Monday qualifying, no nothing," he says. "I even want to go as high as 21 years old."

College provides four years of mostly free tutoring and training. Even Tiger Woods attended Stanford for two years before turning pro, and Uihlein has his eye on a scholarship. With his parents' encouragement, he has accepted to play at Oklahoma State starting in the fall of 2008. Oklahoma State has won eight national college golf championships and counts more players—ten—on the PGA Tour than any other school. Former Cowboys—the Oklahoma nickname for its golfers—include pro standouts Charles Howell III, Scott Verplank, and Hunter Mahan. The school's success has paid off, funding the construction of a shrine of a championship golf course called Karsten Creek. In 2006 T. Boone Pickens, a quail-hunting buddy of Oklahoma State's former golf coach, made a record-breaking $165 million donation to the athletic department. Cowboy golfers now travel by private jet to tournaments and enjoy food prepared by a special chef. The present golf coach, Mike McGraw, an intense, hard-working man, runs a military-style outfit. "Oklahoma State is a good fit for Peter, a round peg for a round hole," his father Wally says, explaining his choice. "Peter needs the structure and discipline."

Before heading to college, Uihlein aims to cap his junior career in glory. The FootJoy tournament at the Forrest Oaks Country Club in Greensboro, North Carolina, represents his first big summer test. Three of the five past FootJoy champions who won the tournament ended up as the Player of the Year.

Uihlein has competed in the FootJoy for the five past years, and this will be his final opportunity to capture the title. The event offers him a perfect opportunity to overcome his reputation for choking. The year before, Uihlein birdied the first two holes on his final round and jumped into the lead. Going into the last hole of the final round, he was tied at ten under par with fifteen-year-old Andrew Yun. The challenger was a serious underdog and felt no pressure. "I was laughing the whole time," Yun said. "I was just having fun." Yun, playing one group ahead of Uihlein, drove down the middle of the fairway. His second shot, a 186-yard four-iron, ended fifteen feet from the pin, and his putt caught the left lip of the cup, falling in for a birdie and a one-shot lead.

Uihlein heard the cheers from the eighteenth green and drilled a perfect drive. His second shot mirrored Yun's approach and offered a birdie putt from a similar location. But his putt rolled just left of the cup. The par left him a shot behind, in second place. Ever since, Uihlein has obsessed about that miss. He wants to prove that he has the nerves to make the big shot at the right moment, to sink the pressure-filled final putt on the final green, overcome the stress of being the favorite, and seal his reputation as America's top-ranked male junior golfer.

———

Nestled in the gently rolling, wooded North Carolina lowlands just south of Greensboro, Forest Oaks Country Club looks uncannily like the clean-cut backdrop to *Leave It to Beaver*. Formerly a tobacco and dairy farm, the property is now flanked by large, two-story colonials and single-level ranch houses. Forest Oaks has eight tennis courts and two swimming pools. "We are a family place," general manager Roger Doyle says.

North Carolina, where many courses are open year-round, is golf country. The famed Pinehurst resort is only about an hour south of Forest Oaks by car. Wake Forest, North Carolina, Duke, and a number of other local colleges boast strong varsity golf teams. Forest Hills's golf course hosts one of the PGA's longest-running events, originally called the Chrysler Classic, and, after the car company dropped the sponsorship, named the Wyndham Championship. In 2006 some 50,000 spectators showed up on the tournament's final Sunday.

Originally built in 1963, the club's golf course was redesigned three decades later by AJGA alumnus and PGA tour player Davis Love III. Love re-sprigged fairways with Tift Sport Bermuda grass, which handles the extremes of summer heat and winter wetness. More important, he toughened the course's defenses, lengthening the layout by more than 500 yards, to 7,280 yards. Instead of attacking greens with simple wedges, even the most advanced players require longer irons. Originally, Forest Hills was a gentle, open layout, with fairways framed only by a few sand bunkers and a few oak trees that blocked few shots. Players felt as if they were rambling through a well-manicured park. Love planted wild fescue along many fairways. The tan-colored, tall, stringy shoots provide a ferocious, jungle-like framing to many holes— and, since balls are almost impossible to find in the deep underbrush— they gobble up errant shots. If players manage to avoid this danger, they are left attacking greens that are perched on the top of a defensive ridge. Instead of allowing iron shots to roll on the green, these false fronts repel balls, blocking them from reaching the flags and requiring players to land and stop their shots with the utmost precision. In addition, Love added difficult-to-read contours and curves to the greens. Many putts now require stinging the ball up a hill to reach the pin, or conversely, caressing it down a slope. Instead of the regulation two putts, these variations turn many greens into potential three-putt minefields. At the FootJoy invitational elite, juniors will play the same course as the adult pros, with a single exception—the sixteenth hole. During the pro tournament, police shut down a road running through the course, forcing players to hit over it and stretching the par four to 467 yards. The police have refused to shut the road for the juniors, so they will play the hole at a short 414 yards.

North Carolina is suffering from a drought that has left fairways dry and kept the rough at a thin two inches. Dry fairways lengthen drives and leave short irons for second shots. Slow greens allow players to fire at the flags because they can stop their balls. "The rough isn't as penal as I would like, and the fairways are going to give a lot of roll," course superintendent Geoffrey Dail worries. He refrains from shaving the grass on the greens for fear that it will burn out later in the summer. Davis Love won the adult tour event the previous year with a four-round total of sixteen under par. The course record is 63. If the weather for the tournament proves fair, the superintendent t fears a mere teenager could challenge those low scores. "I've been watching these kids out on the practice range and they hit it amazing, absolutely amazing," Dail says.

On the FootJoy's opening day, a thick fog covers Forest Oaks, forcing an hour delay to tee offs. The sun appears only around 9:00 a.m., and as the day continues, temperatures rise into the 90s, with humidity climbing. The fairways are rolling well, and the greens are running slow. For this initial round, tournament officials have placed the flags in their easiest positions. The placement of flags varies each day and accounts for much of a course's difficulty. When put in the center of the green, they offer players a direct shot. When placed at the front of the green, or back in the corners, competitors must be prudent. A slight miss will result in the ball heading one minute toward the flag and the next backing off into the sand or rough. On the competition's opening day, the flags are flying from easy, central positions, and the superintendents' worst fears are confirmed. Of the ninety-nine entrants, twenty-nine shoot under par. "They're shooting darts," Dail observes.

Tournament favorite Uihlein produces the first round's biggest surprise. On the par-five, second hole, he reaches the fringe of the green in two shots, chips close, and picks up an easy birdie. He birdies the short par-four sixth hole and arrives at the ninth hole, another par five, with his score at a comfortable two under par. For him and other top players, Forest Oaks's par fives are reachable in two shots, making them good birdie opportunities. But Uihlein tees off far right, into the bushes. When he attempts to chip out into the fairway, he fails to extricate his ball from the intrusive greenery. His second chip touches a tree branch and bounces back onto his golf bag—a two-shot penalty. On his next shot, he caroms his three wood left, giving it a high-arcing trajectory. It takes him another chip to reach the green and two putts to put the ball in the hole.

A bogey, just one over par, represents a disappointment to golfers of Uihlein's level. A double bogey, two over par, signals a catastrophic failure of concentration. A triple bogey is such a damaging stroke that most golfers never can claw back into contention in an AJGA event after committing one. Uihlein closes the ninth hole with a five-over-par quintuple bogey ten. It's his worst score for a single hole in his entire career.

Yet in the face of disastrous play, Uihlein remains remarkably poised. He redoubles his concentration and recovers on the next hole with a birdie. For the entire round, he records thirteen pars and four birdies. Despite the quintuple bogey, his first-round total remains a respectable 73, putting him in a tie for forty-fourth place. When Uihlein arrives in the scoring tent, he sits down and asks, "Hey, did you hear about what I did on number nine?" The scorer shakes her head no. Uihlein chuckles, before offering up the details of his catastrophe.

"It's funny, really," he insists.

———

After the FootJoy's first day of play, sixteen-year-old Cody Gribble leads the tournament, eight shots ahead of Uihlein. Gribble carded a flawless seven-under-par 65. His round starts with four birdies out of the first eight holes. On the par-five thirteenth hole, pitching from about fifty yards from the pin, he manages to get the ball up over the false front mound in front of the green, but still leaves himself a thirty foot putt. He sinks it for a birdie. He walks up the final fairway tied for the lead, facing another long putt. His ball starts off straight and breaks to the right in the last five feet, falling for another birdie. "I wasn't trying to make it, just give it a chance," he admits afterward. "When I saw it drop, I thought, 'Awesome'."

Gribble lives in the Dallas suburb of Highland Park and plays the part of the good ol' Southern boy to perfection. "We're just bubbas," his father, Bill Gribble, offers by way of explanation—the pejorative Texas term for talkative, uneducated, white, working-class men. The

Gribbles actually do not hail from the dry, hardscrabble Texas plains. They don't dig oil, they don't corral cattle, and they are far from poor. Bill Gribble is a fund manager with such high-profile neighbors as the celebrated financial raider and Oklahoma State University financial benefactor T. Boone Pickens. Cody Gribble, for all his Southern accent and charm, trains at a fancy local country club. Randy Smith, the teacher of well-known Texas professionals Justin Leonard and Hunter Mahan, has given Gribble three lessons a month since he was seven years old.

When Gribble was twelve, he quit playing football to concentrate on golf. "I knew I was going to get hurt if I kept trying to battle it out with those big boys," he says. Of modest build, about five foot, nine inches, Cody sports curly light brown hair, a genial smart-ass twinkle in his eyes, and a crooked but welcoming smile. He is polite and considerate, both to the other players and to their parents. "He's no Einstein, but he certainly has a silver tongue," his father stresses.

Like most other junior boy golfers, Gribble's dad serves as his mentor and financial and emotional support system. He encouraged his son to pick up the game, handing him a club to hit wiffle balls in the backyard. Although Gribble grew up as a natural right-hander, he followed pro golfer Phil Mickelson's example and started hitting golf balls left-handed. Even now, he mimics Mickelson with the ability to make the ball draw, swerving left to right, and fade, right to left. "If I play bad, there are a few fights," Cody admits. "My dad is just trying to help me, but it pisses me off." Cody's mom, who remains in Texas with Cody's little sister during the FootJoy, attends tournaments sporadically. The Gribbles never considered moving to Florida or packing off their oldest boy to attend Leadbetter Academy. "Cody is my best buddy and I could never send away my best buddy," Bill Gribble explains.

Gribble, like Peter Uihlein, is a work in progress. The Texan has a habit of making many birdies—and many bogeys. During the previous season he won two events, plus the 2006 Texas State Amateur Championship. It was his first State Amateur, and he was among the youngest of the 144 players. He finished his round strong with four shots under par over the final five holes for a stunning total of 64. When he's on, Gribble is masterful. When he's off, he sprays balls around the course. His swing, normally a picture of flowing grace, breaks down and develops a damaging little wiggle when the club reaches the top of its backswing.

This weakness helps explain why, following his blazing first round, Gribble is careful to avoid overconfidence. He has never captured an invitational. Unlike regular AJGA tournaments, which last three rounds, the FootJoy tests endurance through four grueling days. "It's a marathon," Gribble warns.

He knows that to win he must limit his mental and physical errors. His first round offers some promising signs of progress. On Forest Hills's short par-four sixteenth hole, Gribble's second shot requires a simple, short downhill pitch. The pin, perched at the back of the green, gives him room to roll his ball. In the past, the aggressive Gribble would have fired at the flag, risking a shot that flies over the green and leaves an almost impossible recovery. This time he plays cautiously, leaving the ball at the front of the green. Although too far from the hole for a legitimate chance at a birdie, he earns an easy par. "I'm much more mature than I was a year ago," he says afterward, pointing to his conservative play on the hole.

When playing, Gribble looks anything but conservative. He dresses in bright electric yellows, reds, oranges, and blues. "I like to have fun, and that's a big reason that I'm relaxed on the course," he explains. Golf clothing has gone through ups and downs—literally—through the ages. In the 1700s elaborate coats and hats were common for golfers. Well into the twentieth century, men sported a collared shirt, tie, sweater, and slacks. Bing Crosby wore a fedora on the fairways. Another popular 1930s look, perfected by superstar Bobby Jones, consisted of cropped pants and a sweater over a shirt and tic. Short-sleeved polo shirts, paired with slacks and golf shoes, became a staple on the greens in the 1960s, explaining why writers mocked golf attire for its preppy and prissy stripes, baggy fit, loud plaids, and clashing colors.

Under Tiger Woods's influence, golf clothes have become hip. These days, golf attire can be worn straight from the course to a nice restaurant. There's a new emphasis on performance fabrics and technology. Knits are embedded with moisture-control technology, sweaters have been treated to repel water, and outerwear has become rain-and-wind resistant. Shirts and shorts come with Lycra added for extra comfort. Big-name designers ranging from Calvin Klein to Stella McCartney are putting out collections of sleek tailored golf clothes.

Woods himself replaced collared cotton polo shirts with sleek, collarless shirts developed by Nike. Nike Golf sponsors several junior golfers, Gribble among them. Before every tournament, the company sends him a new set of clothes that cater to his palette. Nike's junior golf field rep, Travis Thompson, is attending the FootJoy tournament, seeing what fashions are popular and eyeing which juniors he wants to sponsor. Although Nike, the world's largest sporting goods company, sponsors Gribble, and of course, Tiger Woods, rival Titleist surpasses it as an equipment supplier to elite golfers. Among young golfers, too, "Titleist is the 400-pound gorilla," Thompson complains.

As one of the AJGA's main sponsors, Titleist has sent two representatives to FootJoy. They set up a stand on the practice tee, where they let the players try out the company's newest drivers and irons. Only players and their parents are allowed near the testing center, and the Titleist representatives refuse to talk about their work. "We don't want to give away our strategy by talking about it," explains Wally Uihlein. Titleist gives promising juniors caps, balls, clubs, and shoes, all free of charge. Outfitting an ambitious junior golfer is an expensive proposition. Sets of Titleist irons retail for $800 or more, and a single Titleist driver, the type with a fancy steel grille and shiny, space age, titanium head, go for up to $500. A box of a dozen souped-up Titleist Pro Vs costs $45. And the equipment matters. When *Golf Magazine* compared a golfer hitting a Titleist Pro V with a new titanium melon-shaped 460-centimeter large driver and a golfer using a hickory-shafted model used a century ago, the average drive with new equipment carried fifty yards longer. When the tester used a generation-old ball, the modern driver smacked the ball almost twice as far as the antique.

Until recently, elite juniors could not take free equipment out of fear of forfeiting their amateur status. In an effort to encourage players from low income families, the United States Golf Association (USGA) and the National Collegiate Athletic Association (NCAA) have loosened the rules so junior golfers can be reimbursed for expenses at tournaments, and many receive free equipment—provided they refrain from selling it or participating in any company advertisements. Although the new rules have done little to increase minority participation, they have launched an expensive race to nab equipment freebies. Ray Popeck estimates that his son John, who is playing in the FootJoy, receives as much as $10,000 worth of clubs and clothes a year from Titleist.

Top-ranked junior golfers do not buy clubs off the rack—they use clubs that are hand fitted and assembled like haute couture. When the Popecks visited San Diego for a tournament the previous year, they also took the time to visit the Titleist fitting center. Technicians measured the correct angle to place the club's blade on the shaft. They clocked Popeck's clubhead speed so they could choose the correct weight and flexibility for the shafts. Weekend duffers struggle with "cavity" irons, which benefit from a round, curved shape that has a wide sweet spot and is forgiving for poor hits. Hotshot kids crave "blades," sharp, flat-headed irons that are hard to hit but allow them to put special spin and control on their shots. Many teenage golfers need to change their clubs two or three times a year, altering the stiffness of their shafts and the weights of their heads to match their growing bodies, or simply to take advantage of updated technology. "Without Titleist, I don't know if we could be here," says a grateful Popeck. For most top junior boys, the fashion of their clubs is much more important than the style of their clothes. Gribble is an exception among the boys, choosing Nike over Titleist, primarily for their clothes rather than their clubs.

———

If Cody Gribble seems relaxed on and off the course, it is not just because of his Nike sponsorship and good fashion sense. It's also because his path forward is well marked in comparison to some of his competitors. Although only a sixteen-year-old high school sophomore, he has already committed to the University of Texas in Austin. His decision has sparked a notable trend to earlier and earlier college choices. At FootJoy, roughly half of the ninety-nine boys competing have already signed with a university.

Officially, recruits are allowed to sign up with a college only in November of their senior year in high school. No commitment is legally valid until coaches receive a recruit's signed paper of intent. In recent years, however, coaches and students have begun to strike earlier, informal arrangements. "It's like everything else in our society —we accelerate the process," Oklahoma State men's golf coach Mike McGraw explains. Both sides are careful about the informal deals. After a coach and player agree, the player is loath to back out, for fear of jeopardizing his or her reputation. The danger for students is that the coach who recruits them early might leave in the interim. Recruiters bombard teen golfers. Cameron Peck, a fifteen-year-old from Tacoma, Washington, who is competing at FootJoy, has already begun visiting colleges. His first choice, after visiting Las Vegas and seeing how golfers had their own chef, dorms, and access to wonderful courses, is the University of Las Vegas. "I tell him there's more to college—there's also the education," his father grumbles. Jim Peck, who wants his son to study engineering, finds it difficult to combine academic achievement with golfing prowess. The Pecks—he is a computer technician and his wife is an accountant for the state of Washington—cannot afford the Leadbetter and disapprove of the academy model's skimpy academics. To play in the FootJoy, Cameron had to skip school just before his exams. When he returns to his hometown, he'll head to school an hour early each day and stay an hour after classes, to make up for the materials he has missed. The Pecks will not even consider the possibility of their child turning pro out of high school. "The girls can go pro, but not the boys—they're not ready," Jim Peck says. "College golf is the best mini tour possible—and it's free."

At the FootJoy tournament, some thirty college coaches are recruiting. College coaches attend most AJGA events, but they converge on invitationals like pilgrims flocking to see the pope. Most big-time college recruiters are present at Forest Oaks—Oklahoma State, Florida, Georgia, Duke, Texas Tech, and Texas. On the course, coaches can decipher players' graduation dates based on the color of their bag tags. During rounds, the recruiters walk along the fairways, observing players, sometimes taking out a little notebook to record a judgment. And they are not just looking at how the players hit the ball. "We're watching little things, how they interact with their parents, their playing partners—all the things that show character," says Duke's assistant men's coach, Brad Sparling. "Remember, we have to live with these kids for four years in college." For most coaches like Sparling, recruiting is a near full-time job during the summer. Coaches will travel nearly as much as the top junior golfers, attempting to entice the best to their schools. If they succeed, their teams will win and their jobs will be secure. If they fail, they are at risk. "It's like buying a car—you don't put down the big check after only one look," says University of Illinois coach Mike Small.

Such cutthroat recruiting is a recent phenomenon. Before the AJGA existed, most college golf coaches went on vacation during the summer, and they attended two or three tournaments a year. The majority of their recruiting was conducted "from behind a desk, with letters or phone calls," says *Golfweek* editor-in-chief Eric Soderstrom. Oklahoma State managed to transform itself into a college golf superpower in large part because then golf coach Mike Holder became one of the first coaches to attend AJGA events and attract its best players. Oklahoma State signed seven of the first nine boy Players of the Year.

Today, the AJGA dominates college recruiting. According to a 2005 study, almost two-thirds of Division I men's golf participants and almost half of Division I women came from its ranks. After each tournament, the organization sends the results to the coaches and offers them access to an extensive Web database, "Coaches Corner," which provides past results and detailed contact information.

While many coaches applaud the creation of a one-stop shop for spotting the best young players, others complain it has professionalized and pressured the process. For decades, coaches had limited access to watching prospective recruits. Now, many complain that they end up viewing the same small group of teenagers over and over. They must bombard the prospects with letters about what a fine-looking swing they have and about all the goodies that can come with picking their university, the sparkling practice pitches, the shimmering championship courses, the restaurants just for the golf team, and yes, even the private jets they will use to hop around the country to tournaments. They rush to nab the best players before they have matured as students or athletes. "I think recruiting earlier and earlier is dangerous," says Jamie Green, men's golf coach at University of North Carolina at Charlotte. "The kids can change so much." Coming from a smaller, less-well known golf school than Duke or Wake Forest, Green has little chance to sign the most celebrated recruits early and prefers anyhow to wait until they are closer to graduation, after they have visited and met their future teammates. His star Corey Nagy, became an honorable mention All-American in 2006, after signing to attend Charlotte only after his high school graduation.

For some less-privileged competitors, the pressure to choose a college is financial. Wesley Graham, the third-ranked Polo boy junior and a legitimate contender for the FootJoy title, shoots a disappointing 72 in the first round, tying for twenty-ninth place. He comes from a middle-class family in Port Orange—his father is a car salesman—and the Grahams are emptying their savings account to allow their son to play a full junior schedule this summer. His mother Tammy rationalizes the decision by saying that her son looks set to win a full scholarship to college and be able to continue his golf education free of charge. "When you work that hard, how can you tell him that you can't go for it?" she wonders aloud. "He is our only child. You dig deep and let him have this summer. He earned it." Graham is one of the longest juniors off the tee and has some of the best touch near the greens. Since starting to play AJGA tournaments a year ago, he never has finished below tenth place. Yet Graham starts his first round at the FootJoy with a bogey on the easy starting hole and finishes with another bogey. The rest of his rounds will follow a similar script: 74, 75, and 73. He ends in fifty-second place, blaming the pressure of college recruiting for his poor performance. "A bunch of people say that when they are getting ready to announce about college," Graham said. "They are right."

For well-off competitors such as Uihlein, the pressure over the choice of college stems less from finances than from choosing the right athletic training ground. The four years at school allow players to hone their game and prepare for the PGA Tour. Some colleges, including Oklahoma State, enjoy a reputation for producing pros; an opportunity to play there increases the odds of eventually making a good living from the sport. With so much at stake for both coaches and players, it's understandable how a recruiting arms race has erupted.

The NCAA has attempted to impose a cease-fire. Each year, it publishes rules of conduct prohibiting direct contacts with high school sophomores and juniors. Coaches may have direct contact with students only after they finish their junior year of high school, and even then, only after July 1. June is mandated as a "dead" period. During the FootJoy tournament, this decree prohibits coaches from talking to contestants. "We may say hello, but if they continue the conversation, we have to walk away," says McGraw, the Oklahoma State coach. An illegal direct contact is defined as "any face-to-face encounter between a prospect or the prospect's parents, relatives or legal guardian(s) and an institutional staff member or athletics representative during which any dialogue occurs in excess of an exchange of a greeting." If a sophomore or junior student e-mails a coach or leaves a message on the coach's answering machine, the coach is forbidden to respond. If a student succeeds in getting the coach on the telephone, however, the two are permitted to speak.

Designed to protect students from harassment, particularly the most-sought-after football and basketball recruits, the NCAA's complex rules end up frustrating both sides. At the FootJoy tournament, players and coaches participate in an elaborate performance: players pretend not to see the coaches and coaches slink along the fairways, observing and judging, without opening their mouths. Neither side interacts and the players must stay on their best behavior. "We used to throw clubs and get red in the face and slap ourselves," recalls Robin Walton, the assistant woman's golf coach at the University of Florida and a twenty-year veteran tour player who scouts at junior tournaments. "You don't see these kids losing their cool." It's a big change from her childhood in the state of Washington. "There were maybe one or two tournaments a year with as much pressure as this," she says.

Walton doesn't think the junior golfers themselves have changed, more that their expectations have shifted. "They are on a faster track," she observes.

Fast-tracked teens may be prodigies, but kids are kids. Before the second day of play at FootJoy, scorers warn players to avoid peeing in the woods. Some club members have complained. Any unauthorized trip to the bathroom during a round will result in a penalty stroke.

Leader Cody Gribble is progressing nicely. Despite a bogey on the opening hole, he reaches the thirteenth at two under par. The next hole tests his mental toughness. He reaches the green in two regulation shots, takes a putt, places a small pin to mark the ball, and cleans it. When he replaces the ball on the green, it seems to inch forward just before he strokes it in. "Right before I was about to hit it, it looked like the ball moved," he said later. "I could no longer see the Nike 4 label on top of the ball. It felt kind of weird, a little different, like it oscillated."

It is easy to understand why Gribble is frightened. If he did hit a moving ball, he faces a two-stroke penalty. All FootJoy competitors are paired with two other golfers in groups, and he asks his partners for their opinion.

"Don't worry about it," they tell him.

But Gribble frets. He calls a penalty on himself and putts a second provisional ball. Through the end of the round, he does not know if he has scored a par or a double bogey. When he finishes his round, his shoulders are slumped and his face is long. In the scoring tent, he asks to talk with a rules official. The official questions Gribbles' playing partners, who say the ball did not move and accepts their explanation. "It's a par," he judges.

Although a relieved Gribble and his certified two-under-par 70 remain in the lead by a shot with a two round total of nine under par, he is stressed over his performance. Neither his shot making nor his putting was sharp, and he acknowledges some nervousness "I was leaking a little oil today," he says. "I've never had the lead in a major tournament like this before, so I guess I'm in new territory. I just have to loosen up tomorrow."

Several players threaten Gribble's lead. His first challenger, Mu Hu, the first young Chinese golfer to come to America to master his sport, sees himself as a pioneer. Born in Shenzhen, near Hong Kong, Mu was only eleven years old when he won the fifteen- to eighteen-year-old division at the 2001 China Junior Golf Open. Later that same year he moved to the United States for schooling at the academy in Bradenton. His father, a businessman, has remained in China. His mother Jenny lives with him in Florida and travels with him to tournaments. When he arrived in the United States, Hu's English was poor, but the Leadbetter Academy was great for golf, and it wasn't long before Hu learned English and made friends. As he integrated within his new culture, he impressed his teachers. "Mu is technically advanced for his age and a quick learner," Leadbetter says. "He's also a good swing imitator. His Tiger [Woods] is first rate, and he does a mean Vijay [Singh, another star pro golfer]—right down to the distinctive high-hands finish."

At Leadbetter's invitation, mother and son left the academy in Bradenton for Orlando, so that he could train directly with the guru. It is rare that Leadbetter himself offers to give juniors a lesson. Most of his teaching hours are taken by counseling tour professionals. "It was great at the Academy with all the kids, but if I would go to Orlando, Leadbetter said he would teach me and you can't resist that," Mu said. Hu enrolled in a public high school. His natural shyness receded and his golf scores fell. He now still speaks idiomatic English in soft, calm tones, and could be mistaken for a native-born American, except that he remains first and foremost Chinese. "I came to the United States to learn golf, nothing else," he insists. "If it was not for golf, I would go back to China."

The seventeen-year-old Hu already packs star power in his homeland, returning two to three times a year to burnish his budding image. During the 2007 Shanghai Open, he outscored Tiger Woods in the first round, only to collapse during the second round and miss the cut for the final weekend. After finishing his junior career, Hu plans to attend the University of Florida. His parents will return home to China. "He will be a man, able to take care of himself," his mother Jenny says. If he makes the PGA Tour, he will stay in the United States. If he fails, he will try to play the European tour, which also runs tournaments in Asia.

Day by day, round by round, Hu's confidence mounts. On FootJoy's first day, he fires a stunning 66. On the second day, he keeps up with a 71, including a long birdie putt on the final hole. This puts him at seven under par and in second place. He is satisfied. "I grinded throughout the entire day," he says. "I didn't hit the ball well and I still scored well." Even though the squat Chinese player stands several inches shorter than his main American competitor, Uihlein, he hits the ball just as far. Regular physical training has strengthened his legs and firmed his abdomen. "I speak English now. My swing has gotten a lot more in control. I have way more experience playing AJGA tournaments," he says after his second round. "Now when I am playing bad, one good shot can get me back into good form. That's experience."

Even though they hail from half a world apart, Peter Uihlein and Mu Hu have a good deal in common. Both are the sons of self-made men. Both train full-year in Florida. In that sense, they fit the common mold of AJGA players. But a few contenders grow up in less-rarified circumstances. One is Titleist-sponsored John Popeck from Washington, Pennsylvania. Popeck started the tournament with a solid 69 and followed with a second-round 68, leaving him two shots off the lead. The Pennsylvania hopeful is delighted with his new "baby," a sparkling Titleist 907D2, a $400 bulb-headed driver, with which he claims he cannot miss a fairway.

John Popeck wants to show those fancy Floridians that he belongs. He frowns as he makes his way down the fairways. Despite his stylish clothes, the staccato tempo and the sharp vowels of his speech give away his less-than-rarefied background. Within the junior golf's rarified ranks, the Popecks consider themselves, with some reason, gritty, working-class outsiders. "We're hicks," Ray acknowledges with a chuckle.

Ray Popeck's father's family emigrated from Poland and originally worked in the steel mills. Ray escaped Washington's decline by training as an accountant. He's a partner in a local firm, an articulate man with a straightforward Pennsylvania accent. Washington is a place where residents dig deep roots, and the Popecks insist they will never leave. Pittsburgh, Ray says, is too big, too crowded. "Sandy and I grew up in Washington," he explains. In town, he seems to know everybody, greeting each of them with a genial "Howdy, how are you doing?"

Philadelphia and Pittsburgh are home to fancy country clubs, Merion and Oakmont, which host the country's most prestigious professional tournament, the United States Open. Elsewhere in Pennsylvania, the sport is played in less rarified air. The Popecks belong to The Golf Club of Washington. Despite the fancy moniker, it's a modest affair, a nine-hole course squeezed in by Interstate 79 on one side and sliced in two by an access road. Golfers must hit their drives on the first hole over the road. Tees are placed in different areas to allow some variety when playing a second set of nine holes. Ray Popeck's father taught him golf, and Ray taught John. To this day, father and son play together. When John Popeck was eight years old, his father took him to see local driving range golf pro Bill Kurz. From the start, the two got along, like a grandfather with his prized grandchild. Little Popeck "was a natural," Kurz recalled. Many kids are born with a fluid golf swing. Popeck's determination distinguished him from other youngsters. "He has the eye of the tiger, the will to win," Kurz says. The gentle, sixty-six-year-old, silver-haired Kurz remains Popeck's coach. Kurz shares both the highs and lows of raising a teenage talent, and projects some of his own lost fairway dreams through his star student. "I want to see John walking up the eighteenth hole at the United States Open," Kurz says.

Both the coach's and the player's dream remains a long shot. Although John Popeck has grown into a solid six-footer who hits the ball as far as any junior golfer, he faces stiff competition from the academy-trained players. Neither he nor his coach can remember the last Pennsylvania golfer who was recruited to a major college. "Leadbetter produces robots—they all hit the ball the same way" Ray Popeck insists. "Bill Kurz sculpts individuals." During his young career, Popeck has won almost every local junior golf tournament. He has qualified three times for the United States Junior Amateur event. But he has never won a major junior event, and he plays with an overly aggressive, swashbuckling style, almost as if he wants to punch the little golf ball inside a boxing ring. He smacks his drives, knocks his irons, and whacks even his putts. When they fall, they knock against the back of the hole. When they miss, they shoot past by at least several feet. The gritty Popeck needs to learn to calm down and caress the ball, particularly when pressure mounts. "John just hasn't broken through yet," his father acknowledges.

During the winter, Popeck is one of the few top junior golfers to compete at a high level in another sport, in his case, basketball. He came close to all-state as a junior, scoring more than fifty points in two games in the state finals, and was named most valuable player. Basketball keeps him in shape, and his exceptional athleticism helps explain how he has overcome his handicaps to reach the top echelons of junior golf.

After golf courses in Pennsylvania close, however, Popeck practices only once a week at an indoor facility in Pittsburgh, where he can only chip and hit short irons. There's not enough room to smack 300-yard drives. The cold 2007 winter only allowed him to get back on the course in mid-April. When the fairways thaw, he comes out of hibernation and tries to make up for lost time by spending entire days playing. During the summer, he will arrive at 8:00 a.m. and stay until sunset, playing upwards of thirty-six holes a day. Sometimes he takes a couple of bites of dinner and continues on. He once completed a total sixty-three holes in a day. "We would have kept on going, but it finally got dark," Popeck says. On one memorable day, he crushed the course record by shooting an eleven-under-par 60. He downed two eagles and seven birdies, shooting 30 on both the front and back nines.

The Popecks spend tens of thousands of dollars a year on John's golf, even though they try to save as much as possible. They drive their silver Toyota Camry back and forth from golf tournaments. If John does not make the cut after two days, they can return home right away. With a flight, they are obliged to stay around and pay for a hotel room and restaurants, until the end of the tournament. The Popecks drove close to ten hours straight on the highway to North Carolina, and they're tired. But with John playing well, at least they don't have to head back north right away. Maybe the FootJoy will be his big, long-awaited breakthrough.

After two days of hot, humid weather, clouds and drizzle greet the competitors and end the streak of low scores. During the dry first two rounds, balls rolled along the hard fairways. Both long and short hitters needed only two shots to reach the green of the 555-yard, par-five fifteenth hole. During the third round, the wet fairway forces almost all players to use three shots to get to the green.

Only four players break 70 in the third round. Chinese hopeful Mu Hu drops out of the running, shooting a poor 76, which he blames on bad putting. Leader Cody Gribble misses a short putt on the par-three seventeenth and finishes with a two-over-par 74. "I just couldn't get anything started," he says. Gribble falls to second place, a shot behind John Popeck, who notches three successive birdies on holes five, six, and seven and ends with a one-under-par 71. "I just hope I can put another good round together tomorrow, keep my head on straight and play steady," Popeck says. "I'd be jumping for joy if I win."

Peter Uihlein once again provides the round's biggest surprise. After a 66 in the second round, he keeps up the pressure with a third-round 70, leaving him tied for second place at seven under par.

"Did you ever feel out of it after your quintuple bogey?" a journalist asks.

"No, if I can't give up five shots to the field, I shouldn't be here," he insists. "I had 54 holes and I was only eight back."

When play finishes for the day, the scoreboard looks crammed: a half-dozen players are stacked within a few shots of the top and feel they have good a chance at winning. "The final round is going to be a crapshoot," Ray Popeck predicts.

Tournament organizers reserve the toughest pin placements for the decisive, fourth day. No flag is set more than six feet from the edge of the green. Officials perch the pin on the fifteenth hole on the top of the ridge, at the beginning of the green. Anyone who dares to fire at the hole risks one of the most depressing sights in golf: watching his ball land on the green tantalizingly close to its target, only to retreat back down a hill into the fairway. Smart players aim for the middle of the green, even though this tactic leaves two long putts just for par.

Cody Gribble stumbles right out of the starting blocks, bogeying the easy second and third holes. Bill Gribble starts to slouch along the fairways as he watches his son lose composure. On the twelfth hole, a 189-yard par three, Cody shanks a five-iron: instead of flying forward, his ball veers almost straight right into the woods and out of bounds. Gribble buries his head in his yellow cap and lets out a poignant Texas-infused squeal, "Gawd dang it!" Gribble hits a second ball and ends with a double bogey five. As the round progresses, Gribble's swing becomes looser. "Uhhh, oh, he's got that little wiggle on top of his backswing," his worried father laments on the sidelines. Gribble finishes with a five-over-par 77, and ties for twenty-first place.

John Popeck is the next front-runner to falter. On both the tenth and eleventh holes, he misses short par puts. Popeck chips his ball into the false front on the par-five thirteenth, and it rolls back into the fairway. He takes a bogey on the hole, ends with a 77, and ties for nineteenth place.

As the leaders come unstuck, an unknown named David Sanders races forward with a string of birdies. The seventeen-year-old Sanders hails from Mount Laurel, New Jersey. He has spent the last year at the International Junior Golf Academy on Hilton Head, and this is his first season playing elite junior golf. Sanders does not look the part of a Tiger wannabe: he is middling in size and somewhat squat. His swing—a series of semi-jerky mechanical motions—looks clunky, but Sanders displays a rare dedication to the game. The son of a Korean mother and an American father, he began hitting balls almost as soon as he could walk, and scored a 92 at age four on an eighteen-hole shortened "executive" course, according to his father. Sanders enjoys playing tournaments and over the past winter has competed in an almost unheard of thirty-four events. "He's just a competitor, a winner," says his Hilton Head teacher, Matt Fields, who has followed Sanders to Greensboro to assist him. There's a fearlessness about Sanders verging on recklessness. He steps up to the ball and hits. Fields has been working with him to slow down and weigh each shot's options.

Starting out in the fourth and final round, Sanders is tied for sixth place at five under par. He birdies the tenth hole to go two under for the day and seven under for the tournament. On the par-five fifteenth, with the flag placed right at the dangerous front edge, Sanders caresses an open-faced, 52-degree gap wedge from ninety yards just beyond the flag. Instead of retreating back down the hill, it heads straight into the cup for an eagle. He drops to nine under par and surges into a tie for the lead with Peter Uihlein.

In contrast to the aggressive Sanders, former Player of the Year Uihlein chooses a conservative approach and starts with six consecutive pars. He birdies the seventh, a par four, only to bogey the following hole. "My strategy was to hit to the center of the green and make pars and to make sure that they come after you," Uihlein says. "I feel like I did that all right." Even as the pressure mounts on the final nine holes, Uihlein remains calm and controlled, continuing to aim at the center of green. He pars all the par threes and fours and reaches the two par fives in two shots for tap-in birdies.

Sanders, one group ahead of Uihlein, ignores the leaderboard and shoots for birdies. On the 222-yard par-three seventeenth, he hits a draw over a dangerous sand trap roughly twelve feet from the flag. His putt speeds toward the hole and looks ready to drop before it slides by the target. On the eighteenth, Sanders knows he is tied for the lead. He wants to win. His drive splits the fairway, leaving him only an eight-iron to the green. The pin is placed on the far right front of the green, just over a sand bunker. The safe and smart play is to the center of the green. Instead, Sanders flies at the flag and ends up in the front bunker, leaving himself little green to navigate. His bunker shot flies out of the sand and stays in the fringe. Swiftly, he chips. "Too fast," his coach Fields whispers under his breath as he watches his student from the sideline. His putt heads right at the hole before stopping three inches short, and Sanders drops to eight under par for the tournament.

Uihlein is playing in the threesome behind Sanders. He cannot see his opponent, but he learns about Sanders's error while he is putting on the seventeenth green. "I heard he missed a short birdie on 17 and bogeyed 18, so I knew what I had to do," he says later. His drive on the final hole drifts right toward a bunker, ending up in the fescue. "I killed my tee shot and thought it was going to carry the bunker to be perfect," he laments. "I guess it hit the bunker and bounced out." The ball lies 140 yards from pin, but lying on top of, not buried in, the tall grass. Uihlein figures he has a good chance to reach the green with a solid pitching wedge. Unlike Sanders, he aims at the center of the green, not the flag. As often happens from the rough, the ball flies off his club and lands sixty feet long behind the hole at the back of the green. Calmly, Uihlein strokes his putt to within eighteen inches of the hole and taps in for his first-ever invitational triumph. "It feels great to finally win one," Uihlein says. "I have been close so many times and to finally come out on top is nice."

After a chuckle, he credits "clutch" putting for his victory. During the entire tournament, he three-putted a single green. The experience walking down the final fairway in the lead is what he has practiced for since he started to play golf. "I like one man sports—you kind of want to have that shot coming down the eighteenth hole. You don't want to have anyone taking it for you."

Maybe Uihlein has matured enough to dominate junior golf like Tiger Woods. His rivals congratulate him, with many acknowledging the fear that they will be outclassed for the rest of the summer "Best man won," says Cody Gribble, "I have to take notes on how he kept his calm and patience."

While character counts in almost all activities, it plays a particularly important role in golf. No other sport requires so much concentration over such a long period, more than four hours for a single round. Golfers with bad tempers tend to flame out. During a round of eighteen holes, a single mistake on a single hole can prove fatal.

Almost all champion golfers display formidable concentration and level headedness. Tiger Woods represents the ideal combination of hard work, constant concentration, and even temperament. He never seems to lose his cool. In contrast, Cody Gribble, John Popeck, and David Sanders all demonstrated lapses in one or more of these areas during the FootJoy. Under pressure, each came unhinged. Some foundered under the watchful eyes of so many college coaches. Others cracked under the pressure of sensing victory. For whatever reason, all demonstrated a lack of maturity at the most crucial moments.

Until this tournament, Peter Uihlein had suffered from similar failings. But this week he kept calm and overcame a disastrous quintuple bogey. He is a curious mixture of grown-up beyond his years and child lurking within. His goal of equaling Tiger Woods's junior record, or at least coming close to matching it, no longer seems like a fantasy, particularly if his newfound display of maturity signals a longer-lasting trend.

After the awards ceremony, Uihlein signs his autograph for several young fans, before heading to Massachusetts to visit his dad. On June 19 he has a crucial date in West Virginia, where he will attempt to qualify for the single most important junior tournament of the year, the U.S. Junior Amateur. One of the nation's oldest junior tournaments, it enjoys unrivalled prestige and determines the national junior champion. Uihlein has long dreamed about winning the U.S. Junior, only to be knocked out each year in the early rounds. This year is his final opportunity. The U.S. Junior is not an AJGA event. It is run by the venerable USGA, and true to the organization's form, the qualifying procedure is, to say the least, idiosyncratic.

CHAPTER 6

The Qualifier

Devin Komline is an underdog challenger
from Vermont.

URING THE MONTH OF JUNE, the nation's top-ranked junior golfers take a break from the glamorous elite junior venues and travel to some strange places. Mu Hu and his mom make their way to Murfreesboro, Tennessee. John Popeck and his dad drive to the Naval Academy in Annapolis, Maryland. Peter Uihlein and his mother visit the Glade Springs Resort in Daniels, West Virginia. Others go to Bakker Crossing Golf Course in Sioux Falls, South Dakota. Girls undertake similar journeys. Kyung Kim of Hawaii travels to Fargo Country Club in Fargo, North Dakota, and Cheyenne Hickle of Arizona journeys to Tacoma Country Club in Washington State. Others visit the Red Rock Country Club in Rapid City, South Dakota, the Green Meadow Country Club in Montana, and the Shadow Hills Country Club in Junction City, Oregon.

By traveling to these far-flung destinations, players are attempting to win a spot in the United States Junior Amateur and the United States

Junior Girls Championships at special one-day events called qualifiers. The United States Golf Association (USGA), which sponsors the two events, demands that almost everyone play his or her way into its sole annual junior competition. For boys, it holds thirty-nine one-day, thirty-six-hole playoffs throughout the United States. For the girls, the USGA holds one-day, eighteen-hole events across the country.

For the elite who receive invitations to American Junior Golf Association (AJGA) events, these qualifiers are a painful process. They inject additional uncertainty into what already is a long, rocky road. Only the top two or three players at each qualifier make it into the finals; the rest go home empty-handed. One poor shot, or fatigue during the long day, may mean the end of the dream of becoming a national champion. By visiting small towns in Tennessee or West Virginia or South Dakota, the elite aim to improve their chances by competing in places with few strong homegrown players.

Both the boys' and girls' junior amateur national championships stand separate from, and in many ways above, the main junior season. They are the only junior golf tournaments sponsored by the august USGA. They are more demanding than even the AJGA junior events such as Mirasol and FootJoy. They offer the most points for national rankings to the winner, and they carry the most prestige, conferring the distinctive tile of national champion. Tiger Woods, who was fifteen years, six months, and twenty-eight days old when he won in 1991, remains the youngest ever champion, and for much of his career, he cited this first victory in a national championship as his greatest golf achievement.

The USGA, golf's governing body in North America, initially ignored junior golfers. In 1914 it allowed the Western Golf Association, a grouping of eleven Chicago-area golf clubs, to launch the country's first major championship for young golfers. Three decades later, in 1946, two additional competitions appeared, each with a claim on the national title. The Junior Chamber of Commerce sponsored one, and

Hearst Newspapers backed the other. Only then did the USGA join the fray, organizing its first U.S. Junior Amateur in 1948.

A golf icon named Francis Ouimet offered decisive support for the initiative. As a twenty-year-old amateur, Ouimet had captured the 1913 United States Open in a stunning upset over the top British pros of the era, Harry Vardon and Ted Ray. The victory, later immortalized in the book and movie *The Greatest Game Ever Played*, changed golf in America forever, and, some have argued, changed America in the process. "His dethroning of the great British golfers of the day, paralleled America's relationship with Great Britain," argues Douglas Stark, the USGA's education curator. "In 1913, the balance of power in the world was shifting. Great Britain, long a powerful empire, found its dominance challenged by an upstart, the United States." At the time, golf in America "was still Scottish in its appearance, manner and sensibility," Stark adds. "There was little that was uniquely American about the game." Before Ouimet's victory, no public courses existed in America, and the game was confined to the wealthy. Within a decade of his historic victory, the number of golfers had tripled in America.

Ouimet's own story reads like something out of a Dickens novel. He grew up across the street from The Country Club in Brookline, Massachusetts, in a working-class home and learned the game with one old club, building three makeshift holes in his backyard, incorporating a gravel pit, a swamp, a brook, and a patch of long, rough grass. Sunken tomato cans substituted as cups. USGA organizers invited Ouimet to play in the Open only because they were lacking one player. Since no caddie was available, an eleven-year-old named Eddie Lowery toted his bag. The morning of the playoff, the tournament organizers deemed that Francis should have a real assistant. In a celebrated scene Ouimet, already a gentleman, simply replied, "No thank you. I'll stick with Eddie." Since the day he insisted that Eddie Lowery carry his bag in the 1913 U.S. Open, Ouimet had been known for his interest in helping young people. In 1949 he set up the Ouimet Fund to award a college scholarship to youths who had worked either as caddies, in a pro shop, or in greenkeeping in Massachusetts.

Ouimet never turned pro. When he opened a sporting-goods store in Boston in 1916, the USGA stripped him of his amateur status. A public outcry ensued. After the Army inducted Ouimet in 1918, the ban was lifted and the USGA reinstated him as an amateur. Not one to hold a grudge, Ouimet won the United States Amateur at age thirty-eight in 1931 and later served for many years on the USGA executive committee.

During a committee meeting on September 8, 1947, Ouimet proposed a "Junior Championship for players who have not reached their eighteenth birthday and to inaugurate the event as soon as possible." The first U.S. Junior Amateur Championship took place at the University of Michigan Golf Course and drew 495 entries. Forty-one qualifiers were held to select the starting field of 128 players. In the evenings during the tournament, courses were held on the rules and history of the game. Dean Lind of Rockford, Illinois, became the first champion, beating Ken Venturi of San Francisco, a future U.S. Open men's champion, in the final. The USGA's executive committee, meeting in August 1948, judged the championship "a most successful and interesting event," and voted to allow the victor immediate entry into the adult U.S. Amateur Championship.

In January 1949 the executive committee agreed to host a separate U.S. Girls' Junior Championship. Glenna Collett Vare, a four-time U.S. Amateur champion and female golf legend, lobbied for the event and arranged for the Philadelphia Country Club to host it. Entry fee for both the boys' and girls' championships was fixed at $3. The inaugural Girls' Junior drew a starting field of twenty-eight girls from seventeen states; ten of the players were from the Philadelphia area. Since then, Girls' Junior Am has helped launch the careers of such outstanding players as Mickey Wright, who won in 1952 and later captured four

U.S. Women's Open championships, and JoAnne Gunderson Carner, who won the first of her eight national titles in the 1956 Girls' Junior.

Both boys' and girls' junior championships soon expanded. By 1963, entries to the boys' junior had reached 2,230. In 1964 a handicap limit of ten strokes was introduced to trim the field. Once the players qualified, they played two stroke rounds, with the lowest sixty-four scores qualifying for the decisive matches. The champion then needed to win six straight duels. With the exception of the 1978 Boys' and Girls' Junior Amateurs, which were held on different courses at the same golf club, the two championships have been held in different locations. In 2007 the girls were scheduled to play from July 23 through July 28 in Tacoma Country and Golf Club in Washington State, and the boys from July 23 through July 29 in Boone Valley, Missouri, outside St. Louis.

Most famous American golfers have participated in the Junior Amateur. It was the only national championship Jack Nicklaus ever contested and failed to win. Only five players have reached the finals more than once, and only Tiger Woods has won more than once: in 1991, 1992, and 1993.

Although the AJGA and the USGA are nonprofits, they approach their missions differently. The upstart junior association purrs like a smooth, professional vehicle. The venerable adult association long operated as a volunteer-driven sedan. While ambitious paid staff members direct the AJGA events, unpaid volunteer golf enthusiasts man USGA events. Historically, the two organizations have wrangled over a variety of issues. The USGA has criticized the AJGA for commercializing the junior game, and for its part, it has barred eighteen-year-olds from participating in its events. Since British golf authorities used the seventeen-year-old limit for their boys' championship and eighteen-year-olds are allowed to drive and travel by themselves, the USGA argues they should be considered adults. "To raise the age limit would create two classes of players who would be competing under different rules in the same tournament," argued Richard Tufts, the chairman of the organization's Championship Committee, in the *USGA Journal* of August 1948. The AJGA, which distinguishes its mission as a preparatory ground for college, insists that eighteen-year-olds enrolled in high school should be able to compete.

But lately the two associations have begun to resemble each other more closely. The USGA's former "please don't talk to me about money" attitude has vanished. It has transformed the job of overseeing amateur golf into a commercial juggernaut, amassing a balance sheet of $250 million, up from less than $50 million in 1990. Marketing- and media-savvy professionals have replaced the former volunteers. American Express, Lexus, IBM, and the Royal Bank of Scotland have signed on as sponsors.

The modernized USGA cooperates in many areas with the AJGA, though the two organizations remain separated by a conflicting raison d'être. The AJGA is open only to the best performers, while the USGA, despite its aristocratic heritage, sees its mission as that of promoting the game in its purest, most democratic, and most affordable incarnation. Even the U.S. Open, its signature adult event, holds qualifiers in which any golfer with a low handicap is allowed a chance to get into the field. Only a few players are offered automatic entry. Similarly, qualifiers for the Junior Am are held all across the country, because the USGA believes that the event should be truly national. For the U.S. Junior Am, all boys who have not reached their eighteenth birthday with a handicap less than 6.4 can enter. The girl's handicap limit is a more generous 18.4. Entry fees are a minimal $25.

Besides its belief in allowing everybody an equal chance, the USGA sees its mission to be the selection of a national champion. It knows that champions represent a special breed, and that the victor in its championship enjoys a unique pedigree for the rest of his or her life, becoming the champion for the entire country. In the USGA's view a champion must display remarkable talent, along with exceptional endurance, character, and courage. The USGA is famed for setting up its courses in the toughest possible arrangements, with the thickest rough, the narrowest fairways, and the fastest greens. Top professionals often complain about the severity of USGA layouts, and the U.S. Open winner often shoots over par. The philosophy remains the same at the U.S. Junior Amateur: no AJGA performance points assure entry. After fighting through the qualifier, the finalists must endure a full-week-long championship consisting first of two rounds of stroke play, with the top sixty-four finishers then engaging in winner-take-all matches. The USGA crowns champions only after forcing them to their knees.

The grueling process of sorting out the nation's junior champions begins in backwaters, such as Loudonville, New York, where the Shaker Ridge Country Club held a boys' qualifier on June 27, 2007. Shaker Ridge is located far from the suntanned, well-groomed fairways of Florida or North Carolina. It hosts no professional tournaments. Its golf course overlooks the Albany International Airport, and airplanes fly low overhead. Rugged forested Adirondack Mountains lurk in the distance. Since its fairways are frozen during the winter, the course is open only about six months a year, beginning in mid-April.

At Shaker Ridge, a certain cold New England austerity reigns. Shakers, a severe Puritan sect known for their elegant, simple furniture designs, built their first settlement in the deep forests next to the club. A meetinghouse dating from 1848, residences, and a barnyard are preserved next to the golf course as a museum. Jewish immigrants first built a nine-hole course in 1929 on the farmland after they were excluded from the nearby, exclusive Mohawk Club.

Since then, the Shaker Ridge course has been extended to eighteen holes and 6,800-plus yards from its hardest, black tees. For the junior hopefuls, greenkeeper Jim Sieman has allowed the rough to grow to six inches high and trimmed the greens to run eleven feet on the Stimpmeter, the device employed for measuring the speed that a ball travels on the green. For everyday play on a well-groomed municipal course, the greens roll on the Stimpmeter about nine feet. Stimpmeter readings of ten and higher are considered fast, and professional tournaments clock in at about twelve feet. Shaker Ridge's resident pro, Chaz Conrad, deems the club's course "a solid track."

Shaker Ridge's 320 members are solidly middle class and no longer predominantly Jewish, but rather are drawn from all ethnic groups. Many work at a nearby General Electric factory in Schenectady or in the government offices in Albany. They pay $5,000 a year in fees, and they get much for their money: a well-maintained, fun-to-play golf course, a few tennis courts, a large swimming pool, and a comfortable clubhouse. "This is a *Caddyshack* type of place," says club pro Conrad, referring to the country club setting of the 1980s Bill Murray and Chevy Chase comedy flick. And indeed, fifty-eight-year-old Conrad typifies the sort of working-class bonhomie exhibited in *Caddyshack's* humorous spoof on golf. One of ten children, he played more basketball and football than golf as a kid.

Junior tournament organizations forbid golf carts, ruling that walking is an integral part of the sport. The AJGA, which sees caddies as an unnecessary expense, obliges teenagers to carry their own clubs. The USGA allows caddies other than parents for the Junior Am. Most who are carrying bags at Shaker Ridge are family friends. Some are fellow teenage school buddies who have never played a round. Quietly, without offering any advice to the players they accompany, these caddies plod mulelike around the course. Others are adult golfers, who come equipped with towels to clean clubs and balls, mini tongues to fix ball marks in greens, and other utensils of the trade. These veterans help choose the right clubs to hit and read the correct break for their players' putts. Each player decides whether to engage a caddie. About half of the qualifiers at Shaker Ridge will lug their own clubs. While the USGA recently allowed brothers and sisters to carry the clubs, the ban against parents remains. If the parents intervene and offer advice or protest an official call, their child receives a two-stroke penalty. "We don't want to become like Little League baseball, where the parents get too involved, arguing with the coaches and yelling and screaming at the kids," explains Mark Fitzgerald, the USGA volunteer organizing the Shaker Ridge qualifier. "Our premise is to keep the parents out of this game and let the kids play." He demands that parents come out to the first tee, where he can warn them against talking to their children. If Fitzgerald sees any parent giving a kid advice on the course, he threatens to impose a two-stroke penalty. But most parents, according to Fitzgerald, "stay in the woods."

Fitzgerald is a sixty-seven-year-old, cigar-chomping, deep-voiced, beer-bellied man who himself never played junior golf. He grew up in Albany and caddied as a kid at Wolferts Roost Country Club in Albany. "They let us play on caddies' day, but we would just go out and bang the ball around," he says. Fitzgerald learned the game during his Marine service in the 1950s, at Camp Lejeune in North Carolina, where many of his superiors played. He found golf a good social and career skill and credits golf for keeping him out of trouble.

For the past twenty-five years, Fitzgerald has volunteered and officiated at the USGA's finals. When he started running the qualifiers, only a dozen or so players showed up. In the past two decades, he has seen marked improvement in the quality of play. "These kids can flat out hit it," he says. "They don't care where you put the hole locations on the green—the better ones will go right at it." He credits the increase in the number of junior tournaments "for creating a better young golfer." In 1992 he worked Tiger Woods's second Junior Am final, where he saw what he believes was the largest ever turnout at a junior golf tournament. At the Shaker Ridge qualifier, in contrast, he expects almost no spectators.

In the past, some top-rated outsiders have crashed Fitzgerald's northern New York qualifiers. The most prominent was a Columbian boy named Camilio Villegas, who shot a 66 and 71, qualified for the main event, and made it all the way to the finals in 1999. Villegas has matured into a prominent PGA tour player. In 2007 no well-known junior player has signed up for the Shaker Ridge duel, and Fitzgerald knows few of the contestants. In the field of thirty-seven hopeful teenagers, the youngest is fourteen years old.

The forecast is for hot and humid weather, with a chance of thundershowers. The qualifier starts near dawn because players need to finish thirty-six holes in a single day. With temperatures predicted in excess of 100 degrees Fahrenheit, the qualifier looks set to resemble an Iron Man competition.

Contestants begin checking in at Shaker Ridge before 7:00 a.m. for the 7:30 tee time. Unlike most exclusive junior events, where players practice for hours before their round, many contestants show up only a few minutes before their start time. Some, to save money, have driven directly to the course from their homes. Devlin Conrad left his home in Montrose, Pennsylvania, at four in the morning. He slept in the car for the two-and-a-half-hour drive. The seventeen-year-old hopes to play golf in college but still has not been recruited. His last-minute strategy backfires. Without a chance to see the course, he hits a couple of balls out of bounds and shoots an 86, de facto eliminating himself after the first round. "It was my worst round in a long time," he admits.

If a favorite exists at Shaker Ridge, it is fifteen-year-old Andrew De Forest, whose father is a local club pro who once played on the tour. Andrew's older brother Chris qualified the previous year and continues to compete in AJGA events but is too old to play in this year's USGA national championship. A family friend of the De Forests named Ed Ardzone carries De Forest's bag. Ardzone acts like a true professional, wiping the clubs clean with a towel after each shot, pulling the flag on his shots, and helping De Forest read the path of putts. His main role, however, is to keep his charge under control. De Forest acts like Rambo on the golf course. He steps up and whacks the ball, lacking much reflection or strategy. He hasn't bothered to play a practice round. Despite his best efforts, De Forest sticks to his aggressive machine-gun tactics. On the ninth hole, he hits his ball clear over the green. Many of his putts run by the hole, some as far as twenty feet. De Forest ends the first round with a score of 81, putting him, except in the most optimistic of scenarios, out of contention.

"I went for the pins and it just didn't work," De Forest says of his poor play.

Many share De Forest's frustration, as scores fly ten or more strokes over a par 72 into the 80s. Donald Kim, a seventeen-year-old from New Jersey who spends much of the winter in Florida, is furious with his 78. On one hole, he took four putts. "The greens were slick, but this was horrible," he complains. The heat strikes down even physically fit players. After John Davies shoots a disappointing 79, he predicts that the qualifier's eventual winner "will pay a pound of flesh."

Amid the carnage, a diminutive left-hander, Devin Komline from Dorsett, Vermont, emerges in the lead after the first round with a two-under-par 70. The Komlines benefit from a deep golf bloodline. Brian Komline, a cousin to Devon, is the New Jersey amateur champion. After giving up professional tennis, Devin's father, Keith Komline, became a single-digit handicapper, a sign of a strong player. The Komlines moved from New Jersey to live in the New England countryside, where they joined the local Dorsett Country Club. Devon's father has served as his son's golf teacher and encourages his son's golf dreams. His mother Patti, a Vermont legislator, would prefer her son concentrate on school. Devon satisfies her by studying hard during the winter.

At a Junior Am qualifier during the previous year, Komline shot two rounds of 86 and didn't come close to qualifying. The slender Vermont native stands a mere five feet, six inches tall. As he walks on the fairways, a cough shakes his slight frame. The cough, which Komline says he cannot seem to get rid of even though the weather has turned warm, lingers from the winter. With his frail appearance, Komline is one of the shorter hitters in the event. But he is accurate. During his first round he hits every fairway. His short drives travel fifty yards less than most of his competitors, leaving him with long iron second shots, while his opponents caress lofted pitching wedges at the flag. "That's my game, hit the driver down the middle, long iron to the green, take two putts, and get out of there," he confides after his first round.

Komline has entered a few AJGA events over the past few years. In his best outing, he shot five under par for three rounds, and lost by eleven strokes. "When I saw that, I was a little discouraged," he admits. Several times he stood in the lead in the final round of a tournament, only to reach the fifteenth or sixteenth hole, triple bogey, and end up losing. "That's why I am so cautious about my chances here," he says following his first eighteen holes. If he qualifies at this event, he feels he will take a giant step toward winning a scholarship to a college "somewhere in the south."

After the first round, almost a dozen players are bunched within a few shots of Komline. They gobble down hamburgers and hot dogs and head out for the second round. The day is stiflingly hot and humid. Sweat plasters players' shirts, and even the freshest pubescent face turns tomato red. Tempers flare. The skies darken. Around four in the afternoon, bursts of thunder sound a dramatic warning and a torrid thundershower ensues. Fitzgerald blows his horn to stop play.

Instead, chaos erupts.

New Yorker Alex Andruskevich finds himself in the middle of the ninth-hole green. After shooting a 79 in the first round, he is only one over par in the next round, putting him "in the hunt." He steps up to the ball on the green. His playing partners warn him to stop after Fitzgerald's call, but Alex does not like to be told what to do. Since the ninth green is located in front of the clubhouse, Fitzgerald spots the infraction. He calls over Andruskevich and disqualifies him. "This is crap," the angry Andruskevich says, as he and his mother head to the parking lot for what promises to be a long ride back home.

Donald Kim and his father, who have driven to Shaker Ridge from New Jersey, are similarly fuming. Kim's father has accused his son's playing partners of cheating. "They hit balls into the forest and placed replacements in the rough," he complains. "And they didn't count missed putts." Fitzgerald calls the players into the golf pro shop's office, where after interrogating them, he finds insufficient evidence and delivers a not guilty verdict. "One side says they sunk the putts, and the other says they did not," he explains. "The USGA is not a serious organization," Donald Kim's father complains, as he walks to the parking lot. From Fitzgerald's point of view, this is yet another case of an overbearing father. "It is just a parent complaining," he insists.

As play is delayed on account of rain, other players with little hope of qualifying drop out. Andrew De Forest has only finished the sixteenth hole and decides he has had enough. Soon only the dozen or so top scorers are left mulling about the clubhouse, snacking, chitchatting, and wondering what will happen. Devin Komline considers whether to reserve a hotel room or drive back and forth to Vermont if the rest of the qualifier is postponed until tomorrow. But Fitzgerald wants to avoid this scenario. "We're going to try to finish it, even if we have to stay until it is dark," he vows.

Around 6:30 p.m., the rain subsides and the players are sent back onto the course. It's dusk when the leaders approach the eighteenth hole. The first contender to finish is Pennsylvanian Connor Cronkhite, who shot a 76 in his first round and is only three over par for his second round. Cronkhite has never made it into a major junior tournament. "He's in the ballgame," his excited mom Jane explains. But Cronkhite leaves his approach to the eighteenth green short of the hole and bogeys, for a total score of 152. Mother and son embrace on the sidelines and wait to see if his result is low enough to qualify.

By the time Devin Komline reaches the last hole, he is coughing harder and louder than ever and struggling to see his ball in the dark. Fitzgerald, sitting in a golf cart and watching out on the course, urges him to speed up. It is 7:30 p.m. and Komline has fallen to seven over par for his second round. On the eighteenth hole, he chips long and takes yet another bogey. He finishes with a 79. "My hands were shaking at the end," he says.

Komline, Cronkhite, and the other finishers straggle into the clubhouse to count up their scores. Fitzgerald's gray hair is matted, his polo shirt is soaked with sweat, and his voice is hoarse. "This the first time anything like this has happened," he says on the sidelines of the accusations of cheating and the disqualifications. "Next year, I'm going to recruit a lot of volunteers and they will follow the kids around the course."

Connor Cronkhite's total score is 152. The second-place finisher's total is 151. Cronkhite has failed to qualify by a single stroke. "This is like *Desperate Housewives* or the ultimate soccer mom tragedy," his dejected mother says ruefully as she attempts to comfort her son, who is in tears at her side.

Devin Komline's first place score of 149 qualifies him for the finals of the U.S. Junior Amateur Final in St. Louis. Ecstatic, he calls his father in China to relay the news. When the euphoria subsides, he is asked what his odds are for the main event. "A kid from Vermont has no chance," Komline says. "I'm just going to go, play my best and see what happens."

A quick look at scores from the top-ranked players supports his pessimism. Mu Hu, the budding Chinese star, qualified a few days earlier, shooting 62 and 69 on an easy Tennessee course. Even though he lost his concentration at the end of the second round and bogeyed and triple bogeyed the final two holes, the Chinese phenom won his qualifier by nine strokes. It was his sixth and only successful attempt at getting into the national championship. In previous years he had played in Florida. "It's a big tournament and I wanted it so much that I put a lot of pressure on myself," Hu explains. "There are so many great players in Florida that one can go ahead and shoot a 67 and keep you out." Peter Uihlein qualified for the Junior Am playing in West Virginia and finished with a thirty-six-hole score of 136, a full ten strokes lower than Komline.

The USGA's national championship is the one opportunity during the summer for outsiders like the short Vermont native to compete against the nation's best. Even if Komline fails to do well in the national championship, the experience offers him a lifetime of memories. Later in life he will be able to look back and will carry a badge of honor for playing against the world's best golfer. Before heading to Missouri for the Junior Am finals, though, the true Tiger wannabees, Uihlein, Mu, and the other top-ranked juniors, are heading to Ohio, where they will compete in the AJGA's Rolex Tournament of Champions at Ohio State University. Devin Komline receives no invitation.

CHAPTER 7

Burning Out

Courtney Ellenboggen, far left, Vicky Hurst, middle, and Kristen Park, right, formed the final threesome at the Rolex Tournament of Champions.

IT IS EARLY EVENING, and the sun is low over the Ohio State University Golf Club, when John's Popeck's mother Sandy observes what she considers a disturbing scene. Several dozen players continue to practice on the putting green. Almost all are Korean Americans. Their parents watch from a nearby grassy mound. Many mothers ward off the heat by sitting sheltered under dainty umbrellas, chitchatting in Korean. A tournament official will soon close the practice area. Otherwise, the Koreans would keep on putting into the darkness.

Most serious junior golfers practice hours a day—when they finish a round, they head to the driving range or the putting green—but the parent-enforced diligence of many Korean players surprises even the mother of a son who plays up to seventy-two holes in a single day. "I've seen Asian parents tell their kids 'stay on the practice green until you make five putts in a row,'" Sandy Popeck says. During rounds, Korean fathers scout out ahead of their children, while the mothers follow the children from behind. Popeck says that once, when a thunderstorm erupted, she watched a mother run over to open an umbrella over her child.

Almost all of the Korean golfers on the junior circuit hail from California, and for many, the trip to Columbus, Ohio, is the summer's first voyage east of the Mississippi River. Ohio State University's Golf Club is hosting the Rolex Tournament of Champions from July 2 to 6. Historically, the Rolex was the American Junior Golf Association's (AJGA) first major tournament, and this year it is marking its thirtieth anniversary. Although the organization now hosts half a dozen other invitationals each year, the Rolex remains its signature event. Only the top-ranked 143 junior players are allowed to enter, and winners have a good shot at being named Player of the Year. No one who is invited to an invitational is obliged to compete, but few decline the offer to play in the best competition before so many college coaches.

Unlike most invitationals, which are single sex, the Rolex hosts both boys and girls. On the tournament's second night, a gala dinner is held. All AJGA events mimic adult Professional Golf Association (PGA) Tour tournaments, but the Rolex does so in particular. The Nationwide Tour, the PGA's version of the Triple AAA Minor League baseball, is holding a tournament with $700,000 in prize money at the Ohio State club during the following week, and portable stands and television cranes have been erected around the eighteenth green on the Scarlet Course. The par-71 course extends 7,346 yards for the boys and 6,188 yards for the girls. AJGA executive director Stephen Hamblin says he chose the venue so the juniors could benefit from the Nationwide's infrastructure. "This is BIG TIME," he declares with relish.

On the night before the first round at Rolex, associate tournament director Gus Montano—who ran the Mirasol Birks & Meyer Junior Championship—holds a players' meeting at the tournament hotel, a nondescript Holiday Inn on the Ohio State campus. Montano warns the players about a few of the course's particularities. Golfers may pick up their balls without penalty from flower beds, because organizers are unsure whether they represent burial resting grounds. But if balls fall into a pile of bird droppings, they must be hit from where they lie. Boys must tuck in their shirts. Girls must not bare their midriffs. Montano cautions players against withdrawing from the event even if they're doing poorly. "All the college coaches—and a lot are here—will see that you are a quitter," he explains.

Of the 143 players invited to attend this year's Rolex, about forty are Korean. Some were born in the States. Others moved as little children. Chinese players like Mu Hu may represent the future of golf, but young Korean golfers often occupy the front lines of the game. After SeRi Pak helped put Korea on the map by winning the 1998 United States Women's Open, Korean women discovered a new path to success and an obsession became training daughters to become professional golfers. "Golf sort of matches the Asian mindset," with its emphasis on practice and repetition, insists David Leadbetter, who has traveled frequently to Asia and taught the Korean national team. "It requires not just pure physical exertion, but also a lot of mind control. It requires practice. Koreans train eight to ten hours a day, with only one day off in two weeks. It is [a] game in which parents can get involved with, where parents must travel with kids. For the Asians, doctors, lawyers, pianist, dancer, you have to give it 110 percent from the word go."

What Americans see as negative pushing, Koreans often consider right and proper parenting. Among Koreans, little time or temptation is left for kids to be kids. Wasted moments are seen as irresponsible, just as leaving children to make their own decisions is considered disastrous. A child's schedule is a serious affair. Children are in school, in an after-school tutoring program, or in a sports activity until it's time to go to bed. The parent's role is to teach the child to be successful in a tough world. Many Korean parents scorn the American idea of creative and well-rounded kids. Instead, they see the need for children to succeed.

After the Rolex's first day of play, the Korean players pack the top of the scoreboard. Kristen Park of Buena Park, California, leads the girls with a three-under-par 68. Jane Rah of Torrance, California, is tied for second place with a one-over-par 72. Neither Californian participated at Mirasol, both judging the trip to Florida too far during the school year. Just behind them is half-Korean Vicky Hurst, in fifth place with a two-over-par 73.

Kristen Park, an incoming freshman at Sunny Hills High School, is a shy, razor-thin teenager who steps back slightly when strangers shake her hand. Her father runs a Korean restaurant, and her mom travels with her to tournaments. She took up the game only three years ago and until this spring was unknown among the junior golf elite. "I was actually in tennis and then my grandpa got me into golf," she says. "For the first six months, I kind of wanted to quit, but then I started getting competitive and decided to stick with it." Her parents were skeptical. "They saw that golf takes lots of money, but I wanted to play." In her first significant tournament as a seventh grader in 2005, Park took a nine-stroke lead into the final round, shot 81, and lost in a playoff. Since then she has worked on course management. She lacks the muscles to power the ball, instead relying on a smooth, graceful swing to provide consistency and accuracy. In May, at the prestigious Kathy Whitworth Invitational in Fort Worth, Texas, she beat the defending U.S. Women's Amateur champion—another Korean named Kimberly Kim. "I didn't expect to be at these tournaments," Park admits. "The Whitworth win surprised me. It felt good." Unlike other players, no equipment manufacturer represents her, and she plays with old-fashioned "cavity" clubs bought from a golf shop.

Second-place Jane Rah, a stocky five foot, one inch tall, overcomes her small stature and a jerky, awkward-looking swing with course intelligence and a ferocious bulldog competitive will. "I would love to get some more distance like Vicky Hurst, but you have to work with what you have," she says. "I just have to stay consistent." Rah was invited to participate in her first adult Ladies Professional Golf Association (LPGA) event when she was only thirteen. Just two weeks before, she led from the first through the final day to capture an AJGA Invitational in Colorado. Most girls struggled to play in the high elevation of the Rocky Mountains and to keep their balls on the hard mountain greens. But Rah adapted her game and won with a conservative strategy of keeping the ball straight and aiming to score pars rather than birdies.

Rah grew up in Chicago, where she originally trained as a figure skater. "I was on the rink before six o'clock in the morning and there were such strict rules," she says. "In golf you can have these flaws and you can still make it." By the age of seven and a half, Rah had abandoned the rink. Her parents—her father is a high-school math teacher, and her mother is a homemaker—relocated to Southern California so she could play golf year-round.

In the boys' division another Korean, Alex Shi Yup Kim, leads with a one-under-par 70, followed in third place by Korean Sihwan Kim. Alex hails from Fullerton, California, and Sihwan, who's from Buena Park, the same town as Kristen Park, is a ten-minute drive away. Sihwan graduated a few weeks earlier from Sunny Hills High, which Kristen will attend in the fall. In 2004 Sihwan Kim burst upon the scene unexpectedly, becoming the second-youngest U.S. Junior Amateur champion, behind Tiger Woods.

Neither Alex nor Sihwan played in the FootJoy Invitational in North Carolina in June because they had to cram for final exams. "Studies come first," Alex explains. Although he has not yet chosen his university, he sees himself enrolling somewhere other than at Oklahoma State. "Wherever I go has to be strong academically and golf-wise," he says. Kim was born and raised in Korea until he was eight years old. His dad emigrated first and set up a business importing wigs. His mom now accompanies him to golf tournaments, while his father remains at home working.

Like most Koreans, Kim says he never considered attending a Florida golf academy, both for hard-edged monetary reasons—his parents would find it difficult to pay the tuition—and for family reasons. "My goal is to be a pro golfer, but I need a backup plan," he explains.

Tight organization is required to compete at such a high level and avoid a structured academy lifestyle. Alex Kim's school starts at 7:40 a.m. and lasts until 2:00 p.m. His mom then picks him up and takes him to the golf courses, where he practices until the shadows grow long. This wisp of a teenager stands a mere five feet, seven inches tall, and he is thin and angular. His methodical, well-proportioned swing lacks the punch and power of his rivals. But what Alex loses in distance, he makes up in steadiness and accuracy. He almost never drives off line. He makes few mistakes. "People look at Peter Uihlein who is six foot two inches and some say I cannot succeed in golf because I am too skinny and weak," Kim acknowledges. "This only motivates me to try harder." In the Rolex's first round, Alex "Little" Kim said his putting saved him. He required only twenty-seven putts for the full eighteen holes.

Sihwan Kim, by contrast, sports an unblemished baby face and stands a strapping six feet, one inch tall and weighs 200 pounds. He hits the ball as far as any other junior, and appropriately, his favorite golfer is South Africa's giant, Ernie Els.

Born in Korea, Sihwan "Big" Kim started playing golf at age nine. "I was kind of chubby back then," he recalls. "I couldn't run and my parents thought golf would be a good sport for me." With his mother and two sisters, Kim moved to the United States when he was twelve. His father, a clothing manufacturer, stayed in Korea. His mother, who still doesn't speak English, enrolled her son in an American elementary school that had few other Korean students. It was rough, but it worked," Kim admits. "I learned fast." As a fifteen-year-old high school sophomore, he won the U.S. Junior Amateur at the historic Olympic Club near San Francisco. Since then he has struggled to stay at the top of the junior game, in large part, he says, because he was worrying about his applications to college. Recently Kim was accepted at Stanford, and he seems more relaxed.

As Ohio State golf coach Jim Brown watches the contestants practice, he reflects on the dramatic generational change overtaking his sport. Brown, a thin, tall, balding sixty-three-year-old, who has coached Ohio State University's golf team since 1974, will retire at the end of the 2009 season. A native of Martins Ferry, Ohio, he learned golf by caddying at the local country club. He attended Ohio State, playing backup as a freshman on the basketball team to the likes of senior John Havlicek, Jerry Lucas, and Bobby Knight. Jack Nicklaus had left the year before Brown arrived, so Brown roomed with another future pro great, Tom Weiskopf, and graduated in 1965. To this day, Brown believes his former college mates could hold their own against today's best. "Tom and Jack were as long as these kids and they had garbage as equipment," he says, referring to the old steel-shafted, wood-headed drivers.

As a recruiter, Brown wooed high school golfers by speaking about pride of playing at THE Ohio State University. He never forgets to refer to the legendary Buckeye Jack Nicklaus, who remains an active alumnus, attending almost every Ohio State home football game. In his thirty-five seasons as Ohio State coach, Brown led the Buckeyes to eleven top-ten National Collegiate Athletic Association (NCAA) championship finishes. More than a dozen of his players have gone on tour.

Despite this formidable record, Brown and Ohio State have struggled in recent years. The Buckeyes won their last national championship in 1979. Increasingly, the nation's best young golfers aim to attend sun-drenched universities that offer nine solid months of golf weather "It is this modern idea that you must play golf year-round," Brown laments, pointing out that although weather prohibits outdoor play, that Ohio State boasts an indoor driving and chipping range. A universe in which young golfers engage in physical fitness and see sports psychologists makes him uncomfortable. "Kids still should have fun," he insists.

California-based Korean prospects have few links to Ohio and little reason to consider playing for Brown's team. Columbus is the quintessential

clean and calm Midwestern city of 1.7 million, with the height of excitement consisting of an Ohio State football game. Ohioans practice golf as
democratic middle-class sport, and Columbus is peppered with superb
private layouts such as Scioto, Muirfield Village, Longaberger, and The
Golf Club. The city counts six courses rated in *Golf Digest's* Top 100.
High-class public courses such as Foxfire Golf Club, where greens fees
run to a modest $32, are scattered throughout the region. "Columbus is as
close to golf heaven as you can get," Brown insists.

Famed golf architect Alistair MacKenzie—the designer of the
Masters' course in Augusta, Georgia, and the famed Cyprus Point in
California—drew up the plans for Ohio State's Scarlett course in 1931.
It was one of MacKenzie's last designs, and he died before it was completed in 1938. Until then, only a handful of universities had golf facilities, and most of those were eastern schools. Even though MacKenzie
could only work with flat farmland in Columbus, the course contains
many of his signature touches: deep bunkers and undulating greens.
All the holes are accessible by open fronts, allowing the average golfer
to roll the ball up to the greens. In 2006 Jack Nicklaus, who donated his
design fee, completed a $4.2 million facelift. He added almost 200 yards
to the course, building nine new tees and bringing the length to 7,455
yards from the back tees. "We're maxed out on every hole now," Brown
says. Where fairway bunkers used to measure 230 to 240 yards off the
tee, they now are often situated about 285 to 320 yards off, making it
much more difficult for long hitters to carry them.

MacKenzie-style sand traps become steeper as they get closer to the
green, so players attempting to carry them will struggle if they come up
short. "The bunker guy was a real artist," Brown explains. Besides the
bunkers, some of the most dramatic changes were made to the fourth hole,
which Nicklaus rerouted around the lake, and to the fourteenth, which
was changed from a par five to a par four and now has a larger green.

For traditionalist Brown, the odds-on Rolex favorite is academy-
bred, Oklahoma-bound, newly crowned FootJoy champion Peter Uih-

lein. "He's long off the tee, got good fundamentals, and a really good short game," Brown says. "It is just the way he approaches the shots he has to hit. He knows when to go for it and when not to." Sure enough, after the first day, Uihlein ends near the top of the scoreboard amid the Korean leaders, tied for fourth place with an even-par 71. His round resembles a roller coaster, with a double bogey eleventh followed by an eagle on the twelfth hole. On the short dogleg right fifteenth hole, a poor chip shot leaves a five-foot put for a par—which he misses. Two holes later, Uihlein defies a pin placed just above a trap and fires straight at the flag. It is a bold shot. Some might say too bold, but the ball stops ten feet from the pin, and Uihlein sinks the birdie. He finishes with a birdie on the par-four eighteenth.

Other favorites are less fortunate on the Columbus course. During practice before the tournament, Mu Hu injures his wrist, tearing ligaments. "I was hitting a left-handed shot on the range, goofing round, and I stuck it in the ground," he says. At first he almost fails to notice the injury. He swings without pain, but poorly. In the first round, he shoots a six-over-par 77. On subsequent days, he fails to recover his form, finishing tied for twenty-seventh place, and heads back to Orlando for some appointments: with his doctor to examine his wrist, with his golf teacher David Leadbetter to analyze his swing, and with his sports psychologist to restore his battered confidence.

Cody Gribble, the Texas bubba, comes to Columbus believing he finally has overcome his top-of-the-swing wobble. Two weeks after his collapse at the FootJoy, he flew to Des Moines, Iowa, to participate in the oldest national junior tournament, the 90th Western Junior Championship, at the Wakonda Club. This time, with his father caddying for him, his nerve held. With two holes left, a golfer named Clayton Rotz birdied to tie him. "I thought I would tense up, but I just looked at the fairway and felt calm," he recalls. Gribble responded on the seventeenth hole by hitting an eight-iron to nine feet. He nailed the putt for a birdie to recapture the lead. On the final hole, he hit a sand wedge to within a foot of the hole and birdied again. "It feels great to put my name on that trophy with all the great professionals who have won the championship," the University of Texas-bound Gribble said. "This gives me a lot of confidence." His proud father e-mailed acquaintances newspaper clippings about his son's victory.

In Columbus, the silver-haired Bill Gribble accepts congratulations from other parents. But the Gribbles' celebration is short-lived. Cody double bogeys his first hole in the first round. He ends up with a six-over-par 77, tying him for forty-sixth place. His other three rounds consist of mediocre scores of 74, 74, and a final 78. Afterward, Gribble cites the stress of traveling so many weeks in a row with his father. He's eager to return to Dallas and plans to take a few weeks off before the USGA's Junior Amateur. "Otherwise, I am going to burn out," he warns.

———

Girls confront an equal, if not even greater, danger of burnout than their male counterparts throughout the intensity of the summer season. Most of the boys compete only in junior events. A few sometimes attempt adult amateur events, but almost none plays against male professionals on the PGA Tour. The PGA rarely extends an invitation to a junior golfer, and it is almost unheard of for a boy under age eighteen to qualify for the annual United States Men's Open. But many young female golfers are combining junior tournaments with professional ones. Seven girls at Rolex completed the woman's qualifiers to make the final draw for the U.S. Women's Open, the premier adult women's tournament, which was held the previous week in Southern Pines, North Carolina.

Vicky Hurst qualifies. More surprisingly, at the tender age of twelve years, four months, and one day, seventh grader Alexis Thompson—the same temper-tantrum Thompson from Mirasol—surpassed Morgan Pressel as the youngest player to qualify for the U.S. Women's

Open. Thompson survived the thirty-six-hole, one-day qualifier in Orlando to earn her spot. In Southern Pines large crowds followed Thompson. Even though she shot 76-82 and missed the cut by ten strokes, journalists demanded she give a press conference.

"What about signing autographs, what's fun about that?" one journalist inquired.

"I like seeing kids my age coming up to me asking for my autograph. It's really cool. I like it," she responded.

"What are you going to do to kill the time and not let the nerves build up?" a journalist continued.

"Probably sleep in, eat breakfast, and maybe go to PetSmart. I've gone there every day now."

"What's the attraction of PetSmart?"

"Cats," Thompson answered. "I have two."

"Did you buy toys? What did you buy for them, anything?"

"Nothing, I go to pet the cats and hold them.

"What are your cats' names?"

"Angel and Smelly."

The psychological and financial costs and challenges of becoming a professional golfer are immense. More than a thousand girls compete each year on the AJGA, and fewer than half a dozen each year end up on the LPGA tour. Of these, even fewer lucky ones end up as teenage multimillionaires. If they manage to maintain their passion for the game, these girls can look forward to a long career. Golfers are able to play at a top level well into their forties, and senior tours allow them to compete until retirement. For boys, multiply the odds against success several hundred times. Many aspiring pros must start out on minor league tours for minor league purses and try to play themselves up into the big leagues. This may translate into years of financial struggles. Costs of travel and paying for a caddy add up.

The Thompson family golf team sees both the potential bonanza and the difficulty of cashing in. Alexis's brother Nicholas graduated from Georgia Tech and started out on the main PGA tour in 2006, but did not play well enough to qualify for the best events in 2007 and ended up competing in minor league tournaments. "He thought it was easy and found out it was hard," his father says. (In 2008, Thompson recovered and rejoined the PGA Tour, and his career earnings by the end of the year reached $2.2 million.)

In North Carolina, none of the teenage girl prodigies proved mature enough to make the cut against the adults. Mirasol champion Vicky Hurst shot an eight-over-par 150 and finished in a thirteen-way tie for eightieth place. Both of Hurst's playing partners, Kris Tamulis and Song Hee Kim, survived even though Hurst hit the ball farther than they did from the tee. The woman pros displayed superior short games around the greens, chipping and putting better than the junior upstart. Even so, Hurst ended eight shots lower than her previous showing at the U.S. Women's Open. "I was ready for the crowds and the course," she says. "I could have easily made the cut if I played my game."

Since July 1, 2007, the date when golf coaches are allowed to contact incoming seniors, Hurst had received dozens of e-mails expressing interest in her. "I don't need to impress the coaches," she explains. "The way I am playing, I can pretty much go where I want." Her real dilemma remains whether to turn pro.

Among the cautionary examples of going too far too fast, Michelle Wie stands out for the velocity of her rise and downfall. Wie grew up in Hawaii and attracted early attention for her height (she was six feet, one inch tall by her mid-teens), and for the rare length of her drives. When Wie was fourteen, Ernie Els observed that she'd be ready for the PGA Tour with a few solid years of practice. When she was only fifteen, Wie averaged drives of about 280 yards, almost as long as most male professionals. "It's just the scariest thing you've ever seen," pro Fred Couples noted of Wie. "She's probably going to influence the golfing scene as much as Tiger," added Arnold Palmer. A week before her sixteenth birthday, Wie turned professional, signing sponsorship contracts with Nike and Sony worth totaling more than $10 million per year.

But almost as soon as she jumped into the spotlight, Wie imploded. Just two months before the Rolex Tournament, playing in Orlando at the women's Ginn Tribute, she withdrew after sixteen holes, blaming her early exit on a wrist injury. When Wie pulled out, she was close to breaking the so-called Rule 88—any non-LPGA member who shoots 88 or more is barred from competing on the tour for the rest of the year. Two days later, journalists spotted her practicing at the site of the LPGA championship in Bulle Rock, Maryland.

At the U.S. Women's Open, Wie's play continued to deteriorate, and by the middle of the second round she had dropped out. It was her second withdrawal in a month. She missed seven fairways in seven tries, and shooting six over par through her opening nine holes to put her at seventeen over par for the championship. Once again, she blamed her wrist. "I definitely want to compete because that's what I like to do, but I have to think about my health," she said afterward.

Wie's fate is a regular subject of conversation at the Rolex Tournament. Many juniors and parents react with skepticism to her injury claims, blaming pressure and burnout for her poor play. "Michelle has lost interest," Andrea Watts, the second-place finisher at Mirasol, observes. "She is hounded by the media, grilled by her parents and she doesn't want to play. Yes, she's injured and she needs time off. But I think she's burnt out. She felt she was too good for junior golf, she felt she was too good for college golf, and she jumped into the pros. It was too much too soon."

Watts relates to these feelings. Her strong showing at Mirasol proved exhilarating, but her following tournament in Colorado, the AJGA Invitational, was a true challenge. Hard dried-out Colorado greens proved much more difficult than soft, accommodating Florida greens. "It was like war," she said afterward. "I was so used to attacking aggressively, in Florida, where everything is plush and soft on the greens and you can land it close to the flags. In Colorado, I needed to hit from downhill slopes to elevated greens and it didn't feel like golf." Watts three-putted seven times in her first round and ended up shooting a 77. The next two days were equally mediocre, 77 and 78, and she finished tied for twenty-first place.

From Colorado, the talented seven junior girls who qualified for the U.S. Women's Open flew to North Carolina. Andrea insists she felt no jealousy. "I think that I needed a little time to catch up to their level," she says. "Remember, I started late. I didn't get great instruction. These girls start since they were four, five, and six, and it makes a difference." Instead of North Carolina, she and her mother jetted to Texas for another junior event. They expected hot and dry weather. Instead, rain pummeled them. Balls did not roll; they plugged. On the first day, Andrea hit a series of shots twenty to thirty yards short of the green. She ended the round with a 79. The following day she recovered, scoring a two-under-par 34 for the first nine holes, moving her into fifth place— only to be caught in a torrential rainstorm, which forced the rest of the tournament to be cancelled.

Right after the washout, mother and daughter boarded another plane, to Ohio. They arrived a day before the start of the Rolex, and Andrea managed to play only a single practice round. For most tournaments, particularly important ones, she preferred two practices to map out the courses and prepare her strategy.

As Andrea's stress mounts, she and her mom quarrel over how to manage the Ohio State course. Andrea insists she should plot a conservative strategy, using accurate fairway woods off many tees. "My mom keeps telling me to hit a driver," Andrea complained. "She doesn't calculate risk. She doesn't understand that it's all right to gamble on a practice round but difficult to deliver precision on tournament day."

Behind the debate over golf course strategy lies a deeper power struggle, which Andrea believes stems from the conflict between her
mother's Asian heritage and her own American upbringing. "We're
fighting a lot, which makes me question whether my mom's love is dependent on how I play," Andrea says. "Korean moms teach you that
you are their princess. When you play bad, or disappoint them, you are
no longer their kid. They watch every move you make and they are the
only person other than yourself that knows your mistakes."

On the Rolex's opening day, Andrea follows her mother's advice.
She plays aggressively—and emerges bloodied. On the fourth hole, a
short par five that Nicklaus redesigned to wind its way around a lake,
she attempts to reach the green on her second shot, a dangerous
prospect. The small green tucked around water offers a tiny target
zone, making it difficult to attack with a long iron or fairway wood.
The smart, if conservative, play is to lay up in front of the water and
pitch onto the green with the third shot. Andrea Watts attempts to
reach the green on her second shot and ends up hitting two balls into
the water before finishing with a catastrophic quadruple bogey nine.
"I was fried," she admits.

Watts's penalty shots take a long time to play out. Twice she must
walk back and forth between the spot on the fourth hole where her
ball entered the water back and her dropping zone. An official dis-
penses a red card for slow play: unless she speeds up, Hurst will face
a penalty. Andrea begins rushing between shots and takes five more
bogeys. By the end of the first round, she shoots herself out of contention with an 85, the highest score she has recorded in a tournament in three years.

Sunee Watts sweats on the sidelines. Her daughter, as she sees it, is
"just fried." Their decision to move to Florida from Colorado may have
been an error. The new club motion taught at the Leadbetter Academy—the mechanical wrist cock—may not fit her daughter. "I don't
care for her new swing," Sunee says. "The wrist thing seems fine with

boys, but it makes girls who are not as athletic look constricted." In Sunee Watts's opinion, Vicky Hurst benefits from the best motion among the juniors: smooth, fluid, and natural, not academy-toned and too mechanical.

Mother and daughter squabble over how to proceed. Andrea has entered two tournaments over the following two weeks, and Sunee insists that she follow through. A vacation without golf will be fine, perhaps even a tour of Europe or Asia, Sunee says, but only after the tournament at the end of July or in August. "I definitely need a break," Andrea tells her mother. "I need a day to sit in my bed and read a book." She would like to curl up with the final installment of Harry Potter. Instead she is reading Earl Woods's treatise *Training a Tiger*. Long term, Vicky says she is happy with her decision to concentrate on golf. Short term, she is frustrated and tends to blame her mom. "My mother's idea of a break is like, to go practice putting," she complains.

Even some of the most pedigree-rich competitors struggle with mid-season burnout. Ivan Lendl, the tennis great, is accompanying his daughters Marika and Isabelle during the summer season. High school junior Marika is recovering from mononucleosis; she looks fatigued and drawn lugging her bag around the course at Rolex. Isabelle, a high school sophomore, is suffering from a fault in her swing. She brings her club back in too steep a line, a defect that leaves her smashing balls all over the course. Throughout the spring at the academy, Isabelle hit the ball well and felt well armed for the summer season. But all of a sudden, something goes awry. On the first hole at the Rolex, she slices her drive. On the next hole, she hooks. "I have never seen anything like that, I do NOT exaggerate," Ivan Lendl admits when he describes the disaster in a clipped, machine-gun-style staccato tempo, his English flavored with a light Slavic accent.

Lendl won three consecutive United States Tennis Opens, propelling him to the number one rank in the world for more than three years in a row. His superior fitness, discipline, and preparation wore his opponents down with repetitive cannon shots from baseline. He picked up an image as a sourpuss champion, a dour East European who played and talked like a robot. Lendl retired at the age of thirty-four with a permanent back injury caused by the intense combat on the courts. "People will sometimes ask me, 'How much talent did you have in tennis?' I say, 'Well, how do you measure talent?' Sure, McEnroe had more feel for the ball. But I knew how to work, and I worked harder than he did. Is that a talent in itself? I think it is.'"

Lendl now is thicker around the middle than he was in his tennis years and acknowledges continued back pain that often makes him feel crippled. If he ever really was a sourpuss, he no longer is, exhibiting a warm, witty—if often ribald and rough—personality. Quick with quips, he dishes out generous helpings of love and demands near total obedience from his kids. He literally pushed his kids from the time they were toddlers. "When they were crawling," his wife Samantha told a reporter "he would say, 'OK, who can get to the top of the stairs first?' And he would sort of push them, and they went up the stairs. Marika would throw her sisters out of the way so she could beat them. I would say, 'Ivan, you're going to kill them. Relax a little,' and he would say, 'No, no, no, this is good—it's how you teach them to compete.'"

Both Marika and Isabelle started out playing tennis. By the time they reached age ten, they had abandoned the game. Neither liked the idea of being compared with her father. "I was like six years old and everybody was asking me, are you going to be as good as your dad?" Marika recalls. "It was so much pressure. I couldn't be in his shadow."

Once they dropped their father's profession, Marika spent several months without a sport. Lendl hated how she would plop herself before the television or computer and urged her to try golf. "He bribed me," Marika recalls. Marika wanted a dog. Lendl offered her a deal. If she took some golf lessons—and practiced hard for three months—she could get her dog. The family now owns three German shepherds.

Marika ended up loving the game. Her younger sisters Isabelle and Daniela soon took it up. All three golf-playing Lendls play elite-level tournaments. According to her older sisters, Daniela may be the most talented. But at age thirteen and a full head shorter than her older sisters, she cannot hit the ball long enough to qualify for the elite invitational events and has stayed behind in Florida.

After his daughters took up golf, Lendl made them study a single golf rule a week and write a report on it. Every time they finish a round, he orders them to write a hole-by-hole, shot-by-shot description, detailing what they aimed to do and what they ended up doing. Until last year, he set their curfew at 9:00 p.m. His wife Samantha intervened and warned him that his girls would end up hating him. In response, Lendl extended the curfew to 10:00 p.m., but was insistent the girls put their phones by the back door every night before they went to sleep. He also continued to monitor his daughters' whereabouts through remote control over the mobile phones, though Marika has discovered how to trick him. In March 2006 Marika quit the game for a month, a bold attempt to push back her dad's control. Both now say that their relationship has improved.

The two oldest Lendl girls arrive at Ohio State with strong golf resumes. Isabelle ranks tenth among junior girls in the AJGA. She earned a second-team Rolex Junior All-American, finishing sixth or better in all the AJGA events that she competed in during the previous year. Marika won the 2006 McDonald's Betsy Rawls Girls Championship and Ringgold Telephone Company Junior Classic and received honorable mention in the Rolex Junior All-American. Both Lendl girls sport long, light-brown hair that falls below their shoulders. At five foot eight, Marika stands two inches shorter than her younger sister, and she projects a more feminine image. She wears pink laces in her golf shoes and decorates most of her golf clubs with pink paint. Isabelle is the picture of an athlete. Her father says he would have a hard time beating her in arm wrestling. Marika and Isabelle, who are tanned from many hours on the driving range and on the course, frighten other academy students with their diligence. Each morning they arrive well in advance of the start of their lesson. If many Americans fear and admire Asian discipline and determination, they are equally awed by what they perceive as the pushy East European drive to succeed. "The Lendls are task masters. They know what it takes to be champions," says Larry Alger, the father of AJGA junior golfer Elizabeth Alger.

Ivan Lendl has long loved golf. On the day of his 1986 U.S. Open semifinal, he played nine holes. He won the tennis match and the Open. After he retired, he attempted to play the game professionally, bringing the same single-minded determination to his new passion. After a round, he would skip rope 100 times for each stroke over par. He once told a reporter that he played 300 rounds of golf in a single year, though he now amends the total to a mere 250. He holds the record at his home Lake Waramaug, Connecticut, course with a score of 64. Even so, he turned in mediocre performances as a golf professional, never qualifying for the U.S. Open, and finished near the bottom in the five top-class professional events he entered, demonstrating, as basketball star Michael Jordan discovered when he failed to play Major League baseball, just how difficult it can be to transfer exceptional athletic ability from one sport to another.

These days Ivan Lendl spends most of his time with his daughters at golf tournaments. The family summers in Greenwich, Connecticut, and heads to Bradenton for the winter. "You can't just stop for six months to let the snow melt," Lendl explains. He has transferred much of his intensity to training his daughters, supervising them like a bodyguard, forgoing cozy pep talks and instead issuing commands uttered in Marine-style barks.

"Tuck in your shirt or you don't start," he warns Isabelle.

"Dad, stop," she protests.

"Don't give me that Dad stuff," Ivan responds, watching his daughter until she obeys.

"Fix your hair," he tells Marika, who promptly puts it in a neat ponytail.

Lendl carries a folding chair at tournaments—his back injury makes it difficult for him to stand for long periods. As Isabelle makes her way around the course, he plants the chair beside a fairway when she drives and behind a green when she putts. Sometimes he takes out a pair of binoculars to scrutinize his daughters. He isn't upset when his girls hit a poor shot, but mental mistakes such as failing to follow through with the regular pre-shot routine or failing to line up a putt incense him.

Marika, fatigued from her mononucleosis, comes undone on the same par-five fifth hole as Andrea Watts. After her drive, her ball sits only about a tantalizing 200 yards from the flag. But the shot must carry almost entirely over a wide body of water, and through two large sand traps to the right and left of the green. An aggressive shot must be perfectly positioned. Like Watts before her, Marika gambles and goes for the green in two shots. Her first ball plops into the water. Instead of playing a defensive shot, she again chooses to be bold, and sinks a second shot in the water. She ends the hole with a quadruple bogey nine. On the sidelines, Lendl scowls, folds his chair, and moves on to the next hole. "Instead of recouping, she tried to hit a crazy shot and it snowballed from there," he later acknowledges. Marika caroms toward a catastrophic 47 for the first nine holes and an 84 for eighteen holes, leaving her in fifty-fourth place. The next day, she shoots 80 and misses the cut. "I was tired; I couldn't hit it straight for my life," she admits.

Like her sister, Isabelle Lendl drags herself around the course, her shoulders drooping and her walk slowing as she advances. "She's giving away a lot of shots," says a worried Tim Sheredy, her teacher from the Leadbetter Academy, who is watching her play. Isabelle ends with rounds of 81 and 79, and also misses the cut. Ivan Lendl issues a harsher judgment. "It is crazy—these girls want to go pro, but there's no way playing like this," he says. "It is a bad situation."

———

During the Rolex championship's second and third days, players jockey for position like boxers sizing up the course and their opponents. The fourth and final day of play will prove decisive.

In the girls' draw, Kristen Park, Vicky Hurst, and a diminutive Virginian named Courtney Ellenbogen form the lead trio and will play together in the last threesome to tee off. During the two previous rounds, the other Korean contender, Jane Rah, fell back to fourth place and is in the second-to-last group. By all measurements, Vicky Hurst sizes up as the favorite. The veteran of the threesome, she is four years older than Park and a year older than Ellenbogen. She stands a full head taller than either of her rivals and hits the ball sixty to seventy yards farther off the tee. During the tournament's first three rounds, she displays steady shot-making, shooting 73, 71, and 71 Hurst manages to reach the par fives, even the dangerous fourth, in two shots, seemingly, as Ivan Lendl points out, "without breaking a sweat." Although Hurst starts out the final round in second place, three shots behind Ellenbogen, Lendl predicts her length will give her an advantage over her smaller, short-shooting rivals.

Hurst brims with confidence. At Mirasol, she similarly lurked just behind the leader before teeing off on the final day. "There's more pressure if you are in first place," she says. "If you are in second, you have nothing to lose. You can just go for it."

Neither Ellenbogen nor Park met before the tournament, evidence of their newfound status at the top level of junior golf. The previous year, the sixteen-year-old Ellenbogen played so poorly that she considered dropping the sport. Instead, she worked hard on her swing over the winter, and her results so far show the payoff. She won an AJGA

Invitational over Easter in Georgia and then qualified for the U.S. Women's Open.

Ellenbogen hails from Blacksburg, Virginia. Her dad, Bill, graduated from Virginia Tech in 1973, where he starred as a defensive lineman. He played as a guard and tackle with the New York Giants in the mid-1970s, lasting through eight seasons and four surgeries. He weighs 260 pounds and stands six feet, four inches tall. In contrast, his light-brown-haired, fresh-faced daughter measures a diminutive five feet, two inches and weighs a mere 110 pounds, making her one of the shorter and lighter hitters among top-ranked juniors. At the U.S. Women's Open in North Carolina the previous week, many spectators asking for her autograph confused her for the twelve-year-old Alexis Thompson. During the winter, Ellenbogen rose at 5:00 a.m. three mornings each week to weight lift with her father in the basement. She also is working on adding distance by developing a little "lag" to her swing on tee shots.

Even so, Ellenbogen drives the ball shorter distances than the thirteen-year-old Park. Ellenbogen makes up for the deficit by keeping the ball straight. She almost never misses a fairway. Though she must hit long irons or fairway woods into greens, she pitches and putts with confidence. At 6,700 yards, the U.S. Women Open's Pine Needles course makes her distance disadvantage almost insurmountable. At less than 6,200 yards, the Ohio State course falls within her reach. During the Rolex's second round, Ellenbogen hit seventeen greens in regulation and avoided bogeys, for a two-under-par 69. This gave her a one-shot advantage over Park and a three-shot lead over Hurst. In the third round she continues her solid play, shooting even par and solidifying the distance between her and both Park and Hurst to three shots.

Ellenbogen might have gone down the academy path, but her father resisted. He and his wife didn't want to split up the family—in addition to Courtney, they have an eighteen-year-old son, a tennis player—and they didn't buy into the teenager-in-training pro athlete.

"There's a part of growing up and being a kid and experiencing all the things young people experience that I think is important," Bill Ellenbogen explained. "Some of these young kids get skewed values based on the emphasis placed on athletics."

His daughter plays on the Blacksburg High School golf team with the boys, since there's no girls' team. Ellenbogen is also a committed pianist and a straight-A student who must make up for the days of school she misses in order to play tournaments. "It's a public school—they can't single out individual students and help them," Ellenbogen explains. Unlike Vicky Hurst, Ellenbogen opposes a jump from high school to the pros. She wants to attend college. "I feel I could go out and compete out there on the pro tour, but I could use the extra four years to get ready," she says. Her goal is a school "with good academics and a good golf team." Although this rules out the Ivy League because "they don't have the best golf teams," it allows her to shoot for excellent universities like Duke and Stanford.

Ellenbogen's football star dad, now a successful real-estate developer, is a curious mixture of environmentalist and hard-nosed businessman—he lobbied hard in favor of preserving the Huckleberry nature trail in the Appalachian Mountains around Blacksburg, and simultaneously pushed to allow Wal-Mart to build a store in the town. In contrast to her father, Courtney is soft-spoken and well-mannered, with a light Southern accent. But behind the sweet, unassuming façade, she shares a great deal with her tough football star dad. Both are fearless, fierce competitors. Courtney marches down fairways, focused, intent, sure of herself. "I've been working to keep an even keel, but I still have more of a temper than a golfer needs," she admits.

Despite sometimes losing her cool, Ellenbogen never seems to lose her concentration, displaying a ferocious determination and drive. "She plays much better in tournaments than just for fun," says her uncle, Mark Hawley, who caddied for her the previous week at the U.S. Open and chauffeured her to the Rolex in Ohio. "She puts her game face on and starts grinding." At the Open, Ellenbogen beat Vicky Hurst and missed the cut by a single stroke. "She sleeps fine and always seems so calm," says Hawley. "I thought she would be nervous before the Open, but she just wasn't." Although three strokes ahead, Ellenbogen believes she must stay aggressive in the final round. "The other girls are really good," she says. "I must take the win, not just let it come to me."

By playing together in the final group of girls to tee off, Ellenbogen, Park, and Hurst guarantee a duel-like match-play atmosphere. On the seventh hole, a straightforward par four, Hurst enjoys an opportunity to make up ground. She needs only a short iron to reach the green, while Ellenbogen must hit a fairway wood. Ellenbogen leaves her ball well short of the target and takes a bogey. Hurst puts her ball close to the flag and putts for a birdie—only to miss. Instead of closing to a single shot, she remains two behind.

All three girls par three the eighth hole. On the ninth, they line up birdie putts, ranging from ten to fifteen feet. Hurst misses. Ellenbogen and Park sink their putts. Park stays two shots behind, and Hurst falls three behind. Her usually erect shoulders slump and her face turns sour; she knows it will be difficult to make up four shots in the remaining nine holes. Park is left as Ellenbogen's final challenger entering the back nine.

The tenth hole, a short, straightforward par four, plays at a little over 220 yards. Its main difficulty lies in a narrow fairway bordered by a large sand trap shaped like an O. Both Ellenbogen and Park avoid this danger and are left with pitching wedges. The flag is positioned at the back of the green. Ellenbogen lands her approach about thirty feet short. She is disappointed and will be forced to concentrate on saving her par with two good putts. Park has an opportunity to claw back a shot on the leader and strikes her ball straight on target, landing it about ten feet from the pin, directly in the line of Ellenbogen's putt.

As is customary in such situations, Ellenbogen asks Park to move her ball mark. Park picks up her ball, measures a putter's length to the right, and replaces her mark. Since Ellenbogen is farther from the hole than her playing partner and rival, she must putt first. Ellenbogen proceeds to hit a poor putt, leaving herself with six feet for par. Park replaces her ball and two-putts for a par. Ellenbogen misses and finishes with a bogey.

As Park prepares to move to the next hole, a rules official sees something suspicious.

"Did you move the ball back?" he asks Park. Under the rules, Park should have putted from her ball's original resting spot on the green, not where she had moved it to allow Ellenbogen a clear path. Park hesitates, reflects, acknowledges her error—and receives a punitive two-stroke penalty. A comfortable par is transformed into a disastrous double bogey, and what should have become a single-shot Ellenbogen lead instead turns into a yawning three-shot gap. Park looks as if she has been punched in the gut. She loses her concentration, bogeys the next hole, and stumbles to a 40 for the back nine for a total three-over-par 74. Ellenbogen steadies in for a one-over-par 72 and a five-stroke victory.

At the award ceremony at the end of the day, no one mentions the ball-moving two-stroke penalty. Courtney Ellenbogen may not hit the ball long, but "none of the other girls use their brains as much," says an admiring Scott Thompson, Alexis's father. When he is told about the penalty, and that Ellenbogen failed to warn Park of her error, however, he is outraged. "If that happened to my daughter, I don't know what I would have done."

In front of the crowd, Ellenbogen goes through the traditional litany of thank-yous, while a dejected Park only says afterward that she "learned a lesson." Ellenbogen later says she did not notice the error until after Park putted. "I feel bad about it, but it's not my responsibility to tell her to put the ball back," she says. "It's her responsibility."

Vicky Hurst stands off to the side looking dejected. Instead of "going for it" as she had vowed, she lost her concentration and looked frightened out on the course. Though she merits her reputation as a dominant junior player, Hurst has yet to win an AJGA Junior Invitational. She is scheduled to play in two days' time in another tournament in Ohio and then head to Philadelphia for the Betsy Rawls Invitational, where she finished second last year behind Marika Lendl.

For now, Hurst would prefer a pause from golf. But her mother, disappointed by her performance, has other plans. "She insists we go to the driving range—that's her idea of a break," Hurst laments as evening falls in Columbus.

The boys at Rolex endure a similar bruising emotional roller coaster ride that also challenges golf's tradition of etiquette and fair play. The Korean challengers stumble in the second round. First-round leader Alex "Little" Kim shoots a one-over-par 73 for a two-round total 143 that drops him to fourth place. Sihwan "Big" Kim finds himself a further stroke back, tied for eighth.

Two Floridians replace the Kims at the top of the leaderboard. Under the watchful eye of his future Oklahoma State golf coach, Mike McGraw, Peter Uihlein birdies two of the final three holes for a one-under-par 141. If he continues playing with this steadiness, he believes he can win. "It is a major this week," Uihlein says. "The leaders should be around even par or one under par. A course like this takes the 63s out of the equation. I would be happy with 18 pars out there."

Alongside Uihlein at one under par stands Wesley Graham, who has recovered from his college recruiting jitters at FootJoy. He has accepted a scholarship at Florida State, and the peace of mind has helped his game recover its lost sparkle. If Peter Uihlein was born and nurtured to play golf, the seventeen-year-old Graham grabbed onto the game as a way out of a middle-class upbringing and to help conquer his ferocious shyness. Graham hails from Port Orange, an undistinguished suburb of Daytona Beach, where his father sells cars. When he was eight years old, his parents took him to a junior golf clinic. "Wes is one of the old-fashioned, public school kids. His parents have no money, so he can't go to the Academy," says his mother Tammy. "He's our only child and he only started playing AJGA events extremely late, a year ago because of finances." Graham never has seen a nutritionist or sports psychologist. His only "swing doctor" is a little-known local pro called Lawson Mitchell, who teaches at the River Bend club located on Airport Road in Port Orange.

Graham played with his father George when he started out in the game. At age fourteen, Wes beat his father and he hasn't lost since. "All of George's friends ask if it bothers him. George says, 'as a dad, it makes him proud,'" says mom Tammy. She occasionally shares nine holes with her son, though not often. "On a Sunday afternoon if he has nothing to do, he says, 'come on mom, let's do nine holes,'" she says. "But it's frustrating for both of us. He is just so good and I'm a recreational player."

Tall, thin, and angular, Graham's face is sprinkled with freckles. When he does speak, Graham tends to look down at his shoes and mumble, his slow, soft drawl elongating o's and a's to transform the word golf into gaaalf. "You will not get two words out of Wesley Graham," predicts Mac Thayer, the founder of the *Junior Golf Scoreboard* Web site.

Yet behind Graham's shy façade is a quiet confidence. "Every time I step out on the course, I feel I am going to win," he says. No one frightens him, not even Peter Uihlein. "I've played with Peter a million times and I don't feel intimidated by him at all," Graham insists. When golf teachers ordered him to do something without explaining themselves, he dropped them. Little-known Lawson Mitchell pleased him because he "explained why" he needed to do something, according to his mother. Graham does exhibit some weaknesses. He is streaky, notching lots of birdies and lots of bogeys. He takes foolish chances, going for greens when instead he should play the ball safely into the fairways. "His rounds are like seesaws," his mom comments.

On the tournament's third day Graham tees off in the same group as Peter Uihlein. A light drizzle softens the greens and allows players to stop and spin their balls near flags. Wes Graham cruises along until the eleventh hole, a modest par four, which he triple bogeys. Despite a birdie on the following hole—he reaches the green in two shots—he ends with a three-over-par 74 and finds himself in third place. "I played all the other holes just fine and just blew up once," he says, disappointed. "I'm confident that I can still win, but I could have been in a lot better position."

Uihlein suffers more serious regrets. While Graham exhibits a lapse of concentration, Uihlein's temper torpedoes his chances. On the twelfth hole, a par five, he faces what looks like an easy pitch to the green. He hits an average shot to the middle of the green. Angry, he twirls around and whips his club to the ground. Uihlein proceeds to sink a putt for what looks like an ordinary par and moves on to the next tee box, when tournament director Walker Hill approaches him. Without discussion, or any opportunity to appeal, Hill announces an on-the-spot one-stroke penalty for poor sportsmanship. Uihlein offers no resistance and makes no comment, standing still for several seconds.

His tee shot on the next hole, a par three, flies left into a bunker. Although he manages to save par, he slices his drive right into the woods on the fourteenth hole and once again slams his club down onto his bag in disgust. This time, fortunately for him, Walker Hill is not watching. Even though he escapes a penalty, Uihlein is forced to chip out and hit his third shot onto the green. He takes another bogey and finishes with a 74, leaving him in third place with a bruised image. "A spoiled kid," judges one college coach. When journalists ask him later if he has five minutes to discuss his round, Uihlein denies the request. His future Oklahoma State coach, Mike McGraw, is mortified. "Peter should have asked for a couple of minutes to gather his thoughts and then come '

back and answered questions," says McGraw. "He still has some growing up to do."

In the evening, Ohio State greenkeeper Dennis Bowsher surveys his
course. The juniors' golf skill impresses him. He expects the pros coming the following week for the Nationwide Tour event will fail to score
lower than the teenagers. "The kids hit the same 300-yard drives," he
says with awe. But the same kids left his course looking close to a horse
pasture, with unfilled holes pocking up the fairways. "I was disappointed," he laments. "These kids know the fundamentals and mechanics of the game, but they haven't learned the etiquette and the
history." In fairness, the AJGA makes a real effort to teach respect to
their hosts and their environment. It trains winners to give thank-you
speeches. It also conducts "Care for the Course" campaigns during each
event. At the end of each afternoon of play, the AJGA orders all players out onto the fairways, where they pile moist soil over the most glaring divots. Yet so many divots crater the Ohio State fairways that
Bowsher commands his own staff into action.

––––––

The next day, in the tournament's final and fourth round, junior
golf's golden boy fails to recover. Although Uihlein avoids glaring
mental errors—and throws no penalty-invoking temper tantrums—
he struggles with his concentration and his game. His father, Wally,
has flown in from Massachusetts to watch the final round. Uihlein
stands even par through the fourteenth hole, within striking distance
of the lead, when he proceeds to bogey three holes in a row and finishes with a 73, tied for fourth place at five over par for the tournament. On the sixteenth hole, a short par four, Uihlein smacks his
second shot over the green onto the next tee box. He chips back
straight at the flag. "Sit, sit, sit," his mother, Tina, mutters on the sidelines. The ball rolls well beyond the flag. Once again, Uihlein declines

to give any post-match interviews, and the Uihleins leave before the prizes are awarded.

Wesley Graham's hopes soon vanish as well. He gambles on the 378-yard par-four sixteenth hole dogleg, which swerves left around a clump of trees to a sloped green guarded by four bunkers. When played as designed, it requires only a short drive followed by a short iron. Graham instead attempts to go over the trees and to drive the green with a single wham-bam shot, the equivalent of a half-court heave in basketball. The tee shot falls short, into the trees. Graham punches out into the fairway, reaches the green with his third shot, takes a bogey, and finishes with a 76, tied for tenth place.

As the Floridians falter, the Korean players gather momentum. Alex "Little" Kim birdies two holes on the front nine. He birdies the twelfth, putting him three under par for the day. But he proceeds to bogey the fourteenth and fifteenth, and his even-par 71 leaves him tied with Uihlein in fourth place.

Sihwan "Big" Kim, starting from fourth place after consecutive one-over-par 72s in the first three rounds, is paired with Uihlein and Graham and sneaks up on the leaders. He launches his round with a thud, three-putting on the first hole for a bogey. "I was chunking and hooking everything—the angle on my swing was too steep—so I tried something that my coach talked to me about over the phone and it started me straight." After nine holes Kim is one under par for the day. "The hole locations today were really hard, and we all had no choice but to play it safe and to the middle of the greens," he points out. He keeps plugging away, and his putts begin to fall. On the fifteenth hole, he sinks an eight-foot putt for a birdie, bringing him to four under par for the day.

On the sixteenth tee box, Graham tells Kim the course record is four under par. "If I make a birdie, I could go to five under," Kim recalls. "But I didn't want to push it." On the seventeenth, a long par three, he had hit a five-iron during the first three rounds. With the wind against him, he takes out a four-iron. His adrenalin-filled tee shot flies over the green into a bunker, and with it, his best chance of breaking the course record. Avoid a blowup, he tells himself. Kim blasts out to six feet and sinks his par putt. He finishes with a four-under-par 67 for the tournament, three shots ahead of his closest challenger.

At the award ceremony, Kim seems subdued, partly overtaken by a rare calmness, partly with renewed confidence and by a strange sense of freedom. This is his last major junior golf tournament. He plans to spend most of the summer before Stanford playing adult amateur tournaments. "I don't feel as much pressure as I did a long time ago when I was really young," he acknowledges.

The Korean players are not one-dimensional stock characters. Some, like Jane Rah, are spunky and sparkle. Others, like Kristen Park, are shy and soft spoken. Some are big and broad chested, like Sihwan Kim. Others are thin and whispy, like little Alex Kim. Some raise their voices against their parents, and others do not. Yet in Korean culture, one trait seems to dominate: parents will do whatever is needed to cultivate their children to ripen and reach the top. They serve as chauffeur, counselor, and critic all at once. Once successful, the reactions from the offspring seem to diverge depending on sex.

Although many Korean women star on the pro tour—of the 120 players on the LPGA tour, some 45 hail from South Korea—few Korean men do. "Once the boys are released and allowed to experience something new, they find golf is not everything," explains Rah. "We girls stick with it." When asked, Sihwan "Big" Kim says his goal is "to get done with school, get a diploma and go to the PGA." If pressed, though, he seems to express some doubts. He wants to "relax and fish." His parents are pressing him to study engineering, or become a doctor or lawyer. "I don't want to take such a hard major and screw myself," he says. Although Korean parents may seem to push their children harder than other parents, even hard-driving techniques cannot ensure results or prevent an eventual teenage rebellion.

Americans and Europeans may allow their children to leave the nest earlier than Koreans do, but many, like their Korean counterparts, leave their jobs to accompany their children on the junior golf circuit. By definition, such behavior propels young players onto a fast track, where they are judged by excellence, not by their well-roundedness or their social skills.

No one parenting style ensures success, and each child requires a different level of support and has a different need for independence. Bill Ellenbogen has left his daughter alone to compete and triumph. Courtney Ellenbogen, who benefits from her father's athleticism, is driven by her own desire to succeed and does not seem to need the additional pressure of a parent. The Lendl girls benefit and suffer from the close attention of their champion dad. For their part, the parentally pressured Koreans score impressive results. Although too much pressure from parents seems to backfire, the appropriate amount of attention requires of parents a complicated balancing act—one that demands just enough, but not too much, encouragement.

Sihwan "Big" Kim triumphs at the moment when he manages to gain enough self-confidence to fly on his own. As Kim holds up his Rolex trophy, his crooked half smile seems to hide a riddle. Does the impressive, relaxed confidence that he demonstrated in his Rolex win underscore a new determination that will drive him to golf stardom? Or once he arrives at Stanford, will he find new interests that literally take his eye off the little white ball?

Kim is too old to defend his title at the U.S. Junior Amateur. He has outgrown the junior game and will leave the boys he has just whipped to chase the Player of the Year award. They have no time to rest. Two decisive tournaments are scheduled for the following week.

CHAPTER 8

Tenuous Ground

An exhausted Marika Lendl leaves the 18th
green at the Betsy Rawls tournament.

ONE OF THE MOST DELICATE and difficult moments of parenting
is deciding when it's time to leave a child to his or her own devices, like a butterfly emerging from a cocoon. Some kids take off earlier by themselves. Some require coddling. When a child encounters
obstacles, should a teacher or parent intervene? When the inevitable
tough times arrive, do parents and children cooperate, or compete?

As the junior golf season reaches the middle of the summer, parents
and players battle to answer these tough questions. Fatigue and fear
are mounting. Even as teenagers, great athletes are able to dig deep into
their guts to overcome most draining moments. But as golfers are tired
by long days of play, the boundary between parental pushing and encouragement often blurs.

By mid-July, with many of the driven teenagers and parents facing
their seventh straight week of tortuous travel, everyone needs a break.
Among the boys, Peter Uihlein and Cody Gribble, and among the girls,

Courtney Ellenbogen, take a week off. Other Player of the Year candidates don't think they can afford the luxury of time off. They redouble their efforts and attempt to break away from the pack.

A group of exhausted girls gather for the McDonald's Betsy Rawls Championship in Malvern, Pennsylvania, at the White Manor Country Club on the leafy Philadelphia Main Line. Philadelphia boasts a long golf history and is home to renowned courses such as Merion Golf Club. Some fifteen golf courses are located within a half hour drive of Malvern. Once an also-ran in this competitive landscape, White Manor completed a redesign of its golf course in 2003, lengthening it, toughening its defenses, and prettifying its appearance. Raw, natural heather now sprouts up on many holes, creating an attractive, wild look and gobbling up errant balls. Gentle, rolling countryside frames the fairways. "We used to live in anonymity," says Jonathan Clay, the club manager. "People now come and say, 'hey, your new course is great. Why have we never heard of you?'" White Manor is shooting to reach the ranks of the *Golf Digest* list of the Top 100 American golf courses and is eager to promote itself by hosting high-profile tournaments. "We blew up the old, dull course and started out over again," says club pro Marc Levine. "This is a great chance to show it off."

The Betsy Rawls junior event stands out in part on account of a living golf legend. Elizabeth Earle "Betsy" Rawls, born in 1928 in Spartanburg, South Carolina, captured fifty-five professional events, including eight major championships during her pro career, which began in the 1950s and stretched into the 1980s. These days, at nearly eighty years old, she remains trim and fit and continues to have a healthy passion for golf. Since her professional playing days ended she has worked for the Ladies Professional Golf Association (LPGA) as a tournament director. McDonald's has long sponsored an adult ladies' pro event, which was played on the White Manor Country Club course until 1987, when it moved to Wilmington, Delaware. Under Rawls's encouragement "to help girls and junior golf," the fast-food company extended the sponsorship to a junior golf tournament.

Rawls serves as chair and director of the tournament and at the driver's wheel of a golf cart is on the course observing every day. "Betsy lent her name and her reputation, which makes this is a special event," tournament director Randi Reed explains. Ever optimistic and positive, yet frank and direct, Rawls dishes out only gentle criticism of the excesses in modern junior golf parenting. In her judgment, Michelle Wie's parents displayed "poor guidance" for encouraging her to compete against men. The gap in strength between the sexes remains too wide. Among parents, she blames fathers more than mothers for pushing too hard. "The fathers are worse, and often make the girls feel they have failed," she observes.

Rawls's father taught her to play when she was seventeen years old. Her parents' pushing consisted of driving her to the local country club and "dropping me off." Rawls attended the University of Texas, where she studied math and physics and graduated Phi Beta Kappa. A tomboy, she played golf as a hobby, becoming so good that in 1950, competing as an amateur, she ended as runner-up to Babe Didrikson Zaharias at the United States Women's Open. The next year, after turning pro, she won the Open.

This first generation of pro golfers learned their trade by playing the tour. The just-launched LPGA left players to make their own way from tournament to tournament. "We didn't get our nice amenities and services like players do now, being picked up at hotels, carting 'em around all week now, with breakfast and lunch in the locker rooms," Rawls recalls. "We were lucky to have a locker room. We changed shoes in the car. There were no leader boards, the fairways weren't roped off and there were no skyboxes for business spectators."

When Rawls was growing up, no organized women's high school or college teams existed. Title IX and its flood of college scholarships for girls have made a big difference, and she advises young golfers to continue their studies, not jump to the pros. "College teaches discipline, concentration—a lot of the mental things you don't learn out here—and it's fun," she says. "If I had [had] this opportunity when I was a kid, I would have died and gone to heaven."

———

At the Rawls Invitational in both 2004 and 2005, Morgan Pressel, one of the teens who successfully jumped to the pro tour from high school, sauntered to victory. In 2006 Marika Lendl took home her first American Junior Golf Association (AJGA) Invitational title after a five-under-par 209. Vicky Hurst finished second. In 2007 sweltering temperatures have been predicted, and the Lendls are back at White Manor for a rematch with Hurst. After his daughters' collapse in Ohio at the Rolex, Ivan Lendl took them to Florida for some rest and some refresher lessons with their Leadbetter teachers. Marika is sleeping nine to ten hours a day in an effort to shake off the mononucleosis. "It is a long process with mono—If she wants to go out to one party, she could have a relapse. One relapse and you are back where you started," her father says. Marika still often plays twelve or thirteen holes fine before feeling fatigued.

At White Manor Marika opens the first round with what she describes as a "stupid" double bogey on the par-three third. Her tee shot flies into the bunker. She "chunks" her next shot over the green, leaving her a long chip back. She hits to seven feet, only to miss the putt. Early in the summer, her game collapsed after such a poor hole. Today she focuses intently and stands one over par when she arrives at the final hole, which requires a steep uphill climb to the clubhouse. When she reaches the green, she is grinning even though her face is covered with sweat. "Wow, the hill was something," she exclaims, her satisfaction surpassing her fatigue.

The next two days test her vigor. As Marika tires, her shots lose their precision. She shoots a 74 on the second day and a 76 on the final day, to tie for twenty-second place. Her putting proves poisonous. She three-putts a total of eight greens in the final round. Though far from last year's victory, the performance represents an improvement, and Marika appears upbeat. "I putted like Steve Wonder," she jokes. "But I felt fine walking down the final fairway."

The eldest Lendl daughter is looking forward to a break. Marika will play only two additional tournaments for the rest of the summer and is putting her dreams of joining the pro tour on hold. "I am not ready to play the LPGA," she acknowledges. "I need to go to college." She will attend nearby University of Central Florida in Orlando starting in the fall of 2009 because "it's close to home" and because former pro standout Emilee Klein has signed on as golf coach there. Klein, who has come to White Manor to watch her play, spends much of her time chatting with Ivan Lendl. "Marika is going to be just fine," Klein reassures him.

Although Ivan Lendl seems encouraged by Marika's recovery, he remains concerned about Isabelle. The tallest and strongest Lendl daughter reminds Ivan of himself as a child. She exhibits the most ambition and works the hardest. "I didn't need any pushing from my parents to play tennis," he recalls. "The worst thing was when I had to take a day off. I wanted to play every day. If my mom came home and cooked lunch, I considered it a waste of time." In his opinion, Isabelle shares his determination. She works hard. But unlike him, she worries too much. "Isabelle is not just discouraged—she is frustrated," Ivan Lendl explains. "The problem is much more in the head than in the heart, and nobody knows what is there."

Isabelle has responded to her erratic shot making by spending extra hours on the practice range. Instead of berating her, her taskmaster father has displayed sensitivity and understanding, even attempting to get her to reduce her practice time in an effort to lower her stress. He knows firsthand about what he describes as a sophomore slump. When he joined the pro tour in 1979, he was an immediate sensation, winning seven singles titles. But he lost four straight Grand Slam finals before breaking through to win the French Open in 1984. At the start of his career, Lendl played a weak, sliced backhand, and he needed several years to replace it with a strong, topspin backhand. "This is the first time it has ever happened in her life and it is part of growing up—it happens [in] every sport. Tiger went through a two-year slump and I did too," he says. At White Manor Isabelle starts on a positive note, hitting her first six fairways. Then, without warning, her shots start spraying. A drive on the tenth hole heads straight right. Two holes later, another drive lifts only inches off the ground and travels less than 100 yards. Isabelle's shoulders slump, and her tall, imposing frame turns inward. She ends with a disastrous 85. After the round, she walks over to the side and breaks down in tears, while her father embraces her. The competitive champion suddenly transforms into a warm, comforting father. Isabelle stumbles in with an 85 for her second round and a 77 for her final round, leaving her tied for seventy-third out of a field of seventy-six. "This is part of growing up," Ivan Lendl explains. "When she comes out, her mind will be better, stronger. She just cannot see it right now."

During the tournament another golf father, Larry Alger, attempts to commiserate with Lendl. Alger's daughter Elizabeth is struggling in the tournament, shooting 82, 74, and 85 to finish tied for seventy-first place. Elizabeth is scheduled to play with Marika at the University of Central Florida and is "studying" this summer at the Leadbetter Academy in Bradenton. The Leadbetter teachers had changed her swing, infuriating the cigar-chomping, overweight Larry Alger.

"You pay all that money and it doesn't do any good," Alger complains.

"Give it time—think long-term," Lendl advises. "When I changed my backhand, it went bad and it took me a long time to get comfortable. Tiger took almost two years when he changed his swing. First, you are comfortable on the range, then on the course, and only finally in a tournament."

Throughout the tournament, Lendl watches his daughters and surfs the Web from his Blackberry to review the results of the British Open, being played in Carnoustie, Scotland. Lendl recognizes that it will soon become necessary to pull back from his children. In the debate over encouraging and pushing children, Lendl has thought long and hard about his role as a parent. "Encouraging is when they are having trouble, like how I must encourage Marika and Isabelle now when they face difficulties," he says. As he sees it, there's good and bad pushing. Don't make kids do something they don't want to do, he argues. If they don't want to play golf, then you shouldn't push them. If they do want to play golf, they must be pushed to practice. If they want to go to a certain school, they must study. This positive pushing teaches them, he argues, "how to kick butt.'"

Behind every ambitious athlete, Lendl sees a parent or teacher. Without Earl Woods, Tiger would never have become Tiger. But Lendl thinks that at a certain moment the parent must withdraw and free the child. When Earl moved into the background, Tiger, from Lendl's perspective, took off as a golfer. When Lendl was a child, his parents never needed to push him to play tennis. He loved the game. His parents took him to only a few tournaments. At his tennis club, one of the parents would take an entire group of children to the tournament. When he went to the state-run tennis academy, teachers took care of the students. Isabelle went without her father as part of the American team to Wales the year before to play in the Junior Ryder Cup. If she is picked this year for the Solheim Cup in Sweden, Lendl says he will be happy to sit home and watch the United States Tennis Championship. "She doesn't need anybody else to look over her shoulder," he says. If his children finally make it as professional golfers, he vows to "stay home, play some more senior golf tournaments and if a daughter has a chance to win on Sunday, fly in to watch."

———

What the Ryder Cup—a biannual match-play event pitting Europe's best golfers against America's best—is to men, the Solheim is to women. No money is at stake, only goose bumps full of prestige. Each player represents her country, or in some cases, continent, and many see it as the highlight of their golf career. Media scrutiny is intense. National passions become inflamed. The 2007 event has been scheduled for September in southern Sweden. Two days before the main Solheim Women's Cup begins, the best twelve European golfers under age nineteen face off against the best twelve American juniors. Donna Andrews, the U.S. coach for Solheim, must announce her choices on July 31, and the Rawls tournament is one of the final opportunities for the players to score points, move up in the rankings, and impress her.

Ten of the dozen American players are chosen by a mathematical formula based on their rankings. The coach is allowed two wild-card picks. Golf club manufacturer Ping, the AJGA, and the United States Golf Association (USGA) are sponsoring the American team. Travel expenses will be paid for the dozen girls who are chosen to represent their country. Until their recent slump, both Lendl girls looked sure to qualify. But Andrews sees their chances fading as they struggle to get out from under their father's shadow. "Their daddy is putting a lot of pressure on them," she notes. "On the other hand, they are lucky to have him. He understands the mental side of things." She marvels how, after each round, Lendl encourages his children to write down their feelings about each of their shots. "A lot of these girls have all the raw talent in the world, just no course management," she observes.

Andrews, a powerful-looking, dark-haired, forty-year-old, played fifteen years on tour and earned six tournament victories. She represented the United States in the Solheim Cup in 1994 and 1998 and has since retired to teach at the Pine Needles Resort, run a golf fitness lab, and have a child. At White Manor, the competitors' fitness and focus surprise her. "When I was 18, I didn't spend time in the gym," she recalls. "These girls have chosen golf as a path. I played tennis, basketball and golf in high school."

Since she works at Pine Needles, the site of the U.S. Women's Open, Andrews has seen many of her teenage prospects play. Short-hitter Courtney Ellenbogen impressed her most. "I can relate to Courtney's game," Andrews says. "I was never long, but always straight and on the green in two." Ellenbogen stands eleventh in the junior rankings, one away from automatic selection to the American Solheim team. Andrews would have liked her to be playing at White Manor to pick up needed points. But she understands why Ellenbogen decided to skip the event. "A lot of these kids need to take a week off," she says. "They have as grueling a schedule as [we do] on the LPGA."

As she watches and grades prospects from the sidelines, Andrews sees worrying signs of immaturity on the course. The girls display poor nutritional habits, downing sugary sports drinks and sodas, which provide a quick high but are often accompanied by a crash in energy levels. Many neglect to eat bananas, which are helpful in maintaining potassium levels, or protein bars, which offer valuable doses of needed energy.

On the course, even some of the top-ranked juniors display what Andrews describes as poor course management. She points out a green protected by a "false front," an elevated mound of earth. Most girls are pitching the ball high at the flag with a sand wedge. If they miss by a millimeter, the ball comes rolling back, almost to their feet. A wiser, higher percentage shot is a low chip to the beginning of the green that releases the ball to run toward its target.

Vicky Hurst's smooth swing and crisp ball-striking skills wow Andrews. But her natural talent is matched by what Andrews considers an almost unthinking, blind insouciance. On the tenth hole, a short, narrow par four that glides downhill, Hurst bombs her tee shot toward the green in what, at first glance, looks like a stroke of brilliance. The blast, as Andrews sees it, carries maximum risk for limited reward. Hurst's ball lies half a wedge away from the green. If she hit a three wood, she would have needed a full wedge. The three wood benefits from a larger landing area—and reduced room for error—than the driver. "Vicky Hurst wants to hit her driver everywhere," Andrews criticizes. "She doesn't really need it." If Hurst goes to Sweden—and her ranking almost ensures that she will be chosen—Andrews says she will pair her with a "smarter player" who "can help her with course management."

In contrast, Andrews judges the Lendls, despite their poor showing at the Rawls tournament, as mature shot makers. Before each swing, both Marika and Isabelle consult a book that shows them the distance to their target. Almost all golf clubs publish such yardage books, which measure the distance from various points on the course. Most pro golfers read the small publications with religious fervor, yet few juniors have the patience or skill to use them effectively. "The Lendls really can read those yardage books," Andrews says. "I never have seen Vicky pull out her yardage book." Her conclusion is sobering. Vicky Hurst has "the raw talent" to play professional golf. But she will achieve success only "with the right leadership."

In Andrews's opinion, young players shouldn't go pro right away. Most teenagers who come onto the LPGA Tour face a struggle weaning themselves from their parents. "They become used to their mommies and daddies holding their hands," says Andrews. "Many cannot check into hotels by themselves." As long as their parents accompany them, some of the kid phenoms do well. Once their parents step into the background, however, many of the same teenage whizzes turn to busts. As evidence, she points to her contemporary, Michelle McGann, the

1989 rookie of the year who notched up seven wins on the tour in the dozen years her parents stayed alongside her. When McGann turned thirty she started traveling alone, and her golf game collapsed.

Although it is unnecessary, many parents will accompany their children to Sweden for the Solheim, a factor that worries Andrews. "The parents all tell me how great their kids are," she says. "I want to hear from the kids themselves." She wants to know if the kids spend hours on the golf course and practice range because they love the sport or because they want to please their parents. In her mind, a stark contrast exists between the modern generation and her own father and mother, who played more of a supportive role.

Twelve-year-old Alexis Thompson shined at the U.S. Women's Open, but remains too low in the junior rankings to warrant an automatic selection for Solheim. Andrews watches her closely and spends time talking to her father, Scott, who acknowledges that his daughter's temper was on display earlier in the summer at Mirasol. At one tournament, Scott Thompson became so upset with Alexis's "acting up" that he pulled her out of the event and made her sit in the hotel for two days. He says that since then her behavior has improved. "You need a little fire to play well, and it is OK to slap yourself in the side," he says. "But the fire has to be under control."

At the Betsy Rawls event, Thompson demonstrates a newfound maturity. She says she doesn't even remember what went wrong at the Mirasol tournament. "I'm learning if you don't get flustered, your game goes better," she says. During the first round Thompson hits most greens in regulation and looks at thirteen putts for birdies to shoot a solid 72. Thompson felt she could have done much better if she putted well, and under her father's watchful gaze, heads straight to the practice putting green after her round. During the next two days, Alexis scores 73 and 74 to tie for eleventh place. Attitude is a key criterion in selection for the Solheim. After a bad hole, does a player continue downhill? Or does she pull herself up and fight back?

When Andrews tells Scott Thompson that she will select an older player for Solheim, he seems relieved. A trip across the Atlantic by herself may be a step too far, too fast. "I didn't want her traveling all by herself to Europe," he admits. Unlike Michelle Wie's father, Scott Thompson believes his precocious daughter must take her time and "avoid skipping the needed steps" on the road to becoming a professional golfer. Alexis Thompson will concentrate on junior, not adult, events, he says. She will attend college. She will stick to girl tournaments because it is unrealistic to compete against much stronger boys. Until now, her schedule consisted of at least two tournaments a month, year-round. "I will cut back a little next year," Thompson says. "My daughter needs a little down time."

Many of the latent tensions between teenagers and adults rise to the surface during the tournament season particularly, it seems, in single-parent relationships. "We have our moments," Andrea Watts says about her mother, Sunee. "We fight and make up. We fight and make up." During the Rawls Tournament, the Watts lodge with a family from the White Manor club to save money and enjoy some home cooking. Andrea's performances improve in Philadelphia. She shoots 73, 75, and 73 for a total of 221 and ties for sixteenth place. That's eleven strokes better than the previous year at the same tournament played on the same course. "I was scared to be here last year, so if you compare since last summer, I've taken a huge step forward," she says. "I came this year with a goal, a purpose. I know where I am and I know where I am going."

At the same time, Watts acknowledges that she has failed to live up to the promise she showed at the opening tournament of the year at Mirasol. "I've taken a step backwards since June," she admits. "I haven't seen my coach in a long time. I've been on the road a long time and I haven't done as well as I should." After each round, she looks exhausted. Once the Rawls event finishes, mother and daughter will drive back to Ohio, where they will return a rental car, then fly on to Seattle for the United States Girls Junior. At least they will spend a night with friends—and play no golf—before heading to the West Coast.

For her part, Sunee Watts seems tense. Her business in Colorado importing beauty products is struggling in her absence, and she has difficulty delegating authority. She feels guilty because the stop in Ohio means her daughter will miss one practice round before the national championship. And she often wonders whether her late husband would have handled his daughter in a more positive way. "My husband, he was a good encourager," she points out. "He had more confidence in me than I did in myself."

In an unguarded moment, Andrea says she is not yet ready to go to college, without even mentioning the pro tour. She is frightened of leaving her mom, and to her surprise, relieved that she will spend another year in high school at the Leadbetter Academy. "I had always thought I wanted to get out and go to university right away," she says. "Now I am a little apprehensive about it. I have always had my mom at my side, and it is going to be a big change." For her self-esteem and for her game, she needs time. Often she reflects on the final round at Mirasol, where she dueled against Vicky Hurst, only to collapse in the final few holes. "I will beat Vicky, eventually," she insists. "It will happen. I just don't know when. After all, I played pretty average at this tournament and did OK. I can see how much I have improved since last year."

As stress and strain level the playing field, Vicky Hurst seems to have rediscovered her superhuman powers. A week after her tear-filled collapse at the Rolex, she bombed out of contention for the PGA Junior in Westfield, Ohio, with a ten-over-par 82. "I was timid at those tournaments," she says. "I wasn't attacking the pins." In Pennsylvania she has regained the signature confident Hurst strut down the fairways. Her drives crackle. Her approach shots resemble darts, landing near flags and stopping still or rolling backward at their target with spin. She warms up in the first round with a one-under-par 70. The next day she improves to a 67. On the third and final day she shows up wearing a Superman belt buckle. A friend gave it to her that morning, and although she sees little symbolism, the gesture provokes many comments "She's just amazing the way she hits the ball," Marika Lendl notes. "If she managed the course, she would beat everyone here by fifteen strokes."

The conclusive round of the Rawls event shows Vicky Hurst at her best and worst. Dressed in electric blue shorts, a tight white polo shirt, and a blue beret, Hurst makes a slow start and falls back into a tie for the lead at the ninth hole. Her closest challenger is Kristen Park, who is forced to roll her balls onto the green, while the long-hitting Hurst hits with enough spin to shoot straight at the pin. The only question is whether the powerful Hurst will panic. She stays calm. "When it got close, I just stayed focused in the moment," she says. She drops three birdies in a row on the tenth, eleventh, and twelfth holes. Her tee shot on the par-three twelfth threatens to fall for a hole in one.

The final five holes turn into a formality. Hurst finishes with a two-under-par 69, running away with the championship by five strokes. Over fifty-four holes, she totaled fourteen birdies and one eagle. White Manor's managers are awed that a seventeen-year-old girl has proved capable of tearing up their new, toughened course. They want to attract a major LPGA tournament and fear that their layout now will be judged too easy. "Maybe our greens were too receptive," acknowledges club pro Marc Levine. "But that Vicky Hurst—she's a machine!" Betsy Rawls hands the trophy to Vicky and tells her that she is the most impressive young golfer she has seen at her event in years.

"You can truly hit a ball," Rawls says.

"What a compliment," a happy Hurst says afterward, displaying one of her rare smiles. "Betsy Rawls is a legend."

While she acknowledges her good play, Hurst also accepts the criticism that she must become more mature in her play. She must begin to read yardage books and balance her power with wise shot making. "I am aggressive, I always have been that way, but I am learning to play a bit more conservatively," she says. "When I was younger, I went for everything." She greets her long-awaited victory in a major junior tournament with seeming indifference, showing little emotion after holing her final putt. She makes no Tiger-like pump. She displays no graceful, ballerinalike wave of her beret. She doesn't even hug her mother. "I'm not the type of person to show giant emotion," Hurst explains. After the tournament, a journalist asks Hurst what her mother told her after her win.

"My mom said, 'congratulations, but you could have played better'," Hurst admits.

On the junior tour, many of the contestants, even those close to their parents, say they would like to have more free space. The Lendl daughters often squirm under their father's unrelenting oversight. Cody Gribble loves to hunt and fish with his dad, but at tournaments he prefers to hang out with his fellow competitors, whom he calls his best buddies. John Popeck has a girlfriend, Samantha, whom he would like to have watch him play. But he refrains from bringing her to avoid a conflict with his parents. Most times this generational tension goes unspoken, and only rarely does one see the dutiful golfer sons or daughters berate their fathers or mothers. The kids, most of whom are too young to rent a car or hotel room by themselves, have no choice but to accept parental guidance. Deep down, many of them rely heavily on their parents for emotional support through the highs and lows they endure in a particularly demanding sport.

The girls who jump straight from high school to the pro tour often rely on their parents to caddy, coach, chauffeur, and cook. Sometimes golf parents push their children to practice and berate them when they play poorly. Sometimes children resent this parental pressure. But they also realize they need the guidance. It is too difficult to travel the world playing golf tournaments by oneself. College constitutes a bridge between adolescence and adulthood. Without this academic bridge, parents are needed to make the tricky transition.

Koko Hurst is not the type to let her daughter fly away from the cocoon. In her mind, the pressure she puts on her daughter to practice after her dip is the only way to get her back in form. Although her daughter sometimes thinks about rebelling, Vicky Hurst acknowledges that she needs her mom by her side to reach her dreams.

CHAPTER 9

Younger, Better, and More Talented

Cory Whitsett and his professional caddie Ryan Rue march down a fairway at the U.S. Junior Amateur.

MOST CHILDREN COMPETING in top-level golf pick up their first club when they are five or six years old, and in most cases they start playing in tournaments by the age of eight. As a general rule, girls sprint ahead of boys. One would assume that these prodigies would improve as they mature, that seventeen-year-old girls would triumph in the most challenging under-eighteen championships, particularly the most important championship of the season, the United States Girls' Junior Amateur championship.

Strangely enough, this has not been the case during the past few years: girls fifteen and younger have captured the national title. "Most people know the Olympic motto is 'Faster, Higher, Stronger.' Now if the USGA had such a slogan, considering the ages of some of the recent champions, it might be 'Younger, Better and More Talented,'" jokes David Shefter, a United States Golf Association (USGA) official. In the

2006 final, thirteen-year-old Jenny Shin ousted then sixteen-year-old Vicky Hurst. This year, at the Tacoma Country and Golf Club in Lakewood, Washington, Alexis Thompson is only one of three twelve-year-olds in the field. When the long week of golf ends on July 28, Kristen Park, at fourteen years, seven months, and one day, emerges as the fourth-youngest girls' junior national champion.

Explanations vary for the success of ever-younger golfers. Junior high schoolers such as Thompson benefit by virtue of their youth. They remain too young for boyfriends or for university recruiters, less stressed than players attempting to attract attention from the other sex or from interested college coaches. In a few years, many formerly confident players will falter as they face pressure to make life choices.

Sports carry a fierce element of chance, and perhaps more than most sports, golf is unpredictable. With the seeming exception of Tiger Woods, even the strongest young favorites win only a few tournaments in a row. The organization of the USGA's junior championships favors outsiders. The main tournament itself stretches over six full days. The first two rounds consist of stroke play, with the lowest-scoring 64 players qualifying from the original unwieldy 156-contestant pool. This unfamiliar, multiday formula leaves many opportunities for favorites to falter. Just a week after her triumph at the Betsy Rawls Invitational, Vicky Hurst makes an unlikely early exit from the national championship, shooting a 74–79–153 and drops to number three in the Polo Golf Rankings. "She is surprised, I am surprised, you are surprised, everyone is surprised," Dan Mirocha, *Golfweek's* television commentator, gasps. Hurst herself offers no convincing explanation for her collapse, saying she felt well prepared. "Last week, I was making a lot of putts and this course fit me," she says.

Once the two rounds of stroke play are completed, surviving players engage in a grueling head-to-head match play, where an underdog who gets hot for a few holes can beat even the top-ranked players. Stroke play often resembles modern high-tech warfare, in which one cannot see one's enemies. Match play is more like hand-to-hand combat, where the contestants are pitted in the same group. The first round lasts eighteen holes. On subsequent days, winners play against one another twice a day, eighteen holes in the morning and a second eighteen in the afternoon. Before the Junior Girls' event, Kristen Park never experienced this type of close-up combat. Her inexperience proves a blessing. She tees off weighted down by few worries about her opponent.

Among boys, similar, if less-pronounced, trends are visible. Four fifteen-year-olds have captured the U.S. Junior Amateur. In 2004, inexperienced fifteen-year-old Sihwan Kim triumphed, citing his youthful lack of fear as the determining factor. He was only twenty-two days older than Tiger Woods when Woods won the 1991 Junior Amateur, at fifteen years and seven months. Kim defeated fourteen-year-old David Chung of Fayetteville, North Carolina. In 2005 and 2006, however, experience triumphed in the boys' division. Seventeen-year-old Kevin Tway, son of professional Bob Tway, emerged on top in 2005, and seventeen-year-old Rolex Player of the Year Peter Francis dominated in 206.

Kim is too old to compete in 2007, and seventeen-year-old Peter Uihlein sizes up as the favorite. It will be Uihlein's fifth attempt to win the U.S. Junior Amateur—his final opportunity. Uihlein takes a week off to prepare, skipping one of the American Junior Golf Association's (AJGA) main events. Some other top-ranked players also allow themselves to rest. Cody Gribble stays home in Texas.

Most other top-ranked junior boys head to Florida for the Hewlett Packard Junior Championship at Arnold Palmer's Bay Hill Club & Lodge in Orlando. After their thrashing in Ohio by the Koreans, the Florida-based golfers are delighted to be back on their familiar home ground. Chinese-born player Mu Hu enters the tournament with low expectations. His wrist, injured at the Rolex in Ohio, continues to bother him. When he returns to Florida, he consults David Leadbetter about his off-line swing. The solution is "just simple stuff—become more stable with my body," he says. Instead of perching his chest forward, he must keep his feet firmly planted on the ground, balancing his weight equally between his upper and lower body.

Comfortable in Florida, Hu no longer needs his mom to follow him and take care of him. The seventeen-year-old can stay at home, not in a hotel, and drive by himself to the golf course. After each round, he can confer with his sports psychologist. Throughout the four-day Hewlett Packard Invitational, Hu wields the "secret" counseling to keep his calm and composure. In the first round, he leaps out in front with a two-under-par 70. Despite pain from his wrist, he stays in first place the next day, shooting a second 70. Although Hu feels fine the next day, finishing with a one-under-par 71, another Floridian, Wesley Graham, fires a five-under-par 67 in the third round to leap ahead of him. Graham's round includes an eagle on the par-five sixteenth hole. "It was awesome because an eagle really motivates you," Graham recalls.

Before the final round, Hu's injured wrist flares up. "I thought about withdrawing this morning, actually," he says afterward. "But I hit about four range balls this morning and went straight to play." Yet it takes only four holes for the budding Chinese star to capture the lead against Graham. Once ahead, he never relinquishes his advantage. Graham birdies the twelfth hole to get back within a shot of Hu and create some suspense. But he never gets closer. It's good to finish in second place, especially in an Invitational," Graham says, half-satisfied. "One of these tournaments, I'm going to have a good final day and win one of these things."

For Mu Hu, the victory represents a breakthrough. On the final round, he hit fifteen out of eighteen greens, marked seven birdies, and ended with a five-under-par 67. He has shaken off his reputation for final round choking and being a perennial runner-up. "My goal today was to just go out, relax and play my game," he says. "I thought I accomplished that." If he continues on the same path, he believes he will challenge Peter Uihlein for the U.S. Junior Amateur. "I won here with a wrist injury," he says, in a soft, calm voice. "It's obvious that I can play better. If healthy, I can go a long way."

———

When the players arrive for the 2007 U.S. Junior Amateur on July 22 at the Boone Valley Golf Club, about fifty miles southwest of Saint Louis, bull's-eye in the middle of middle America, they find themselves in a place that feels like Florida on steroids. Temperatures spike up into the mid-90s, accompanied by a sultry, sweaty humidity that turns legs into Jello. Pioneer Daniel Boone's historic homestead, now a museum, is located next to the golf club. In this neck of nature, trees grow thick and roads run narrow. Deer and wild turkey continue to patrol where Boone once made tracks.

At the end of the last century, Enterprise Car Rental founder Jack Taylor pursued another civilizing mission, building a world-class, elite golf course in Boone's land. Taylor wanted to play golf at his whim. He and his partner, Doug Albrecht, went searching for a piece of land and bought a farm. Boone Valley counts only 200 men among its members and allows few guests. The Taylor family underwrites a considerable deficit from its own funds, says Albrecht, who serves as tournament chairman, president of the club, and CEO of the Centric Group, part of the Enterprise Car constellation. No homes or condominiums are built around the course. Boone Valley sees itself as a destination in and of itself. More than an hour from St. Louis, the remote club represents an opportunity for a full-day excursion—a retreat for the prominent city elders to repair and socialize, in private. "We're not after publicity or the pros or national rankings," says Albrecht. "We want to help amateur golf, the future of golf."

Golf architects Pete Dye and his son P. B. drew up the Boone Valley layout in 1989. The Dyes design devilishly difficult and deceptive courses. They are responsible for one of golf's most recognizable and demanding holes, the ferociously frightening, seventeenth island green hole at the Tournament Players Club in Sawgrass, Florida. There, the par three measures only 132 yards, but save a small path, the undulating, 78-foot-long green and a tiny bunker in front of it are surrounded by water.

Many Dye traits are visible at Boone Valley: wooden pile mounding around numerous water hazards; fingerlike wetlands; and large, old trees left in play. Players must hit precise tee shots or play around the limbs and branches. Fescue grass, miles of rock walls, and contoured greens challenge even the most accomplished players. The vast elevation changes include dips and rolls as fairways twist through valleys lined with boulders and rocky outcroppings. In other words, as more than one golf writer has remarked, a Pete Dye golf course requires bringing a lot of golf balls. Boone Valley plays at par 71, measures 7,052 yards, and has a slope rating of 146 and a course rating of 75.4—the latter two figures indicating a tough layout.

The USGA has sent its own taskmasters to set up the course for the Junior Amateur tournament, and the club has closed the course for two full weeks to toughen it up. The break allows for fairways to be narrowed to a mere thirty yards, rough to grow to four full inches, and greens to be shaved to Formula One speed.

From the first tee shot, the Junior Am looks like a distinctive junior golf tournament. Television cables string along the fairways and the *Golf Channel* has parked a broadcast studio converted from a mobile home at the far end of the course. The station televises the tournament's final rounds. A press room occupies a wing of the clubhouse, and players are called to press conferences after their rounds. Instead of parents driving their children to the course in rented cars, official vans chaperone the contestants to and from their hotel. "The players are treated as if they are playing for a national championship," Albrecht explains. Several dozen rules officials are mobilized, and hundreds of spectators watch the matches, walking alongside the players. At crucial moments, throngs surround the greens.

For Devin Komline, the short-hitting, left-handed qualifier from Dorset, Vermont, the razzmatazz of the Junior Amateur is a new experience, both exhilarating and overwhelming. He won the qualifier at Shaker Ridge playing in anonymity. This is his first time competing in a high-profile event against junior stars such as Peter Uihlein and Mu Hu.

Komline likes to talk with his playing partners, but the atmosphere at the Junior Amateur is serious, and few competitors engage in conversation. With the exception of parents, tournament rules allow caddies, and players spend most of their time discussing strategic options with their bag haulers. During a practice round, none of the golfers in his group talks to Devin. "He was very upset, he loves to chat on the course," his father, Keith Komline, says. The Komlines put in an urgent call to a friend from his Vermont club to come and caddy. He arrives the night before the first round.

Even in the deep summer heat, Devin is hounded by his continuing cough. After the qualifier at Shaker Ridge, his father again took him to the doctor, who couldn't explain what is wrong. "I don't think it affects his golf," his father says. "But it's so loud that it affects me when I play with him."

Boone Valley is longer and tougher than any other layout Komline has played, and the short-hitter struggles with the golf course's length. Komline needs a fairway wood to carry the water on his second shot on the thirteenth hole, a 474-yard par four. The monster hole, dubbed "Lookout" by the course architects, plays downhill to an undulating fairway that provides few level lies. It requires an all-carry approach over a lake to a wide green. During his first round, Komline's luck falters. His second shot flies into the flower beds ringing the back of the green. Komline asks for an official. In most tournaments, a player would be allowed a free drop to a safer, more stable spot. When he asks if he can remove the ball from the flower bed, he's told by the official that he must hit it from its current position.

Komline squibs the ball a few yards, takes a double bogey, and finishes with a first-round three-over-par 75.

"Devin got a bad break," Keith Komline observes.

An imposing figure who contrasts with his frail-looking son, Komline expresses his desire for Devin to soak up the surroundings and stop worrying about his results. "I just want him to enjoy being here . . .having the chance to spend four and a half hours walking in this beauty," he says. Keith Komline's reactions reflect his own experience as a professional athlete. Unlike Ivan Lendl or Petr Korda, he was a journeyman tennis tour player who spent most of his career competing in second-tier professional tournaments in Europe. "I was a good practice player," he says. "I wasn't a great tournament player." Even though Komline never qualified for the major events, he made a decent living. He appreciated how his athletic ability allowed him to travel the globe, to play a game he loved.

Because of his own experiences as a professional athlete, Keith Komline remains skeptical of the fairway dreams propelling many junior golfers. Many of his best friends, several much higher ranked as tennis players, failed to make fortunes from tennis. Most professional sports generate an income pyramid that would frighten even many hardened capitalists: the number one rakes in 99 percent of the available sponsorships, leaving the crumbs to talented second-place players.

Many of the parents attending the national golf championship upset Komline. When he spots a father chastising his son for chipping rather than putting from the fringe of a green, he cringes. He dislikes the idea of sports academies. "I saw all those kids going off to play tennis at Nick Bollettieri's in Florida, and thought, 'who would send their kids off

like that at age 12, 13 years old—that's the best period of their lives?'"
One of the reasons Komline moved to Vermont was to set up a tennis
academy that would allow kids to practice close to home. Upon his father's insisting that he play a team sport, Devin participated on the soccer team through his freshman year of high school. Unlike most of the
top-ranked players at the U.S. Junior Amateur, Devin has not yet set-
tled on college. He is a good student, but his father wants to avoid putting pressure on him. He does not dream of his son becoming a
journeyman professional golfer.

Devin lacks guidance from a regular coach. No top-ranked pro lives
in Vermont to teach him. A few decades ago, many golf teachers spent
summers in New England and winters in Florida. Today, most make
their homes full time in the south. "Devin spends a lot of time working
by himself, watching the *Golf Channel*," his father explains. During the
winter, he hits balls into an indoor net in the basement, and father and
son travel once a month to Florida to play a few rounds. Keith admits
that Devin might benefit in terms of his mental game by talking to a
sports psychologist. "You make three birdies and you can't be dancing
down the fairways," he says. "You make three bogeys, and you don't
want to be wrapping the club around the trees."

In the second round, Devin figures he needs to shoot another 75 to
survive the cut. He struggles from the start. On the second hole, he
needs to hack his ball out of the deep rough and takes four putts for a
triple bogey. "Uh, oh, the bounce in his step is gone," observes his father,
watching from the sideline. Although Devin pars the next hole—"a
good comeback," his satisfied dad says—he must hit a wood to the
green on the next hole, a long par four. "You miss the green here, and
it is death," Keith says. Devin's ball takes off, following a low trajectory and screaming left to bury deep into the rough. Because the greens
are so hot and hard, his chip rolls well past the flag, and he takes another bogey. Another chip spins by the flag on the next hole, and on
the seventh hole, Devin's shot smashes into the macadam path used by

golf carts and bounces off target, leading to a double bogey. Suddenly
the wind picks up, and Komline's shots fall short of target. By the time
he begins the final nine holes, he needs to shoot three under par to have
a realistic chance of making the cut. Instead, he unravels and slides to
a disastrous 85, a total of fourteen over par, and a tie for last place. He
will be flying home without participating in the decisive match play.

"He's had a good time," Keith Komline assesses. "He's had a fine
week."

"What do you mean, dad?" Devin interrupts. "It's never fun to shoot
an 85. Nothing went right. It's a great experience being here, but not
being able to compete, just hanging in, is really frustrating."

Devin fails to understand how other competitors manage to beat par
on such a difficult golf course. He vows to lift weights in the off-season
to build up his distance. He will see a sports psychologist. "I wasn't focused enough," he explains. "I got to get my head into the game. I got
to step it up."

———

For the top players at the U.S. Junior Amateur, the first two stroke
rounds are a mere warm-up. John Popeck, the Pittsburgh star, hits the
same flower bed on the long thirteenth hole that bedeviled Devin Komline. But his ball bounces back on the green. Popeck shoots 71 and 70
and finishes even par for the two days, tied for sixth place.

Favorites Mu Hu, Cody Gribble, Wesley Graham, and Peter Uihlein qualify easily. In the first round, Hu holes a forty-five-birdie putt
in the eighteenth hole and ends in third place with a two-round two-
under-par total of 140. The temperatures soar into the high 90s, complete with sweltering humidity, yet Hu finds the heat pleasant
compared to Florida. "I'm used to it, so I have an advantage," he says.
Other players and parents are impressed and make him the favorite.
"Mu's on a roll, he's really hot, and it's whoever who gets hot," says Bill

Gribble. His son Cody finishes twelfth with a 144. Wesley Graham ties for twenty-second place with 146. Peter Uihlein stands one stroke worse. On the long fourteenth hole, Uihlein copies Komline and hits into the dreaded flowers, ending up with a nine. Afterward he remains confident, citing his motivating quintuple bogey ten at the FootJoy earlier in the year.

"This is probably a good omen for me," Uihlein jokes.

The top stroke play finisher is sixteen-year-old Korean Sueng Yul Noh, the Korean amateur men's champion, who traveled to the United States to compete in the USGA championship. In the first round, Noh shoots a two-under-par 69. He improves to a four-under-par 67 in the second round, which includes five birdies. Noh speaks no English and wears an air of mystery, hiding his eyes behind dark sunglasses and wearing a thick layer of white sunscreen, answering questions through his caddie, Benny Kim. When Noh turns eighteen in two years, his caddy says, he will probably turn pro.

At the end of thirty-six holes of stroke play, eight players are tied for the final spot. Justin Estrada from Yuba City, California, heads to the driving range to hit a few balls before the scheduled playoff. He arrives at the tee two minutes late and is given a two-stroke penalty. A large gallery crowds around the tee box. Estrada drives in the middle of the fairway and knocks his second shot four feet from the flag. He makes the putt for what would have been a birdie and a step toward a place in match play. Instead, it counts as a tournament-ending bogey. "It's my fault, I missed the tee time," says a disconsolate Estrada, who displays amazing maturity and poise. Estrada follows the rest of the playoff, clapping for good shots. "Now that's real sportsmanship," says the tournament director, Pat McKinney. Two other players, Jackson Beindorf of Vero Beach, Florida, and Ethan Tracy of Hillard, Ohio, advance to the second playoff hole with birdies. Dark is falling fast. Tracy, struggling to see the ball, bogeys the next hole. Beindorf pars and qualifies.

For his extra work, Beindorf ends up facing Noh in the first match at 8:00 the next morning. Although almost all of the top-ranked players have sauntered through the two stroke rounds, they now face sudden-death pressure. Their scores are erased, and everyone starts over. Although players are seeded from one to sixty-four in order of their scores during the first two days, ratings lose much of their meaning. In match play, in which one player is pitted against another, upsets are common. A few lucky birdies can make all the difference, and a single poor hole that can prove catastrophic in regular events becomes a simple misstep, resulting in only a single lost point. "The wonderful thing about this tournament is that unknowns can win," says Bill Gribble. "There are guys who couldn't afford to go to other tournaments. For them, this is the big banana."

Mu Hu, perhaps the hottest player at the Junior Amateur, is paired against little-known Luke Guthrie, who finished sixty-first in the two days of stroke play. Hu finished ten shots ahead of his opponent in stroke play and radiates confidence. Before this event, Guthrie says his biggest victory was in an Illinois tournament held at his home club. "I just need to play steady," Hu insists. "It only gets interesting in the quarter finals when I face players like Peter."

Yet Hu has little experience with match play, and Guthrie holds home-field advantage, growing up in Quincy, Illinois, only two hours by car across the Mississippi River. "I've been down a lot in this area, and I know it," Guthrie says. "Mu is a good player and he is playing well, but I'm not scared of anyone, except perhaps Tiger." Guthrie's family and friends are watching and rooting for him. He takes command of the match from the beginning, carding two birdies on the front nine to go five up by the eighth hole. Even though Mu birdies the next hole, he never catches up. Guthrie closes him out with six holes remaining. "I wasn't feeling any pressure," Guthrie says afterward. A disappointed Hu can only say afterward, "I was ambushed."

Other favorites meet similar early-round surprises. John Popeck comes into the eighteenth hole tied against unranked Will McCurdy.

Boone Valley's eighteenth hole stacks up as a punishing finishing hole, a long par four. On the left, a series of rough-covered mounds and two bunkers line the fairway, and on the right a bunker and vast prairie grass lurk. The second shot must carry over a large lake to an immense green of approximately 25,000 square feet. Appropriately, Dye dubbed the hole "Waterloo."

Today, the pin is tucked up front near the water. Ever aggressive, Popeck shoots right at it and comes up short, his ball falling back into the water. His opponent plays for an easy par. Popeck takes a penalty, bogeys, and is out of the tournament. "Tiger Woods would have gone for it, too," Popeck says defiantly after the match.

Cody Gribble falls in the second round against unknown Tim Honeycutt of Placerville, California. Gribble misses putt after putt. His father attributes his defeat to his son's struggle to overcome pressure on the course.

In contrast, Wesley Graham escapes his initial scare. in the first round. Graham trails throughout the match against David Chang even though he is playing well, hitting every fairway and landing many irons ten feet or closer to the pins. On the seventeenth hole, Chang misses a two-and-a-half foot par putt. "That was a real gift," Graham acknowledges. Instead of teeing off on the final hole behind by a stroke, Graham finds himself all square.

The two players enter into a sudden-death playoff. On the first playoff hole, Graham's five-foot birdie putt lips in and out, without falling. "It actually came back on me," Graham said. The marathon ends only on the next hole, the twentieth contested, when Graham drops a twelve-foot putt for birdie. "This was the most stressful match I've ever played in," Graham says, as he wipes sweat from his brow.

In the next round, Peter Uihlein veers into trouble. With four holes to play, he trails Hunter Hamrick of Montgomery, Alabama, by two. Uihlein inches back with a birdie on the fifteenth hole, then ties the match when he manages par on the 486-yard seventeenth and Hamrick bogeys. On the difficult eighteenth hole, Uihlein chips his third shot to three feet. His par putt proves decisive when Hamrick three-putts from long range for a bogey. "I dodged a huge bullet," Uihlein says afterward.

Only sixteen players remain in contention when Uihlein faces off in the third round against Jeffrey Kang of Fullerton, California. The favorite faces less of a challenge than in the previous round and forges a quick two-hole lead. On the tenth, he maintains his advantage by sinking a twenty-foot par putt, and on the thirteenth, he buries Kang by holing a sand wedge shot from 126 yards for eagle two. "You kind of get the adrenaline going," he explains. His mother and his uncle, who live in St. Louis, are following him during the match. "Peter just didn't give him any air to come up," his uncle observes.

Uihlein is both confident about and fearful of the next day's quarterfinal. "I am ranked number one; at this age, you guys know about each other, everybody knows who you are," he says. "It is a plus, since guys give me a little respect." Each day his play is improving, and he walks with the slight swagger of someone who has overcome his reputation as Mr. Second. In interviews after rounds, Uihlein keeps mentioning his first-round ten at FootJoy and his subsequent comeback and triumph. Yet the year before he lost at the same stage of the tournament. While carrying the favorite tag may frighten the other players, he acknowledges that it generates a certain pressure, particularly since he is playing against an unknown.

Uihlein's opponent is skinny, five-foot-eleven, 135-pound, fourteen-year-old high school freshman Anthony Paolucci from Texas, who entered the tournament ranked 196th in the nation. Paolucci has never contested in a match-play event. He qualified for the Junior Am only by traveling to visit his grandparents in Ohio, where the field was weak. But Paolucci watched how underdog Argentinean Angel Cabrera held off Tiger Woods in the 2007 United States Open. His father, Mike Paolucci, played golf at Ohio State and has spent a lot of time banging balls with his son. "I'm an extra set of eyes on the video screen helping him understand what's going on with his swing." his father says. Despite his lack of experience, Paolucci knows how to string together birdies. Not long before coming to Boone Valley, he posted a 64 in a local Texas tournament.

It is 7:00 a.m. on Friday, July 27, when Paolucci tees off against Uihlein. Wally Uihlein has flown in from Massachusetts for what looks set to become a coronation for his son.

Although the young Texan challenger falls behind on the first few holes, he sinks a par put on the ninth to go one up. "I told myself on nine, 'I can beat this kid'," says Paolucci. Four holes later, Uihlein puts his ball in the water. Paolucci pounces, pushing his advantage by sinking a long birdie putt. On the fourteenth, Paolucci leaves an eight-foot par putt short on the lip and pumps his fist in a mixture of disgust and frustration as he fails to extend his lead. "I told myself, 'Don't choke coming in'," says Paolucci. He proceeds to hook his drive on the fifteenth hole into the ankle-high rough, followed by a thin approach shot that the elevated green repels. Uihlein sculpts a forty-foot chip to within five feet of the hole. He sinks the putt, and Paolucci's lead narrows to a single hole.

"Come on Pete baby, let's go!" Uihlein's caddie belts out as the two head to the next tee.

The sixteenth hole plays as a long, 224-yard par three that slopes downhill to an expansive, two-tiered green. Uihlein strikes his ball at the middle of the green. He barks orders at his ball, yelling "sit, sit, sit." His ball behaves and brakes in the middle of the green. "Nice shot, bud," his mother exclaims, clapping in approval on the sidelines.

Paolucci drives right of the green and hits a poor chip. He takes a bogey four, putting Uihlein in a position to grab back a point. Instead, Uihlein three-putts. When his par effort rolls by the hole, he whips off his hat in disgust. Paolucci remains one up.

The seventeenth hole is a 486-yard par four that plays to a three-tiered green guarded by bunkers and prairie grass. Paolucci's second shot finds the bunker. Uihlein's drive leaves a mere wedge to the green. Though his shot falls a bit short, he chips to within six feet of the hole, while Paolucci faces a seven-footer for par. The young Texan hesitates. He looks over the angles, one, two, three times, before rolling his ball wide right of the cup. It's Uihlein's turn. If he sinks his six-footer, he squares the match. He steps up, caresses the ball, and drops it in.

"Come on!" he screams.

By this time, more than 100 spectators of all ages are crowding around the players. Having pulled even, Uihlein enjoys the momentum. During every round in the tournament, Paolucci missed the eighteenth fairway with his tee shot. This time the underdog drives dead center, leaving about 130 yards to the hole. Uihlein tees off straight to the middle of the fairway. He has 145 yards to go to reach his goal. Uihlein must hit first. His approach flies about twenty feet left of the flag. "I knew he was going to have a tough putt," says Paolucci. "I was trying to get inside his ball." He stops his iron shot within eight feet.

Uihlein steps up first to putt. His read of the ball's trajectory suggests a mild left-to-right break. But his ball bends around the hole.

It's Paolucci's turn. He studies his line, moves over the ball, and makes a measured motion. As he watches his ball head away, he pumps his right fist before it disappears. "I pretty much knew halfway there on mine that it was in the hole," Paolucci says.

An infuriated Uihlein chucks his ball into the water in front of the green and offers a cursory handshake. His dreams of equaling Tiger Woods and grabbing a national championship have vanished. Each day during the tournament, he had politely answered questions after his victories. After this crushing defeat he bolts to the parking lot, where his mom meets him and whisks him away. Back in the locker room, the talk is of David versus Goliath, not only in the sense of the small slaying the big, but in terms of Goliath's lack of mental maturity.

Much of the discussion off the course of the Junior Am concerns caddies. Most participants believe a bag carrier conveys a real advantage, offering soothing consolation after poor shots and continual encouragement in tense situations. A round of golf, even for adults, often resembles a roller coaster of highs and lows. A talented caddie smoothes the ride. Many parents would like to carry their boys' bags, but the tournament rules forbid it. Bill Gribble caddied his son to victory in the Western Invitational earlier in the summer. "We're batting 1,000," he says. "We have our arguments, but on the golf course I'm pretty supportive." A local boy is working for Cody, but Bill Gribble is unimpressed. "I should have brought someone from Dallas," he says wistfully.

Most caddies are either friends of the players or local teenagers. Paolucci has hired a local, sixteen-year-old Gerard Choinka, and is paying him $50 a round. "It's nice money and a lot of fun," Choinka says.

Another Texan, fifteen-year-old Cory Whitsett, looked even further afield for an advantage and hired a professional bag carrier named Ryan Rue. Until a few weeks before the event, Rue caddied for pro standout Chris DiMarco. (DiMarco, who has struggled at his game, has decided he needs to try another assistant.) "It's the perils of the job," Rue explains. When the Junior Am wraps up, he plans to head to the next Professional Golf Association (PGA) Tour stop and attempt to pick up a bag. For him, this junior championship is a stopgap. Even so, he seems to put 100 percent into his work, wiping clean Whitsett's clubs and ball, discussing what club to hit and standing behind his player to line up each shot. When he agrees with the line, he offers Whitsett an encouraging "yup, go get 'em," and walks away to watch. He explains that as a caddie, the first golden rule is "you must always support your player."

Rue is impressed. Whitsett, though only fifteen, carries himself with a maturity beyond his years, responding to questions politely and thoughtfully, always beginning his answers with a gentle, "yes, sir." His father, Geoff Whitsett, is a renowned surgeon who is taking much of the summer off to accompany his son at golf tournaments. "My patients will have to wait," he says. The elder Whitsett, bearded, thin, and taut, looks much more intense than his easygoing son. But the young Whitsett seems to have inherited his father's surgical mind, as he scans and dissects the golf course. "He thinks his way around the golf course," Rue explains.

Whitsett's conservative Polo style distinguishes him as more preppie than rogue: his clothes are prim and pressed, every strand of his shock of black hair perfectly in place, and his walk and his speech are measured and precise. While fellow Texan Cody Gribble's sounds like a cowboy, Whitsett's Southern drawl remains ever so light. He could almost be mistaken for a New England Brahmin.

In the quarterfinals on Thursday, Whitsett faces off against the fearsome Korean Seung Yul Noh, who breezed through the opening rounds with 4&3 and 6&5 victories. By the thirteenth hole Noh leads by two holes. . The precocious Texan recovers one on the next hole with an accurate wedge and birdie. The turning point comes on the fifteenth. Noh looks over a mere four-footer for birdie. If he sinks it, he wins the hole and moves two holes ahead. "It was just one of those putts where you know you're going to make it right when you see it," Whitsett says. Instead, Noh sends his ball sliding by the hole.

The steady, silent Korean continues to hide his emotions behind his Kabuki-style face mask, even as the young Houston native takes a one-hole advantage into the final hole. Whitsett threatens to unravel. He sails a nine-iron over the green and into waist-high fescue. Although he fears his ball has buried deep into the tough brush, it lies up on top of the wiry weeds. "I'm not going to lie to you: I was lucky with that lie," Whitsett says. He pitches his ball to eighteen feet.

Noh's ball sits just off the green after two shots, offering an easy-looking chip. But he clunks his chip, moving the ball only a few feet. After the amateurish shot, Noh's confidence evaporates. He misses the ensuing twelve-foot putt for par. Whitsett now needs only two putts for victory. H e makes no mistake, tapping in his second shot. "I got kind of lucky, but I'll take it," Whitsett says.

"Wow, that was like a bar room brawl," says an exhausted Geoff Whitsett.

The afternoon semifinals shape up as equally bloody: Whitsett against the championship's hottest player, Wesley Graham. In the morning, Graham finished his best match of the tournament, shooting four birdies on the front nine and finishing off Sean Dale of Jacksonville by the thirteenth hole. Graham either has annihilated his opponents, or as in the first-round tussle against David Chung, has displayed a never-say-die attitude.

The young Whitsett expresses no fear about taking on the Floridian, even though the seventeen-year-old Graham benefits from two years of additional experience. "I've been hitting well, getting everything honed in," Whitsett says. "The older kids are just golfers—they can't shoot it any different than the young kids." His recipe looks simple. "Just got to go out and P-L-A-Y," he says, pronouncing each letter.

On the first hole Whitsett gets up and down from a greenside bunker for par. Graham three-putts for a bogey. On the second hole, Graham strikes his approach fast, finding a front bunker. He hooks his drive on the third hole into the rough. Whitsett responds by sinking a fifteen-foot birdie putt to go three holes ahead. Graham sends his next drive far left, and the ball scrambles across a cart path like a frightened jackrabbit, resulting in an unplayable lie and a bogey as Whitsett two-putts for par. "I just couldn't get anything going in the match," Graham says. "I lost the first five holes and I never in my life would have thought that would happen."

Graham wins his only hole on the seventh when Whitsett hits his drive into the water. The Floridian, usually inspired and emotional on the course, seems lifeless. Whitsett tightens the noose with a two-putt for par on the twelfth to restore his five-hole lead. Graham sits off the edge of the green with his back to the action. "I didn't get pumped up like in the morning because I didn't make any putts," he says. "I was out of the match."

Whitsett remains cautious. He remembers the previous year's semifinal match between Richard Lee and Kevin Tway, when Lee erased Tway's four-up lead, wresting away control of the seventeenth hole for the comeback victory. But this scenario never happens. The young Texan wins the next hole to finish off the match. As Whitsett sees it, he's the same kid as the eight-year-old who saw Tiger Woods demolish the field in the 2000 U.S. Open and decided golf would be his lifelong vocation. Now he has an opportunity to match his idol, who won this same tournament for the first time at the same age.

———

The semifinal to determine Whitsett's opponent in the finals pits Anthony Paolucci against a Pennsylvanian named Sean Brannan. Seventeen-year-old Brannan comes from a hardscrabble background, unlike almost all the other Junior Am contestants. His mother brought him up single-handedly, and his grandfather, Scott Stultz, introduced him to golf. The game offers Brannan an unexpected means of escape—which his grandfather finances with his pension. Twice a year Brannan and his grandfather drive to Georgia to visit Brannan's coach. Otherwise, Brannan trains by himself. At the Junior Am, Brannan carries his own bags. Stultz suffers from emphysema and lacks the energy to follow his grandson through his round. Brannan has only played a few major junior tournaments and sneaks through the first rounds, in his own words, "under the radar." Brannan plays two rounds on Wednesday and wins his morning match on Thursday. "I'm not tired," he insists as he prepares to tee off against Paolucci in the semifinals.

Before the semifinals, the tournament organizers offer to pay for a caddie for Brannan, but he refuses. "I don't think it would help, it might even hurt, going this far and then chang[ing], it wouldn't be smart," he says. Brannan admits to having three or four blisters on his feet bothering him. "I have Band-Aids on them and they should be all right," he insists, explaining that he has a bad back that often forces him to play through pain.

The Pennsylvanian gets off to a good start and looks set to end the fairytale Paolucci dream. On the fourteenth, the uphill par five, he reaches the green in two shots. Although his eagle putt rolls by the hole, he sinks the birdie comeback and is two full holes ahead with only four left to play. Both players need only a pitch second shot on the next hole, a narrow par four. Brannan leaves his ball just short of the green. Paolucci veers his shot left of the target. As he chips, Paolucci's twelve-year-old brother Vincent, overcome by emotion, falls on the ground, and his brother's ball drops into the hole for a birdie. The young Texan has narrowed his deficit to a single hole.

Both players par the sixteenth hole, the downhill par three. On the seventeenth, Brannan looks at his first opportunity to finish the match with a ten-foot birdie putt. Paolucci paces back and forth as his opponent prepares to strike his ball. But Brannan's putt rushes by the cup.

On the eighteenth and final regulation hole, Brannan lands his second shot safe on the right side of the green. Once again, he needs only two putts for victory. His first effort stops a couple of feet short of the hole. The return putt looks almost like a tap-in. Brannan stands for several long seconds over his ball. "I had my hat off to shake his hand," Paolucci says afterward. "I was thinking, 'He's not going to miss two putts in a row'."

But Brannan's putt slams against the side of the cup and stays out. Perhaps the fatigue of carrying his bag is catching up. His face thickens with sweat. After his miss, a disappointed Brannan raises his cap, wipes his brow, and looks up to the sky. He stands still for several long seconds, finally picking up his bag and moving to the next hole.

The sudden-death playoff begins on the fourteenth, a 506-yard par five that plays uphill and longer than the announced yardage. Large bunkers and tall prairie grass guard both sides of the fairway, and a long, narrow, two-tiered green sits at the top of a steep hill, protected by bunkers. The skies darken; a storm threatens. Both players hit poor drives. Paolucci finds himself in the deep right rough, and Brannan lands in a trap. Neither can reach the green in two shots. Brannan pitches his third shot to three feet from the flag. Paolucci takes four shots to find the green, and remains eighteen long feet from the hole. As he steps up to putt, his mother turns her back to the unfolding scene and whispers to her younger son to hug her and offer comfort. His father, Mike, manages to keep his eyes open and comments, "good swing" as the ball leaves the club. Sure enough, Paolucci's ball rolls into the hole.

Brannan must only make his short putt for birdie and the win. Paolucci again believes he is doomed "I was thinking, 'He wasn't going to miss again. Three in a row—that's not possible'." Brannan steps up and strikes the ball with a firm touch. It heads straight toward the hole—and hits the lip, turning 90 degrees and coming to a standstill a foot to the right.

By now, rain is falling. Tournament officials have made an exception for Brannan's grandfather, who is watching his grandson's game from his perch in a golf cart. "Sean just needs one more of those little putts and he'll make it," Stultz points out. Several hundred spectators ring the tee box. On the match's twenty-first hole, Paolucci and Brannan both find the green on the 221-yard par three. Brannan's birdie bid from twenty-five feet comes up less than two feet short. Paolucci's twenty-two footer for birdie stops inches from the hole, and he taps in.

The Pennsylvanian must sink his short putt to keep the match alive. Paolucci's mother covers her face. Paolucci turns his back, also unable to watch. Brannan's putt again heads toward the hole, and again rams against its edge before moving away. The marathon is over. In tears,

Paolucci's mom mutters, "unbelievable, unbelievable." Her son has survived and will face off against his fellow Texan in the finals on Saturday. "Coming down the stretch I thought I should have lost the match," Paolucci says. "I got really lucky."

———

After the dramatic semifinal leg of the Junior Amateur, the final proves anticlimactic. Paolucci wakes up nervous. "The morning before the finals, that's when it hit me. I really wasn't ready. I didn't have the same amount of confidence and made some mistakes." After fourteen holes, Whitsett has raced away to a three-hole lead. After the eighteenth, he stands five holes ahead. "I didn't play that bad—he was just too good," Paolucci says.

Whitsett continues to display rifle-sharp accuracy after lunch, splitting the fairways with his drives and keeping his approaches flying at the center of greens. He waits for his inexperienced opponent to make errors, and he soon receives gratification. Paolucci three-putts on the third hole, and Whitsett goes ahead by six holes. Although Whitsett misses a putt on the next hole to fall back one hole—an oddball mistake that leads to a rare curse from the otherwise ultra-polite player—he recovers and goes seven up on the eighth hole. On the tenth, Paolucci misses another short putt and falls eight holes behind. "He just hasn't given himself a chance," says Victor Paolucci, his disappointed brother. Whitsett and Paolucci par the eleventh hole. This anticlimactic finale delivers the national championship to Whitsett, who has built an insurmountable eight-hole lead with only seven to play. It is the largest margin of victory in the national junior boys' championship since 1970.

John Fields of the University of Texas is just about the only college coach left watching. He has already signed Cody Gribble. Now he would like to ingratiate himself with the two finalists from his state. "Whoever wins, it's a good week for Texas," he observes.

"It's a great feeling—it hasn't really sunk in yet, but it's getting there," Whitsett offers. "No matter what I do the rest of my life, I can always look at that trophy and know I won this tournament."

Will he equal Tiger with three victories in a row?

"No doubt—it's in the back of my mind," he admits.

The just-crowned national champion looks exhausted and acknowledges that he is drained. Whitsett would like to return home to Houston, but he has no time to rest. He has agreed to fly to Chattanooga, Tennessee, for the AJGA's version of the Ryder Cup. The so-called Canon Cup—named after its Japanese corporate sponsor—brings together the top-ranked American junior players, girls and boys, and divides them up, depending on their home addresses, into East and West teams. The West team has crushed the East in recent years. But the competition is not the most notable part of the event. For once, the ultra-serious, ultra-driven junior golfers will have some fun.

CHAPTER 10

A Bit of Fun

The West Team's Alex "Little" Kim shows
off his war paint at the Canon Cup.

DURING MOST OF THE SUMMER the top teenage golfers treat their
sport like an intensive Advanced Placement high-school course.
Students must be polite and proper. They must study hard. Practices
serve as long, drilling, dull, and tiring sessions of homework. Tournaments are tests for coaches to grade them. There is little time for
teenage pranks.

At the end of July the forty highest-ranked junior golfers attempt to
rediscover the pure happiness of playing, profiting from the fresh air
and physical activity and hanging out with friends. They converge at
the Honors Course club outside of Chattanooga, built on former
Cherokee Indian land for the American Junior Golf Association's
(AJGA) annual Canon Cup. The invitation-only event pits the top ten
boys and top ten girls from west of the Mississippi River against their
counterparts from the East. Although parents are allowed to attend,
most permit their children to travel and compete by themselves. The
AJGA provides full-time chaperones. Players are picked up at the airport

and shuttled to a hotel and to the golf course. Meals are gratis. Team members board two to a room.

Without strict parental supervision, super-serious, super-stressed, hyper-ambitious, polite, and controlled juniors have a long-awaited opportunity to act like kids. They paint their faces and whoop it up on the course. They flirt. At night, in the hotel, they party.

Removed from the picture, parents display mixed emotions about the goings on at the Canon Cup. Geoff Whitsett, who returns to Houston after Cory's victory at the United States Junior Am, admits his son's need to be a kid again after the intensity of weeks of summer competition. Even as American parents encourage and push their children to achieve, most continue to believe children should be allowed time to be children. In contrast, Ivan Lendl judges the partying a frivolous waste of time. Marika and Isabelle travel to Tennessee by themselves. "The Canon Cup is just a joke," he says.

These parental debates reflect deep cultural differences. Many East European or Asian parents believe their children must stay controlled and focused. Although they will not prevent them from accepting an honor like the Canon Cup, they don't celebrate. The Canon Cup first took place in 1990. AJGA executive director Stephen Hamblin dreamed of creating his own version of the Ryder Cup, the trans-Atlantic extravaganza pitting the top dozen American golfers against the top dozen European golfers. At the Ryder Cup, the teams face off in three days of matches, with three different formulas of match play. They duel at four balls that require each player in a team of two to play his or her own ball, counting only the better score of each team. In foursome match play, teams of two again play against two, with each side playing one ball by alternating shots. On the final day, the format climaxes in singles' match play. Matches count for a single point. If the score is tied at the eighteenth hole, each side gains half a point.

Instead of building a global rivalry, Hamblin stuck to the United States, dividing the giant country in half at the Mississippi River. He also aimed to create an event that the players would enjoy and have fun with rather than engaging in Ryder Cup stress-filled battles. Rather than only a dozen men on each side as in the Ryder Cup, Hamblin wanted teams of twenty players each, evenly divided between boys and girls. In some matches, the boys would pair with girls. Friendships forged at other junior events would strengthen. Canon signed on as the sponsor, and Hamblin seduced prestigious, exclusive country clubs to host the event. The inaugural 1990 Canon Cup took place at the Orlando-based Lake Nona Golf Club. Tiger Woods, then only thirteen, played for the West Team against the East Team, led by future pro stars Stewart Cink and Vicki Goetze. Hamblin, who coached the West team that year, remembered Tiger as a terrific team player who offered instructive putting lessons to his female teammates. But Woods's West team suffered a crushing defeat, thirty-two points to eighteen. As an adult, the otherwise imperial Woods has posted a mediocre record in the Ryder Cup, and Europeans have dominated over the past decade. The Americans finally reclaimed the Cup (notably without Woods) in 2008.

In recent years, for reasons that Hamblin and others find difficult to explain, the West team has dominated the Canon Cup competition. Some suggest the West enjoys an advantage because of its bevy of serious and talented Korean girls. The East includes golf-crazy Florida, but the West benefits from two golf-enthusiast states, Texas and California. More often than not, the Canon Cup has taken place in the eastern half of the country, so location offers little explanation. At the Capital City Club in Atlanta in 2005, the West triumphed 30½ to 19½. At the Conway Farms Golf club in the exclusive Chicago suburb of Lake Forest in 2006, the West waltzed to a 31 to 19 victory.

The Honors Course in Ooltewah, Tennessee, in the hills outside of Chattanooga, is hosting the 2007 version. Pete Dye, the architect of the Junior National Amateur site Boone Valley, drew up the Honors Course layout, working with a client who aimed to challenge even the best golfers. A local industrialist, the owner of an oil-pipeline company,

John Thomas Lupton holds in utter contempt players who believe they can beat a golf course. "No matter the cost," Lupton ordered architect Dye to "design the goddam thing where even the Nicklauses and the Watsons are likely to make an F in the course." Dye obeyed. He moved earth and stones and drilled wells to fill a massive basin to endanger a maximum number of balls on the maximum number of holes. "Out of the rock and clay, out of the Piss Oak Ridges, and in and amongst the catbriers, the Devil's walking sticks, the sourwoods, dogwoods, and scrub pines, emerged a creation somewhat resembling a mutation of the Badlands of South Dakota and an alligator," Lupton's son writes in his introduction to the course. The bunkers were made to resemble "the Devil's Asshole," he writes, and the green was designed to be chock-full of "bumps and troughs.'

The Honors Course bills itself as being as exclusive and elitist as Boone Valley. It counts only about 300 members and refuses all attempts to open up to professional events, sticking instead to amateur tournaments. It's a pure golf club, with no tennis courts or swimming pool. "The owners aim to pay tribute to amateur athletes who play simply because of the love of the game," says club manager Gerard Daly. Since it opened in 1983, the Honors has hosted the U.S. Amateur, the Men's National Collegiate Athletic Association (NCAA) championships, and the Mid-Amateur Championship. In 1995 it held the Canon Cup. The East, led by future pro standouts Cristie Kerr and Charles Howell III, won a narrow twenty-seven to twenty-three victory.

Despite the prospect of a prestigious, all-paid-for, fun week of golf on a fabulously challenging course, many of the highest-ranked players decline to participate in Canon. Some find it difficult to take a week off for "fun" in the middle of their summer season. Others, such as Si-hwan "Big" Kim, opt to use the week to play adult amateur events. At the Rolex Tournament in Columbus, Peter Uihlein announced that he planned to skip the Canon Cup to play in the prestigious adult Western Amateur tournament, but when the Rolex Tournament director and captain of the East team Walker Hill implored him to reconsider, Uih-lein agreed. His mother Tina is one of the few parents to tag along.

———

For the Cup's opening ceremonies, both teams march out behind bag-pipes as their captains read their rosters. The West team players are dressed in blue and the East teammates in red, outfitted with Canon Cup shoes, shorts, shirts, and golf bags. Hill, the East captain, is decked out in a red suit. The captains hit ceremonial tee shots to inaugurate the event. West coach Beth Reuter squibs her drive along the ground far left and out of bounds, and Hill forces photographers to flinch by hooking his into a left fairway bunker, about 170 yards from the green. "That's the worst swing we'll see this week," promises Steve Ethun, the AJGA's director of communications. On the first day of play, the lead bounces back and forth between East and West. Wesley Graham, play-ing with Lion Kim of Lake Mary, Florida, wins the first four ball match of the day, 3&2. "The first point is important," Kim says. Gra-ham has cut his hair into a Mohawk and dyed it red. "He's having a blast," says Tammy Graham, his mother, who has come to Chattanooga to visit friends. "This is no pressure, just fun,"

Later in the morning the West girls, stacked with Koreans, storm back to win several matches. Mina Harigae and Kimberly Kim from the West trump Easterners Courtney Ellenbogen and Allie White 4&3. The top match pits Peter Uihlein and Arnond Vongvanij from the East, against Cory Whitsett and Josh Jones from the West. Uihlein's team rushes out to a two-hole lead, only to decelerate on the back nine. The West's Jones birdies both the thirteenth and fifteenth holes, and the match comes down to the eighteenth hole. Uihlein hits his second shot to four feet from the hole. Both Josh Jones and Cory Whitsett re-main fifteen feet away, and the two Texans leave their putts just short. If Uihlein sinks his putt, the East wins. If he misses, the match will end tied. Uihlein displays no signs of nervousness and drops his birdie like a champion.

"Great job, Peter," shouts team captain Walker Hill. The penalty Hill called on his anchorman during the Rolex Championship is forgotten. Thanks to Uihlein's win, the East holds a narrow one-point lead at lunch break.

In the afternoon, boys team up with girls and the matches stay tight. Alex "Little" Kim and Jenny Shin, paired in the final match, trail Bud Cauley and Courtney Ellenbogen by a hole going to the eighteenth. The other thirty-six players walk alongside them, offering vigorous support as they approach the eighteenth green. Surrounded by youngsters wearing red and blue, Ellenbogen sinks her twelve-foot putt to win the hole and half of the final match of the day. The East red-robed team swarms onto the green and picks her up. "I felt I owed it to the team to make it," she says, surrounded by a huddle of teammates.

Most golf tournaments are tranquil affairs. Spectators speak in hushed voices and offer reverent, polite applause. The Canon Cup is different. Throughout the day, screams, yells, and chants of "Go East" and "Go West" puncture the traditional tranquility of the secluded, elite Honors Club. From the clubhouse, it possible to hear huge roars erupting from the course's far end.

In the evening the kids are housed in the same hotel. They gather in the hallways to chitchat, though they are under an 11:00 p.m. curfew to return to their rooms. Despite monitors placed along the hotel corridors to discourage late night fraternizing, there are rumors of after hours get-togethers.. After the stress and hard work of the U.S. Junior Amateur championship, the Canon Cup is a useful break, according to mother Tammy Graham. As she sees it, the kids are exhausted; they are not getting a lot of sleep, but at Canon, they're having a blast.

On Canon's second day of play, the West team steadily recovers. In the morning Cory Whitsett, Josh Jones, and Alex Kim lead their teams to victories in the single-sex foursome matches. In total, the West gains six points. Courtney Ellenbogen and Marika Lendl generate the only bright news for the East, teaming up to capture the team's sole full point. The two Lendl girls seem to be regaining their lost form in their father's absence.

In the afternoon's mixed four ball matches, the West gains four points to the East's two and ends the day eight points ahead. Cody Gribble overcomes his shaky nerves against an East tandem led by Wesley Graham. On the sixteenth hole, two up, Gribble misses a par putt to give Graham a chance. But the Floridian pushes his next drive into the woods, while Gribble rolls in a long birdie putt. Peter Uihlein, playing with fellow Leadbetter Academy student Kristina Wong, proves the East's sole stand-out. He holes one eagle and six birdies to crush the opposing team of U.S. champions Cory Whitsett and Kristen Park. Uihlein whoops for joy, savoring some revenge for his own collapse at the national championship.

The West enters day three with an eight-point lead and a determination to inject some competitive seriousness into the low-key event. "We told the East, 'No Mercy,'" says Sang Yi of Carrollton, Texas. In general, though, it's the girls, not the boys, who display the most intensity. In match play, players are allowed to give opponents short putts. Boys concede more putts than girls, says Scott Thompson, who is accompanying his twelve-year-old daughter Lexi. (He felt she was too young to come to the event alone, and besides, he needs to drive her the following week from Tennessee to Indiana for the United States Women's Amateur.)

By the beginning of this final day of competition, the West needs a mere six and a half points to claim victory. The East fights back. Vicky Hurst, who lost both her day two morning and evening matches, manages a victory in singles, winning 4&3. "We all went out today and just tried to win it for our Team Captain Walker," she says. Marika Lendl, thought to be a weak link, ties her opponent and wins half a point.

But Isabelle Lendl begins scattering her shots and loses the decisive match. Her opponent, Stephanie Kono, races out a six-hole lead by the twelfth hole. On the thriteenth, Kono hits her approach shot about thirty feet from the hole. Lendl buries hers in the trap. Although she blasts out to ten feet, she misses the par putt and concedes the hole—and the Canon Cup. Kono's West teammates flood the green to congratulate her. The final score lines up West twenty-seven, East twenty-three.

The least spoken about, but perhaps most significant, moment of the entire tournament takes place on the final day, in the grudge match between Peter Uihlein and Josh Jones. Little love exists between the two seventeen-year-olds, who clashed the previous day in a tense match. Uihlein has long been defined by the responsibilities and privileges that come with being the son of the Titleist CEO. In the Uihlein family, emotions are kept under control and opinions are measured. In the Jones family, they are expressed in a brash, straightforward style. Dave Jones, an American Airlines pilot, runs a set of Texas junior golf tournaments meant to provide a showcase for kids who lack the money, or the pedigree, to play at the AJGA events.

Uihlein and Jones face off in one of the final matches of the day, with the ultimate outcome of the Cup still uncertain. Their match stands square after sixteen holes, when Jones hits his second shot to within inches of the hole for a tap-in birdie. Uihlein needs to equal by sinking a long thirty-foot putt. He steps up to his ball. He stands over it for a measured moment. He brings his putter back, strokes the ball, and urges it forward toward the hole with a shout, "Yeah, yeah, let's go, baby." But the ball stops on the edge of the hole. Jones waits several seconds. Uihlein's ball continues to refuse to drop, and Jones makes what he considers an act of sportsmanship, conceding the putt by picking up Uihlein's ball and handing it back to him. Jones believes he has won the hole and captured the lead.

"It's a penalty," Uihlein shouts. "You cannot pick up my ball."

"I don't know that rule," says Jones. "The ball was not going in."

An official is summoned, and Uihlein explains that he should win the hole. The official looks in his thick United States Golf Association (USGA) rulebook, the Talmud of golf, which agrees with Uihlein. Jones loses the hole, and he finds himself one down.

When Jones tees off on the eighteenth hole, he is steaming. His drive flies wide right, and he fails to reach the green in the regulation two shots. Uihlein faces no problem playing the hole in par and securing his victory. When his final putt falls—Jones refuses to concede this one—Uihlein leaps for joy and continues jumping up and down, celebrating, for several long moments. He fails to shake Jones's hand, instead embracing his East teammates.

AJGA executive director Stephen Hamblin watches with dismay. Titleist is his organization's number one sponsor, and the CEO's son is its marquee player. But Hamblin, ramrod straight, the military man's son, knows he must act to retain his own integrity. On the clubhouse patio, he approaches Tina Uihlein.

"Peter must apologize for his actions," he says.

"For what happened on the seventeenth hole, calling for the official?" Mrs. Uihlein asks.

"No, that was fine," Hamblin says. "Peter was just following the rules." The celebration on the eighteenth hole was unsportsmanlike. "Peter should have shaken Josh's hand. He should apologize."

Soon afterward, Uihlein approaches Jones and offers a reluctant handshake. Jones is not convinced whether it is genuine.

"I lost a lot of respect for Peter," Jones admits. "It's a pretty sick way to win. I think he knows he should have lost. He went pretty crazy on the eighteenth."

———

During the festivities, many contestants talk about team spirit and how, in this most individual of sports, they like to compete for a team.

Tournament organizers express satisfaction with the rah-rah atmosphere. "The theme of the day: Team Pride and screams!" Canon Cup Tournament director Andrew Greenfield announces before the final day of play. When Courtney Ellenbogen sinks her closing day first putt, her partner, Bud Cauley, picks her up in a huge hug, and her teammates envelop her with screams and congratulations.

Some of the enthusiasm seems artificial. The East–West rivalry, unlike the Ryder Cup's Europe versus United States, lacks genuine roots. The Ryder Cup revels in drawing out deep-seated nationalism. The Canon Cup pits Americans against one another. Few journalists or college coaches are present at the Canon Cup. Unlike an AJGA invitational or a national championship, the results do not count toward the players' rankings. Of the few parents attending, a scant handful follow their children on the course. Most prefer to socialize in the clubhouse and enjoy the lavish banquet meals.

This is the one time during the summer when players can joke among themselves and let out their feelings without fear of a negative backlash. A moment of poor sportsmanship on Peter Uihlein's part will go almost unnoticed and won't jeopardize his future. Uihlein and the other players are allowed to learn from their mistakes. The Canon Cup serves as a welcome hiatus in what is otherwise a pressure-filled summer. After this short break, the junior players will advance into the realm of adult golf. Many of the Canon Cup participants will soon travel across the Atlantic to participate in a genuine golf battle, and come face to face with a quite different, quite impressive European approach to accompanying talented youngsters over the bridge into adulthood.

CHAPTER 11

Scandinavian Surprise

Sweden's Caroline Hedwall flies the European flag at the Junior Solheim Cup.

At the beginning of September, the twelve members of the United States Girls' Junior Ping Solheim Cup team fly to Sweden to face off against Europe's best junior girl golfers. Stephanie Kono and Kimberly Kim, both from Hawaii, endure a two-day journey. All the girls suffer through at least twelve hours overnight on a plane, and most miss their first week of school. When the United States last sent a team of teenage girls across the Atlantic to play for the Cup, the Europeans crushed them. "Our players were not acclimated to the jet lag, the culture and the food," recalls Donna Andrews, the U.S. head coach. This year, as an antidote, she has packed an ample supply of peanut butter—a snack that can perk her team up when their blood sugar is low.

The Solheim Cup, launched in 1990 and staged every other year, pits Europe's best professional female golfers against America's.[1]

---

1. Starting in 2003, the Solheim Cup has been played only in odd-numbered years.

Played over three days, the Solheim employs the same format as the men's Ryder Cup. For the past three Solheims, the sponsor, Ping, has added a sister event for female junior golfers under the age of eighteen. A Junior Solheim Cup is contested during the two days before the women's version opens, at a golf course near the main tournament.

Neither adult nor junior players compete for money at Solheim. Instead, the Cup represents prestige, visibility, and the privilege of participating in one of the highest-profile, most exciting events in The 2007 Junior Solheim has been scheduled for September 10 and 11 in Båstad, on Sweden's southern coast across the straights from Denmark, and only a half-hour's drive south of Halmstad, where the professional women are playing the adult Solheim Cup from September 14 to 16. Once the juniors finish their competition, they will spend two days watching the pros before flying home. For many members of the teenage American team, this trip is their first time outside the United States. Although a few travel with their mothers and fathers, most are unaccompanied. "What would my parents do here?" jokes Jane Rah. "The signs are not in English."

Home court advantage has proved crucial in the past. The American team captured the two junior Solheims played in the United States, while Europe won the 2003 edition at the Bokskogen Golf Club in Bara, Sweden. The 2003 U.S. junior team, led by future pro stars Paula Creamer and Brittany Lincicome, looked like a shoe-in. But something failed to click. Maybe it was overconfidence. Maybe it was the massive time change. Maybe it was the tough Swedish conditions, including a blustery wind that made some holes play four clubs longer than they would under regular conditions. Perhaps it was that the Europeans marked their distances on the golf course in meters, rather than yards. On the second day of the competition, Europe won four of six singles matches and took the lead for the first time in the Junior Solheim Cup's short history.

Despite the setback, the Americans continued to display telltale signs of overconfidence. "We weren't too worried because we knew we would be strong during singles matches," recalls assistant coach Beth Reuter, who also served as the Canon Cup West coach. "The Europeans laid an ambush in the final day, packing the top of their lineup with their strongest players and winning three of the first four matches. Although the Americans recovered to win five of the last eight matches, their late comeback failed to overcome the early deficit. "I think the girls were surprised and probably not ready to lose," Reuter said afterward. "It took a while to set in, but it was a good eye-opener for them. There was a lot we took for granted like the time change, food, weather, and even playing in meters."

The American team has learned some important lessons from the defeat. This time, the team arrives three full days before the competition begins. Instead of taking a nap as they had done the previous time in Sweden, assistant coach Reuter and head coach Donna Andrews force them to stay up until after dinner. "It helped them adjust," Andrews says. "They're all spry, happy and ready to go."

When Andrews compares junior and adult golfers, she sees the biggest difference in how the adults "know how to travel." The pros pack enough food and clothes. The kids do not. Although Andrews praises the Swedish food at the hotel, some of her players grumble about the breakfast servings of fish paste. Despite turning their noses up at the unfamiliar food, the kids are for the most part in high spirits. In the evenings they gather at the hotel and serenade the village with ecstatic cheers of "One, Two, Three, U.S.A. All the Way!"

For much of the past century, Sweden's fashionable crowd has gathered in Båstad during the summer, turning it into a Swedish version of St. Tropez. In comparison to its French cousin, however, Båstad displays little pretension or overt opulence. The landscape in this part of Sweden remains rugged and well preserved, alternating among jagged perches of coastline; wide, gentle, sandy beaches; and colorful fishing villages. Inland, bright golden-yellow fields of rapeseed are interrupted only by a Swedish panorama of picturesque, red-timber clapboard country cottages and farmhouses. Bright blue and yellow national Swedish flags hang from many buildings.

Fairways slice through most Swedish cities, including the country's largest, Göteborg and Stockholm. Within an hour of Båstad, more than seventy courses pepper the landscape, ranging from traditional seaside links to elegant, forest-framed parklands. The gentle weather (by Swedish standards) allows for a long season, stretching from late March to early December. "This region is like Florida—real golf country," says Paul Elfving, a club staffer at the Vasatorps Golf Club.

Sweden's only three genuine links courses, Ljunghusens, Flommens, and Falsterbo, are located just south of the regional capital of Malmö on a sandy spit of land, which also contains some of the country's best beaches and bird-watching. North of Malmö, rolling hills and long, sandy beaches define the landscape. The most famous course is located along the water in Barsebäck. In the 1980s a local businessman developed the site as a golf resort, and today it boasts a hotel, rental cottages, and a conference center. The unpretentious, utilitarian resort facilities illustrate, in their own way, the prevailing Swedish attitude toward golf: the course matters more than the setting. Bevan Tattersall, Barsebäck's greenkeeper, arrived at the end of 2005 from the Belfry near Birmingham, England, which has hosted the Ryder Cup several times. "The Belfry was a golf resort, where the course supported the hotel," he says. "This is first and foremost a golf club." The course's fairways and greens are in perfect, velvet condition, in large part due to Tattersall's arrival. "Sweden used to be known for great golfers, not great golf courses," he says. "That's changing."

Evidence of this transformation is visible at a nearby club, called Vasatorps. In the 1970s the original eighteen-hole club hosted the Scandinavian Enterprise Open. The long, flat layout, 6,742 yards from the back tees, with numerous gentle doglegs and big, inviting greens that offer little in the way of hazards, is a straightforward course in a beautiful setting devoid of superficial landscaping or artifice. "This is the typical, traditional Swedish course, the type we built when the country first went golf-crazy," says Elfving, the Vasatorps staff member. In June 2007 the club opened new eighteen holes, designed by Americans Arthur Hills and Steve Forrest, who created numerous water hazards and rolling, manicured fairways, in the style of Florida fairways. The new course runs some 7,327 yards, long enough to challenge the world's best players, and the club says its goal is to host the 2018 Ryder Cup. This golf course is "difficult enough, strategic enough and beautiful enough to keep Vasatorps in these championship conversations for many years to come," says Ove Sellberg, manager of golf at Vasatorps and the first Swede to win on the European Tour in the 1980s.

Båstad's Golf Club, site of this year's Junior Solheim competition, opened in 1930. The country's ninth-oldest golf club, it is perched high above the sea on a dramatic cliff. The club benefits from an aristocratic pedigree—Alfred Nobel's nephew Ludwig Nobel financed it, and distinguished British golf architect A. J. H. Taylor designed it. The original layout, called the Old Course, meanders through a gentle, gardenlike landscape; an old windmill stands next to the first tee. The distance between holes is short—the entire course runs only 6,159 yards from the back tees—but they are by no means simple targets. Clever bunkering and slick, multilayered, contoured greens require more patience and strategy than brute force.

In 1990 the Båstad Club built a second course. Unlike the Old Course, which is flat and ringed with trees, the New Course's layout is hilly, hard, and open to the elements. It offers spectacular views of the sea and runs more than 7,217 yards. At the junior Solheim the girls will play it at a much shorter length, about 5,900 yards for a par 71.

Like the rest of southern Sweden, Båstad boasts uncrowded, fine-grained, child-friendly beaches. The countryside surrounding the village includes 100 kilometers of trails. Then there's tennis. The resort hosts the annual Swedish Open, voted the favorite clay court tournament several years in a row by pro players. Björn Borg won the tournament three times. During his tennis career, Ivan Lendl played several times in Båstad, and perhaps an omen, failed to triumph. Although Marika Lendl failed to make the American Solheim team, her younger sister Isabelle squeaked on. Swedes are intrigued by the irony of her return to her father's haunts. "I hear lots of jokes like about when will I give them a tennis lesson," Isabelle Lendl says.

Ivan Lendl has stayed back in the States to comment on television for the United States Tennis Open, and Isabelle Lendl is understandably more concerned about her own faltering golf game than her father's tennis legacy. In August she endured in a strenuous training regime, arriving at the practice range by 6:30 a.m., where she could chip by herself. "In the morning, nobody is there, so I can practice short shots if others are on the range," she says. Her academy school started in the final week of August, so she breaks off her golf training for three hours at midday for regular academic classes before returning to the range, and then after dinner, for more practice. "I think I know now what was going wrong and how to fix it," she says. "My swing action is outwards in rather than inwards out, horizontal rather than vertical."

In addition to corralling her unreliable swing, Isabelle feels pressure to make a positive impression on university recruiters. On September 1 the National Collegiate Athletic Association (NCAA) allowed college coaches to begin contacting high school seniors. They have flooded Lendl and other top prospects with letters promoting their institutions. Isabelle declines to name her suitors and insists that she remains more concerned about the state of her golf game than her prospects of higher education.

Lendl admits that her play during this season has been uneven. "Yup, been there, done that, seen it—it's been a tough summer, but I hope I learned a lot," she says. "My attitude this summer was pretty good. I'm pretty proud of that. I wasn't the one moping around, slamming clubs or feeling sorry for myself. I tried to work through it, keep my head up. Everybody has bad times."

Both her dad, whom Isabelle describes as being "awesome" during her trough, and Solheim junior head coach Donna Andrews encourage her. "You are going to be fine, just fine," Andrews says as she watches Lendl fire practice shots.

"Yes, I just have to relax and feel my shots," Lendl responds, half-convinced.

Andrews exudes American can-do confidence. She believes her team benefits from much more depth than the Europeans. Each of the dozen players shoots lower regular scores than their European counterparts, particularly the Europeans in the bottom half of the European team. "We have consistency and depth," Andrews says. "We have a lot of players who hit a lot of fairways and greens. That's what you want when you play matches." Morale is higher. "I have 12 players that get along," she says.

When the American team arrives at Båstad's practice range, the sky shines bright blue and the temperature reads a comfortable 59 degrees Fahrenheit. Even so, a brisk wind blows in from the ocean, putting a chill in the air. Most of the American girls, used to gentle climes, are bundled up in winter hats.

"Practice the low balls," barks Andrews, as she watches each girl hit. Andrews is dressed in a Solheim Cup jacket, a memento of her participation in the 2003 Cup. Unlike Florida, where the dangers are in the water hazards and other artificial defenses built into a course, golf in frigid northern Europe requires accepting and overcoming the natural elements. The American team moves out onto the course to practice, and Vicky Hurst takes out her normal five-iron on the par-three, 170-yard fourth hole—only to watch the wind blow her ball well over the green.

"Too much club," Andrews cautions.

On a hole facing the other way, into the wind, Hurst plays another five-iron to a green that is perched 170 yards away. Her shot lands 50 yards short of the target.

"Too high," Andrews says, explaining that the trajectory of a shot into the wind must be twenty yards lower. "You should have used a five wood."

"I don't know if I'll be able to trust that shot," Hurst admits, worriedly.

"You'll have to," Andrews says. "You must figure out how to play the wind. We will spend some time on the range working on low shots."

Hurst, judged by her record and her reputation, sizes up as the strongest American player at the junior Solheim. She hits the ball the farthest and enjoys the best record in recent events. But Andrews is worried that her slugger, taken out of her sunny Florida comfort zone, will slump in windy, cold Sweden.

"Vicky will have the hardest time of all my players," she predicts. "She hits the highest ball."

Worse than a high ball, wind and rain are predicted for the coming days.

———

Sweden, an icebox of a country, would be expected to produce great hockey players and skiers. Tennis, another Swedish specialty, can be played indoors. But golf? How does this gentle, outdoor pursuit thrive in this Scandinavian nation of only 8.8 million people and churn out tour pros such as Henrik Stenson and Annika Sorenstam? Notably, green fees are much cheaper in Sweden than in the United Sates, and the Swedish Golf Federation pays for the training of promising young players. The game is promoted as a family sport, and less pressure is put on young players at the elite level to succeed. Here, talented young golfers aren't shut out of the game as a result of prohibitive fees, and they don't burn out before reaching maturity. The contrast with the

Americans, who perfect their skills by attending expensive full-time golf academies, is striking. "Young Americans just do golf, golf, golf and nothing else," observes Bjorn Akesson, the top-ranked Swedish eighteen-and-under player, who attends a regular Swedish high school and cherishes his time off the course. "I want to have some time to see my friends."

Golf got off to a slow start in Sweden. Scottish fishermen played the game on natural links along Sweden's western coast around 1830. Two English-educated Swedes opened the first real golf course in the country's second-largest city, Göteborg, in 1888. The game remained elitist, and by around 1960 the federation counted only thirty-eight clubs and 7,000 members in the country.

But over the past half century, golf has morphed into a favorite family pastime and has attracted legions of talented youngsters. Some 600,000 Swedes sign up for membership each year. By comparison, Scotland counts 250,000 players in its population of 5.5 million, and Germany, with almost 80 million people, has 527,000. It is no accident that Sweden has hosted the Solheim Cup twice in a row. The 2003 event, held at Barsebäck, attracted huge crowds. Four Swedes are included in this year's twelve-woman European adult Solheim Cup team. All told, some 480 golf clubs are spread out across Sweden. Because so many players participate, membership fees are minimal, averaging $500 a year for adults and $200 for children. If that's too much, players may pay a reasonable daily green fee. The number of junior golfers has declined slightly in Sweden in the past couple of years, but many see advantages in the country's approach. In the United States, golf generally isn't thought of as a family sport, and the Florida-based National Golf Foundation, among others, has lamented the damage that high costs have inflicted on the game's popularity. "America has to change the mind-set that golf is an elitist sport," David Leadbetter argues. "In Sweden, golf is a game for the young, and everybody finds it a pleasure to play."

The Swedish Golf Federation requires that a fifth of all club members be under age twenty-one, a move Båstad's club's secretary-general, Jörgen Kjellgren, supports. As he sees it, the kids are, quite literally, the future of his club. Båstad 's club fields a junior team that competes against peers at other clubs. Young players are encouraged to join the club on their own if their parents aren't interested. No restrictions are imposed on junior tee times, and the club offers free lessons to talented young golfers. "It is incredible and wonderful how the Swedes encourage juniors," marvels Stephen Hamblin, the AJGA executive director, who has traveled to Sweden to follow the event. "We should also have a quota for our clubs of junior members. Junior golf is the only part of the industry that continues to grow."

Each year, from March to September, Sweden holds dozens of youth tournaments that attract 10,000 golfers from ages thirteen to seventeen—twice the AJGA's 5,000 members. The top-ranked 144 Swedish juniors meet at the end of the season in the Skandia Cup final.. Entry fees for the Swedish tournaments are minimal, roughly equivalent to about $50. In addition, the National Golf Federation, besides paying for the training of promising young golfers, covers the travel expenses for all contestants in the elite tournaments. Swedish officials also make a conscious effort to avoid putting too much pressure on young players. "We try to always remember to make it fun," says Lennart Larsson, a longtime administrator of junior golf at the Swedish Golf Federation. "I remember Annika Sorenstam as a kid. She just loved hitting golf balls and playing golf. I think that's one reason she's so great."

Parents in Sweden tend to adopt a similarly relaxed approach to their sport. Sorenstam says her parents stopped accompanying her to tournaments when she was a teen, and she worries that too much pressure from parents can take the joy out of the game for a young golfer. "I compare kids to flowers," Sorenstam says. "Some need a lot of water and sun, some grow fast and some grow slow." She says that "parents must be realistic" and "kids must find their own way." Sweden's junior champion, Akesson, agrees. "Parents are too involved in the States," he says. "I travel with my team and we play together."

Other successful European golf nations have adopted a similar curriculum. Assistant coach Marta Figueras-Dotti played two decades on the U.S. professional tour before returning home to Spain to take over that country's women's teams. In contrast to the United States, "where there are three hundred different ways of teaching golf," Spaniards teach according to a unified curriculum. "Our basics here are very good, the technical skills are good, the communication between coaches and players are good and unified," Figueras-Dotti says. "The competition is better in the States—you have so many players—and the conditions of the golf courses are better in the States. But, to be honest, we have nothing to envy." She travels throughout Spain recruiting the most promising youngsters and brings them to Madrid, where the federation is located, for regular training. "Our system produces good players.'

———

Not all European golf federations practice the same democratic, forward-looking policies as those exhibited in Sweden. Many continue to indulge in the elitist standards that reserve the game as a pastime for the wealthy. Consider Belgium. It has a population of ten million people and a climate that, while rainy, allows the game to be played all year-round. Belgium's King Leopold introduced golf in the nineteenth century, and renowned industrialist Edmond Solvay created the Royal Belgian Golf Federation in 1912. English golf architects Harry Colt and Tom Simpson built half a dozen superb "Royal" golf courses around the country. Yet today the country counts a mere seventy-eight clubs and a paltry 47,000 active members.

Sweden allows non-club members to play the game and participate in its federation tournaments. In Belgium, club membership remains a prerequisite. Next door in The Netherlands, the federation opened its ranks to non-club members two decades ago. The number of registered Dutch golfers has soared, from 38,000 in 1988 to 301,000 in 2007. The Dutch Golf Federation has managed to widen golf's appeal and increase its popularity, lowering the costs involved in learning and practicing the game. Today, Dutch golfers benefit from numerous new public courses.

Each year the Dutch hold a national championship open to the best golfers from around the world. In contrast, most of Belgium's junior golf tournaments, including its national championships, are closed to non-Belgians. A mere eleven players contested the 2008 Belgian championship for girls less than fourteen years old, and fourteen competed to be crowned Belgium's sixteen-and-under girl champions. Not surprisingly, no Belgian plays on either the top-ranked European or American pro tours. In contrast, the level of play in the Netherlands is fast improving. Dutch amateurs recently won the world championship, the so-called Eisenhower Cup. The Dutch Golf Federation's secretary general, Hank Heyster, is confident that the improvement in amateur ranks will soon translate into a breakthrough in the professional ranks. For the biannual Ryder Cup in 2012, his goal is to see two Dutch players participate as part of Europe's team.

At the 2007 Junior Solheim, no Belgian players are competing, and more surprisingly, no Dutch ones, either. Europe's team captain is former top Swedish professional Catrin Nilsmark, who confides that the Europeans have been waiting for two years to regain the trophy. The European team's star Spaniard, Carlota Ciganda, looks like Europe's version of Vicky Hurst, complete with her swaggering walk, powerful body, and ability to belt the ball far down the fairway. Ciganda benefits from experience and success in high-profile international events. The seventeen-year-old won the British Women's Amateur earlier in the summer and helped Spain's ladies' team capture the European team's championship. Importantly, unlike the Americans, Ciganda's experience competing on seaside golf courses has taught her how to keep the ball low when hitting into the wind. This skill gives her an advantage over the visitors. Three Swedes, also used to the home conditions, have made the European team, identical twins Caroline and Jacqueline Hedwall, and Nathalie Månsson; followed by two Danes, Charlotte Lorentzen and Sara Monberg; two Germans; two Spaniards; two English; and one Scottish girl, Sally Watson.

With the exception of Watson, none of the Europeans trains away from home. Watson attends the Leadbetter Academy in Florida. Despite Scotland's historic role as the birthplace of golf, it offers little in the way of training or competition for juniors. "I couldn't come close to achieving my goals if I stayed in Scotland," Watson admits. Her recent results are impressive. Like the teenage Americans who played in the United States Women's Open earlier in the summer, Watson qualified for the British Women's Open and proceeded to make the cut. This summer her travel schedule has included four trans-Atlantic and four transcontinental flights. After the Rolex Tournament in Ohio, she flew overnight to Norway, competed in the European team championships, and then flew right back to Seattle for the United States Girls' Junior Amateur. The demanding schedule has, in her words, left her "knackered."

In many ways, the European players seem more mature than the Americans. All are seventeen or eighteen years old, except for the American-trained sixteen-year-old Watson. In contrast, the U.S. team includes two fifteen-year-olds and fourteen-year-old Kristen Park. Physically, most of the Europeans tower over the Americans. Among the Europeans, almost as many boyfriends as parents are attending. The sight of a thirty-something man accompanying English player Florentyna Parker shocks many of the Americans. "He's so oooold," they whisper. "Lots of us have boyfriends," German Nicola Rössler points out. But she also admits that love will not sidetrack her from achieving her golfing destiny. She plans to attend university in the United States.

Surprisingly, almost as many American college coaches are attending the Junior Solheim event as would be present at a regular AJGA tournament. With a dearth of excellent female American prospects, many coaches at American universities recruit among the top foreigners, particularly among the Swedes, who speak good English. In Europe, junior golfers enjoy few such educational opportunities. No European university allows students to pair golf and their studies; at best, English and Scottish schools of higher education have golf teams, but they are much less serious than American college teams. Ironically, while Swedes, Danes, and Spaniards look toward American universities, most English junior golfers tend to turn pro directly and pass up the opportunity to attend college. Neither Florentyna Parker nor the other English Junior Solheim team cup member, Henrietta Brockway, plans to accept a scholarship. Oklahoma State's women's golf coach, Laura Matthews, eyes Sweden's Caroline Hedwall. "We need some international players in order to get our program to the top," she explains. "The Europeans are more mature, they really want the education, and the Swedes in particular are really prepared for American university studies."

Despite their home-field advantage, European players at the Solheim event are less familiar with one another than the Americans are. Unlike American coach Donna Andrews, Europe's Nilsmark has spent little time scouting her team and hardly knows her roster. And unlike the Americans, who have played together all summer, for the most part the Europeans have only a cursory knowledge of each other, and many don't speak the same language. Most muddle by in less-than-fluent English. Players travel with their separate national federation coach and practice among themselves.

The European team's composition reflects its own set of politics. Ten of the American players are chosen from a transparent national ranking system, with only two wild-card "captain's choices." In Europe, seven players are picked from the results of five major junior tournaments, leaving five "captain's choices." A polyglot committee composed of officials from various national golf federations debates the roster's composition. Some suggest that the team would be better off with more Swedes and Spaniards and fewer French, Danes, and Germans. "The bottom of the European list is a lot weaker than the Americans—I think it was picked for national reasons," Sally Watson's father, Graehme, suggests.

On the day of the opening Solheim ceremony, heavy rain turns the course into a mud field. Organizers cancel a planned junior amateur tournament that would have paired the participants with local club members and move the ceremony inside to the clubhouse restaurant. The girls dress up in "business" clothes for the event: the Europeans in demure, gray skirts and checked Scottish-style checked grey sweaters, and the Americans in blue pant suits and Ralph Lauren Polo sweaters. Vicky Hurst's trademark strut softens in high heels. A band belts out the national European anthems—from the French "Marseillaise" to England's "God Save the Queen"—and even whips out bagpipes for the Scottish national tune. Trumpeters sound the ceremony's end, blaring away as the teams depart from the tented banquet hall.

Impressed by the pomp and circumstance, the American players seem both excited and a bit overwhelmed by their surroundings.

————

On the opening day of play at the Solheim, it is cold, overcast, and blustery. The Europeans jump to an early lead in the foursome morning matches. In this format, each team plays only one ball, with teammates hitting alternate shots. Andrews pairs players with similar playing styles. (Long, aggressive hitters are teamed with long, aggressive hitters, and short hitters with short hitters, so that the distances remain similar.) Traditionally, the foursome format proves toughest for individualistic Americans unused to this method of play.

The matches tee off in quick succession. Europe's Nilsmark has picked her strongest player, Spaniard Carlota Ciganda, to tee off first. Paired with German Nicola Rössler, Ciganda captures the opening match, and the two subsequent European teams continue with wins. As the American players pass the eighth hole, U.S. assistant coach Beth Reuter attempts to rouse their morale by handing out peanut butter sandwiches, and the sustenance seems to revive their play. Vicky Hurst and Jane Rah make a comeback against Swede Caroline Hedwall and Dane Sara Monberg. Rah, sporting ear muffs, sinks a ten-foot putt on the ninth hole to put her team in the lead for the first time, and the American pair steamroll the Europeans 4&3.

In the next group, Isabelle Lendl and Courtney Ellenbogen edge by the European team of Henrietta Brockway and Sally Watson. At one point the American team moves ahead by three holes, only to see their advantage whittled away to a single hole by the seventeen. This long par three stretches over water. Lendl sends her tee shot right at the green. "What a good-looking swing," Andrews says in an attempt to pick up Lendl's flagging spirits. Watson puts the European team's tee shot close to the hole, assuring a par. Ellenbogen chips her ball too far and misses the par putt.

The match heads tied into the final hole. Ellenbogen drills her drive down the eighteenth fairway. Europe's Brockway drives into a bunker, making it impossible for her teammate Watson to reach the green. Lendl gives her team an advantage by stopping her iron near the flag. Brockaway chips to within three feet of the hole. Ellenbogen misses her putt, leaving the match riding on Lendl's comeback. If Lendl sinks it, the Americans win a full point. If she misses again, the Americans will tie and take only half a point.

This time Lendl makes no mistake, stroking the ball confidently and cleanly into the hole, and the Americans rejoice in a narrow victory. "I still hit the ball pretty crappy," Lendl says. "But I'm glad my swing held up under pressure."

The final morning match pits Mina Harigae and Kristen Park against Swede Jacqueline Hedwall, Caroline's twin sister, and Dane Charlotte Lorentzen. The Europeans race out to a three-hole lead, leaving Harigae muttering, "this is not fair—they are on the home ground and get all the breaks."

After a peanut butter sandwich break, the Americans are tied going into the eighteenth hole, a long uphill par four. Harigae, who has painted her face red, white, and blue, splits the fairway with her drive. Under Solheim Cup rules, coaches are allowed to confer with players during a match, and Andrews huddles with Kristen Park, who proceeds to hit the second shot to the far end of the green. Andrews applauds.

"I told her, don't be short, because there's a ridge just below the hole," she explains.   Players and spectators crowd around the eighteenth green as the four girls arrive. Teammates who have finished their matches watch, linking their arms in solidarity.

Denmark's Lorentzen blasts her team's second shot over the green into the left rough. Her teammate, Hedwall, chips to five feet. American Harigae putts to within two feet. Lorentzen must sink the comeback putt to keep her team's chances alive. She stands for a long moment over the ball, considering each possible vector. Her putter moves back, not smoothly, but with a slight jerk, and she sends the ball sliding by the hole.

Now it is up to Park to win their match. The youngest player in the event places down her ball. She must make little more than a tap-in, but under this type of pressure, a player's arms often turn to jelly. Unlike Lorentzen, Park does not flinch and strokes her ball into the hole. The American team explodes with excitement, running onto the green to embrace their victorious teammates.

The morning matches end tied for three, a good result for the Americans considering their awful start and the difficult weather. Andrews's strategy has been to keep close on the first day, when she figures the Europeans, who have more experience with match play than the Americans, have the advantage, and then pull ahead on the second day, when, she believes, her team's greater depth gives them the advantage in one-on-one contests. "What a comeback," the American coach exults. "To come out even is great." On the European side, assistant coach Figueras-Dotti sounds discouraged. "The weather is very still, very nice, and it helps the Americans," Andrews insists. "We worked for five hours and we haven't done anything yet."

Since the morning matches last until well past 1:00 p.m., the Swedish organizers rush to launch the afternoon program to catch the final hours of daylight. They change the pin placements, allow the players a quick buffet lunch, and send them back out on the course. These afternoon matches are played in four-ball format, with each golfer playing her own ball and with the best score in a team counting. Unlike the morning, when Andrews teamed up similar players, she now pairs conservative and aggressive players together. For the first match, Andrews pairs her steadiest, most tactically astute players, Jane Rah and Stephanie Kono, the California Koreans, against the two Spaniards, Ciganda and Marta Silva.

The European coaches, in an effort to maximize the compatibility of their partnerships, have placed nationalities together, pairing the two Swedish twins, the two Danes, and the two Spaniards. Although brilliant sunshine lights up the course, the wind has picked up. Off on the sidelines, the AJGA's Hamblin worries about the macho American players' insistence on carrying their own clubs. The Europeans use pull carts.

A crowd of several hundred adult spectators and a greater number of schoolchildren have gathered to watch. Local schools have called off classes. The Swedish Golf Federation has mounted the event as part of its junior outreach. "This is a great chance to introduce kids to the game," the Federation's Larssen explains.

By the middle of the afternoon, the home-field advantage begins to weigh against the Americans. After five holes, Rah and Kono already have fallen three holes behind Spaniards Ciganda and Silva, who never allow the Americans to get close and finish them off by the fourteenth hole.

"I don't know what hit us—we were just buzzed," Kono offers.

The second European team of Florentyna Parker and Nicola Rössler proceeds to crush Americans Sydney Burlison and Courtney Ellenbogen.

Isabelle Lendl provides a glimmer of hope for the American team. She leads her team to victory in the afternoon's third match, over the Danish team of Charlotte Lorentzen and Sara Monberg. In this elevated competition, the Danish duo looks out of their element. Their shots lack precision and punch. On the sixteenth hole, Monberg snaps her drive left out of bounds and begins cursing. Lendl complains of blisters on her feet, but they do not seem to bother her on the course, and her upbeat attitude seems made for team competition. "I'm proud of us—this was a lot of fun," she says afterward.

The European coaches hand out bananas and chocolate power bars after the players pass the ninth hole, and the team appears visibly revived. Sweden's Hedwall twins, playing together, benefit from local cheerleaders and crush Americans Kimberly Kim and Brianna Do 3&2. Another Swede, Nathalie Mânsson, teams with Scot Sally Watson to overcome Asian Americans Brianna Do and Tiffany Lua.

For her final duo Andrews has paired Hurst, her strongest, most powerful, and most erratic team member, with Kristen Park, her steadiest, smoothest, and youngest player. On the first few holes, the Americans fall behind. Hurst quickly captures two holes with two birdies and pulls her team ahead. On the fifth hole, an uphill par five, Hurst needs a mere chip on her third shot to the flag. The American team seals their victory with five holes remaining.

Although the Europeans have picked off 80 percent of the afternoon matches and lead the Cup seven points to five after the first day, their lead remains precarious. Either side can still seize victory in the following day's dozen face-to-face singles matches. The Americans believe they have won a moral victory, overcoming the bad morning weather and almost neutralizing the European home-field advantage. As the matches end, they begin cheering "USA, USA, All the Way."

———

Black, ominous clouds and a vicious wind herald the competition's second and final day. "This is a four-club wind," a worried American player, Sydney Burlison, observes. A steady drizzle falls, threatening at any moment to explode into a torrent. "We didn't plan the date for the weather," insists Swedish Golf Federation's Thorsten Hellmark. "But these are nice conditions for our team."

Favorites on both sides burst out of the starting blocs. Carlota Ciganda, playing second, steamrollers American Allie White. Ciganda, who stands a full head taller than her opponent, knocks in birdie after birdie. By the end of the first nine, she has sprinted three holes ahead. The match ends on the fourteenth hole. Ciganda slams her drive almost to the green, requiring only a chip and tap-in putt for birdie. White hits a decent drive, but still needs a seven-iron to get to the green. She concedes defeat before putting. All told, Ciganda has scored six birdies in fourteen holes. She has not just won all of her three matches; she has decimated her opponents. "Allie was just machine gunned," her father, Tim White, explains.

American cleanup slugger Vicky Hurst steps in to fill the void. Andrews has put her once again in the final match, this time against German Nicola Rössler. Both girls are tall and thin, and both wallop the ball, but Hurst displays an elegant finesse and precision to her swing, which is lacking in the German's game. Under pressure Hurst is unruffled, and by the fifth hole, she is two holes ahead.

For the Americans, another good omen arrives as the sun peeks through the black clouds. Even though a chill continues to slice through warm clothing, and many of the Swedish spectators sip coffee on the sidelines, Isabelle Lendl takes off her rain pants. Lendl, who played well the first day, sizes up as a clear favorite over France's Audrey Goumard, who is playing in her first big international competition. But the untested French girl wins two of the first three holes and proceeds to nail a crisp iron on the third. Lendl lands her ball in the rough above the hole—perhaps she hit too much of a club or perhaps adrenalin pushed her ball beyond the target. She chips below the hole, only to miss her comeback putt. Goumard pockets an easy par and wins the hole. Lendl shakes her head in dismay, and France's Goumard ends her woes on the fourteenth hole.

The Americans are not yet finished. Rah stays ahead of Monberg, and America's Mina Harigae defeats Sweden's Nathalie Månsson, both on the fifteenth hole. To capture the Cup, Kimberly Kim, Courtney Ellenbogen, and Vicky Hurst must win. To tie, two of the three must triumph. As the afternoon wears on, big gusts of wind sweep through the golf course, putting the Americans at an obvious disadvantage. "We don't ever have anything like this in the States," Andrews says.

Kimberly Kim faces off against English player Florentyna Parker. Parker is unflustered by Swedish rain and wind. Behind by one hole, Kim ties the match on the sixteenth and sinks a long put on the seventeenth to keep the score even. Both girls reach the green in two shots and find themselves about twenty-five feet from the final hole. Parker putts first. "I had a good feeling," she says. Her putt rolls right up and over a ridge and into the hole.

The European spectators erupt with cheers. Kim waits for the cheering to die down. She now must sink her own putt to tie the match. She gives the ball a good ride toward the hole, but her ball rolls past. Parker has won the match, and assured the Europeans a tie for the Cup. The crowd begins jumping up and down, waving the blue-and-yellow starred European Union flag, chanting, "Europa, Europa."

Courtney Ellenbogen, pitted against Sweden's Jacqueline Hedwall, must triumph to keep the slim American hopes alive. The match-up favors the American. Hedwall, who is rated the weaker of the Hedwall twins, is playing as a last-minute replacement for injured German Caroline Masson. But the petite American's lack of power soon causes her problems. On the third hole, playing downwind, the Swede outdrives Ellenbogen by fifty yards. Hedwall needs a mere half pitch to the green and puts her ball close to the flag for an easy birdie that narrows Ellenbogen's lead to a single hole. On the fourth hole, the par three, the two girls hit into the wind, forcing Ellenbogen to deploy a large fairway wood, a club that gives her distance but sacrifices accuracy. Hitting an iron, the Swede places her ball close to the hole. Ellenbogen snaps her wood left of the green and is forced to concede the hole.

Ellenbogen surges back in front on the seventh hole, only to struggle on the fourteenth, a long par five. While her European opponent has no problem reaching the green in two shots, Ellenbogen requires a third. Thanks to a laser-sharp pitch right at the flag, Ellenbogen sinks the ball. "Courtney is so serious," comments Allie White's father, Tim, half in awe at her formidable powers of concentration and half concerned that the intense American is putting herself under too much pressure. Even in the lead, Ellenbogen is concentrating too hard to allow for a smile. On the sixteenth hole, Ellenbogen faces a mere two-foot putt to keep her lead. Her ball catches the lip edge and spins out. The match again stands square and comes down to the final hole, the long, uphill par four.

Playing behind Ellenbogen, Vicky Hurst also struggles. After taking a commanding lead on the first nine holes, she three-putts from a mere eight feet on the fourteenth and gives the hole to her German opponent, Rössler. On the next hole, she misses another short putt. The match is even. Although Hurst needs only a wedge to the green on the sixteenth, she floats her ball high, straight into the wind. Rössler hits her ball with a low trajectory and puts herself safe on the green, while Hurst faces a long downhill putt.

Suddenly, a ferocious "Europa, Europa" scream erupts from around the eighteenth green. Ellenbogen, normally the steadiest of putters, has just knocked her ball past the hole. Sweden's Hedwall easily pars for victory. "Jacqueline really came through for us under pressure—that was key," a delighted assistant coach Figueras-Dotti exclaims. Europe has captured the Solheim Junior cup.

Brandishing bright-blue European Union flags, the European team runs in unison to the sixteenth hole, where Hurst and Rössler are engaged in combat. The two girls could declare a truce and stop playing because the cup has been decisively won, and the results of their match no longer matter. But Hurst presses forward. Hurst proceeds to miss her putt and lose the hole. Both girls have two putts for pars on the next hole, a vicious, short par four, which requires a drive down a hill in front of water and then up over the stream to a hilltop, two-level green. Rössler makes her par. Hurst three-putts. Her loss ignites a new round of European celebrations.

At the awards ceremony, Beethoven's Ninth symphony, adopted by the European Union as the continent's anthem, blares over the loudspeaker. In her victory speech, European coach Nilsmark salutes her team's unity and her star players, Caroline Hedwall and Carlota Ciganda, who won all three of their matches. It matters little that the players share no common language.

The disappointed American girls are gracious losers. Nancy Lopez, the celebrated women's golf star from the 1980s, arrives to console the girls in their locker room. "I heard they played very well—and that's all that matters, as long as you go out there and play their best," she says. "They were in good spirits—they felt they played well and just got beat." That evening, their Swedish hosts treat the Americans to an elaborate gourmet dinner.

Afterward the Americans visit in their hotel. Many of the Europeans join them in their room. "We were having the better party, so the Europeans asked to come on over," Andrews says. The cheer lasts well beyond one in the morning, until Andrews orders them, with a chuckle, to turn off their lights.

The next day, under brilliant blue sunny skies, the Swedish hosts offer a sightseeing tour, treating the Americans to a speedboat ride off the rugged coast. (They had hoped to sail, but are stymied by an insufficient breeze.) "Unfortunately, we had to play golf in the wind and now we get to boat in a beautiful day without wind," a despondent Beth Reuter, the American assistant coach, observes. During the lunch after the cruise, Vicky Hurst, the American anchor, sits expressionless. She is disappointed with her play and remains unsure about whether she will attend college or turn professional. Back in Florida, she must discuss the issue yet again with her mother. She hopes to recover on her home territory. Most of the best Europeans are scheduled to play against their American counterparts over Thanksgiving week in the season-ending Polo Golf Junior Classic in Orlando. This time, the contests will be individual, since no teams are entered, and the AJGA will name its players of the year. Hurst hopes she will win the award. "It's something everyone dreams about," she says.

CHAPTER 12

End Game

The AJGA's 2007 Junior All American Team assemble for the annual award banquets; in the first row, sitting, far left, Jane Rah; middle, Alexis Thompson; and to her right, Vicky Hurst. Standing, second from left, Cory Whitsett; fourth from left, Peter Uihlein; and second from right, Cody Gribble.

LIGHTS. CAMERA. ACTION. On November 18, 2007, the American Junior Golf Association (AJGA) holds its annual Academy Awards for junior golf, a giant, black-tie banquet at the Ginn Reunion Resort's conference center in Orlando, Florida. It is the night before the first round of the Polo Golf Junior Classic, conducted annually since 1978, which brings together a 160-player, invitation-only field made up of boys and girls aged twelve to eighteen from twenty-nine states and eleven countries. Like the U.S. junior championships, the Polo consists of two rounds of stroke golf, followed by match play. Officially, the Polo marks the first tournament of the AJGA's 2008 season, and its results count toward the next year's rankings. Unofficially, it represents the final chapter in the 2007 season, an opportunity for the best Americans to face off,

individually, against the best young international players. It is also the
venue for the AJGA to announce its choices for the year's All-Americans
and Players of the Year. The banquet is held before the tournament to
accommodate participants who will not make the cut or who are elim-
inated in early rounds to attend.

The Ginn, which opened in 2005, includes three golf courses, a tennis center, a spa, and a water park. Its main hotel, the Reunion Grande,
soars ten stories high from the flat Florida landscape, its ochre, red, and
white frame looking, particularly when lit up at night, like a scene out
of a Disney movie set. Inside the banquet hall, lights shine. Television
cameras whirl. Triumphal martial music blares. The association dubs
the event "the greatest night in junior golf." Like everything the AJGA
organizes, the awards dinner runs with near-military precision. On cue,
a dozen boys in suits and a dozen girls sporting floor-length dresses
glide into the packed banquet hall. The All-Americans include Cody
Gribble, Sihwan Kim, Cory Whitsett, Peter Uihlein, Courtney Ellenbogen, Vicky Hurst, Kristen Park, Jane Rah, and Alexis Thompson.
After everyone has filed in, AJGA executive director Stephen Hamblin introduces the two Players of the Year. "The 2007 Rolex Girl's
Player of the Year finished first or second five times in nine events," he
begins. "She was a member of the East Canon Cup and Ping Junior
Solheim Cup teams."

Only one girl has earned these accomplishments—Vicky Hurst.

Even Hurst's closest competitors acknowledge that she deserves to
win. "Vicky should get it," fourteen-year-old Kristen Park declares. "I
still have a lot more chances and she is more mature than me." The
lights dim. A video shines on the wall. It shows Vicky Hurst, sporting
her trademark beret, slaying golf ball after golf ball, strutting down
fairway after fairway, and holding trophy after trophy. When the film
ends, Hurst, draped in a long red chiffon robe, her hair down from its
regular pony tale, steps up to the podium. Shy Vicky Hurst, whom
Hamblin remembers looking down at her shoelaces when he first met

her, speaks loud and clear to a packed banquet hall crowded with more than 500 parents and peers.

"When I was just seven years old, I went to watch an LPGA Samsung World Championship at the World Golf Village and for the first time I saw golf professionals playing in real life, surrounded by adoring fans, and cameramen and media all over the place," Hurst begins. "I knew then I wanted to be just like those players." After extending generous thanks to the people who've helped her make it this far in the game, Hurst suggests an answer to whether she'll attend college or head straight to the professional ranks. "It is no secret that I want to play on the LPGA Tour," she says. "My dream always has been to become a professional golfer." Since September, she has been bombarded with dozens of recruiting letters. She has narrowed the list of potential colleges to Duke, Wake Forest, Vanderbilt, Florida, and Georgia. But Hurst says she is "leaning toward turning pro." At the beginning of November she entered the Duramed Futures Tour Q-School event, a qualifier to gain a playing card for the adult tour—and won. "It's like starting my career," she tells her local newspaper. "Playing this qualifier and winning it kind of starts everything with a bang." She promises to make her final decision about turning pro before the New Year.

After Hurst returns to her seat, Walker Hill, the Rolex Tournament director and East Canon Cup coach, introduces the boy's Player of the Year: Peter Uihlein, who is ranked number one in the Polo Junior Golf rankings, has captured the FootJoy Boys Invitational and finished four times in the top ten of ten invitationals. Uihlein has outdistanced his competition, not only during the past year, but for the past three years. Hill recalls how he won his first significant junior tournament at South Padre Island off the coast of Texas in April 2004. During the final day of play, winds gusted to fifty miles an hour. After overcoming such natural obstacles, Uihlein has "earned the right to be considered one of junior golf['s] greats," according to Hill.

The AGJA tournament director makes no mention of Uihlein's temper tantrums, or the incident at the Rolex Tournament of Champions in Ohio when he slapped Uihlein with a penalty stroke. Instead, he emphasizes how the award winner passed up an opportunity to play in an adult tournament "because he realized what playing Canon Cup meant to him and 19 others who were depending on him."

It's Uihlein's turn to mount the podium. For the occasion, the All-American Player of the Year has cut his long, blond hair into a short 1950s style and dressed in a conservative tie and jacket. In his acceptance speech he offers unanticipated thanks to Walker Hill, for his friendship, his guidance, and giving him a "code of conduct." The speech sums up Uihlein's unlikely mixture of precocious talent and sensitivity, a maturity beyond his years that hides, for now, his teenage exuberance and naiveté. If he's relaxed and prepared, as he was at FootJoy early in the summer, Uihlein displays poise. He can poke fun at himself and talk to adults in an adult language. When informed that it is his duty to attend the Canon Cup instead of playing in another tournament, he listens and complies. But if the unexpected intervenes, Uihlein's emotions race out of control. Although he now jokes with Walker Hill about his penalty at the Rolex Tournament of Champions, at the time he was cursing, not laughing. His display of poor sportsmanship at the Canon Cup similarly demonstrates the growing pains Uihlein must endure before he can reach his potential.

After Uihlein and Hurst receive their awards, the spotlight turns to the night's featured speaker, future Hall of Famer Annika Sorenstam. If Tiger Woods brought new levels of physical and mental preparation to the game, Sorenstam injected similar qualities into the women's division. Now she is nearing the end of her career. The day before the Polo Awards dinner, Sorenstam missed the cut for the season-ending $1 million prize tournament in West Palm Beach and accepted an on-the-spot invitation to appear at the junior awards.

The once shy Swedish teenager has blossomed into a mature, articulate woman, and expresses strong, yet gentle, opinions on her sport's evolution, particularly on the trend toward ever-younger professionals. "Without you guys [at the AJGA], we wouldn't have all these great juniors," Sorenstam admits. "I can tell you that because they beat me every week on tour. I used to be the young one, and now I'm called the crusty old veteran."

She closes with an anecdote from her childhood in Sweden and a subtle but unmistakable message to the assembled teenagers about the Darwinian laws of success. "When I was thirteen or fourteen-years old, I was hitting balls at my club in Stockholm and it started to rain and I called my dad," she begins.

"Dad, I want to go home," she said.

"Sure, I'll be there," her dad replied.

Five minutes later, her father arrived.

"Look at those other kids on the range," he told his daughter. "There are no shortcuts to success."

The banquet wraps up well before 10:00 p.m. AJGA clock Nazis are on duty. Award winners face tee times starting at 7:30 a.m. Officially, the Polo Junior Classic kicks off next year's season. Unofficially, it will pass judgment on the Players of the Year. Over the next five days, both Uihlein and Hurst must navigate two days of stroke play, and if they survive the cut, six rounds of matches.

———

After the United States Junior Girls' championship in July, Andrea Watts and her mother Sunee took a couple of weeks off to rest in Colorado. Andrea caught a bug and spent most of the time sleeping. "I got run down, worn out, burnt out," she says. "I didn't touch a club for three weeks. I needed some time to figure if I wanted to continue golf." Andrea thought about applying to an Ivy League college and concentrating on academics. Her mother worried that her daughter was too immature, both on and off the course, and feared that she was wasting her time and money. Since Sunee largely defines her life through her daughter's golf, her doubts swelled into a full-fledged confrontation. "Andrea and I didn't talk for a couple of weeks," she admits. "It was tense," Andrea adds.

Sunee compares her daughter's summer golf woes to managing a volatile business. When sales are soaring, "you feel you are going to stay rich forever." Then, suddenly, there's a poor season. "You fear it is going to be permanent." In the future, Sunee promises to stop "rushing things." Under no circumstances will she ever again schedule a tournament for her daugher each week. "Body, mind needs to regroup," she says, her English punctuated with an Asian rhythm. "When we started, her swing was good, her mental game was good, and her attitude was so good. Eventually, she just got so tired."

When the Wattses returned to the Leadbetter Academy in Florida at the end of August and Andrea resumed intensive training, their lives started to fall back into place. "I went back to school, started practicing again, saw my friends and began hitting the ball well again," Andrea says. "I got back into the rhythm of things, basically, and enjoyed it." She has only three classes left before graduating from high school, and instead of targeting Harvard, has accepted a scholarship to attend the University of Florida. The Naples tournament is only a minor event, but Andrea shot 71 on the first day and 69 on the second day, and swept the field. "These are stepping stones, a way to test my game," she says. "The confident, assured me is coming back. During the summer, I was always panicking, nervous."

By the Polo, mother and daughter have made their peace and have begun to reconstruct their lives. Sunee has sold her Colorado house and has regained a sense of financial stability. "We took a step backward this summer," she says. "It taught us a bit of humble." Mother and daughter have found a church in Florida that they attend regularly. Sunee has adopted a more positive tone about life in Florida and begun to build a life of her own. She has enrolled in college "to polish her English."

Both mother and daughter are excited about the opportunity to take on the world's best junior golfers. They rush from Naples to Orlando without waiting to pick up Andrea's victory trophy. The Wattses arrive too late to attend the awards banquet or play a practice round. Andrea confers with her Leadbetter schoolmates, Isabelle and Marika Lendl, who explain the particularities of the Ginn Reunion's two golf courses. On the first day of play as she tees off in Orlando, Watts's improvement is visible. She advances to the ball with a positive-looking strut, and her shots crackle. "Andrea hits the ball a ton," says University of Florida coach Jill Briles-Hinton. "She just has to become confident in herself."

But the Polo tournament tests the Wattses' newfound serenity. From the sixth hole of her first round, Andrea's shots begin flying to the right, and her mother's calm evaporates. "She's mistargeting herself," Sunee worries. "She's making silly little mistakes," her academy coach, Tim Sheredy, agrees. On the next hole, Andrea chips short of the flag; her mom complains, "she doesn't think, she's going into la la land." A hole later, officials warn Watts and her two playing partners that they are behind schedule. Unless they speed up, they risk a penalty point.

Andrea scrapes by with a four-over-par 76. "Not bad for never seeing the course," Sheredy encourages her. The next day Andrea improves and shoots a 73, straggling in as the second to final qualifier. In the first round of match play, Andrea loses to Danielle Fraser. During post mortems, she acknowledges a respectable, if mediocre, showing. "I know I still have a long way to go," Watts says.

Isabelle and Marika Lendl make similar attempts to recoup from their recent difficulties. Like Andrea, both have redoubled their training schedules, and their results have improved. Both were invited to the Polo. "Isabelle had a rough summer, her driver looked terrible, but she has come back," says Sheredy. In his opinion, the problem was mechanical rather than mental. Instead of bringing back her club in a narrow arc and extending wide through the follow through, she was reversing the pendulum and swinging outside and then inward. Once corrected, her ball flight improves.

But Isabelle's scores refuse to follow. She explodes for a seven-over-par 79 in the first round, eight strokes behind the leader, and skids out of contention. Even though she improves to an even-par 72 the next day, she fails to make the cut. On one hole, she stubs a chip. On another, her slice returns. When she completes her round, she looks near tears. Once again, her taskmaster tennis champion father must console her. But this time he fails to provide comfort, and Isabelle walks off looking upset.

Tension is visible between father and daughter, but it is not just golf-related. Isabelle, who is equal parts hard worker and fun loving, has just received her driving license. Her father has installed GPS in the girls' car to be able to follow his daughters' movements. But according to their friends, the girls have been switching off the locator.

Unlike her sister, Marika, who has recently signed to play for the University of Central Florida, is all smiles. She shoots 74, followed by a 70, and finishes eighth in the stroke play. Seventeen-year-old Marika is shorter than her than the taller, more powerful Isabelle, but she has successfully recovered from the mononucleosis that ravaged her summer season. "She's feeling much better, and the health shows in her game," University of Central Florida coach Emilee Klein observes. "This is the best I've seen her play all year." When Marika finishes her second round, she asks her father about Isabelle's round. Learning that her sister has missed the cut, she shows genuine disappointment.

In match play, Marika continues her strong performance. She defeats Jane Rah, one of the steadiest and savviest competitors on the jun-

ior golf circuit. On the eleventh and twelfth holes, she finds herself
buried in sand traps next to the green. Both times she blasts out of the
bunkers close to the flag and saves par. As Rah walks off the course,
she delivers what must be the ultimate compliment to her opponent.
"Marika played smart," Rah says. "She made great up and downs,"
lingo for chipping close to the flag and saving par.

In the semifinals Marika faces off against Kimberly Kim. With Kim
ahead by twelve holes, Lendl birdies. But Kim storms back to take the
next hole. On the sixteenth Kim, again two holes ahead, sinks a fifty-
foot putt for birdie. Lendl responds by dropping her thirty-footer to
keep the match alive. Both girls hit wedges to the seventeenth green.
Lendl puts her shot left of target. Kim drills her ball six feet from the
flag. Lendl chips, and for a second her coach Sheredy thinks the ball
will go into the hole. It stays out. Kim makes her putt to win. Despite
the defeat, Lendl smiles. "I'm satisfied," she says. Her performance represents a quantum leap forward from her summer struggle just to
climb the eighteenth fairway of the White Manor course at the Betsy
Rawls tournament.

In the final Kim faces off against Vicky Hurst. The Player of the
Year has looked impressive throughout the week. After the two days of
stroke play, Hurst ties for the top spot with a four-under-par 140. Her
second-round 68 includes six birdies. She says it feels good to be back
from windy Sweden. "I've played the front of these courses almost 20
times, so I feel really comfortable," she explains.

Seeded first in match play, Hurst decimates her opponents, winning
by three holes over Joy Kim of Pinhole, California, and then bull-doz-
ing her Solheim Cup teammate Allie White by five holes.

"She smoked me," says a dejected White afterward.

"No, I didn't," Hurst protests.

"Yeah, you did," White insists.

In the quarterfinals Hurst faces her first real challenge. Stacy Kim of
Columbus, Georgia, stands a hole ahead going into the seventeen hole.

Hurst finds herself off the green chipping, but puts her ball so close as to require only a tap-in. Kim misses her putt, and the match is tied. Even though Hurst three-putts the eighteenth hole, Kim also bogeys, and the match goes into extra time. On the second sudden-death hole, a short dogleg par five, Hurst hits an iron to twelve feet. Kim bangs her ball inside of her rival, to within six feet of the hole. Hurst drains the putt for a birdie. Kim slides hers by. "You played incredible," a gracious Hurst tells her tearful opponent.

Hurst's semifinal against Stephanie Kono proves an even tougher test. On the eighteenth hole, Kono lips out a twenty-five-foot birdie putt, which would have given her the victory. The two girls continue battling in sudden death overtime as darkness falls. When they reach their fourth extra hole at 5:45 p.m., they are illuminated by moonlight. Kono faces a long putt from the back of the green. Hurst needs to chip from the rough. She sends the ball straight at the flag and comes close to holing out. After she taps in for her par, Kono also pars. Officials finally suspend the match—it's too dark to continue.

At 7:30 the next morning, the girls' epic semifinal resumes. For five more holes, they trade pars. Finally, on the twenty-eighth hole, Hurst birdies for victory in what organizers dub the longest match in the history of the AJGA. "It was a great match—Stephanie and I were talking and laughing and just happy to be there," Hurst says.

Hurst benefits from her early-morning workout in the final, which starts right after the end of the semifinal. She birdies the first hole and is three up by the tenth. A group of hometown fans from the Suntree Country Club in Melbourne have made the trip to the Orlando and are following her progress. After each hole Dennis Dahlman, the Suntree president, calls the club to report the result. "We love the Hursts and will do anything to help them," he says. He doesn't want to see Hurst go pro—"she has all the time in the world for that, later," he says—and has told Koko Hurst that the club would help finance her daughter's junior tournament season, if necessary. But Koko Hurst has declined the offer.

On the twelfth hole Hurst widens the lead to four, and she finishes off her opponent on the fifteenth. Hurst's victory is her third "major" of the season, the most AJGA Invitationals won by any single girl since current adult pro Morgan Pressel took four in 2004. Most college recruiters believe she will abandon any idea of attending college. "Vicky's going to go pro; she's got that ambition and belief," says Kirsti Coggins, the University of South Carolina's women's golf coach.

One thing is sure: the Polo tournament will mark Hurst's final junior event. Even if she decides to stay amateur, she will only enter adult tournaments from now on. "It's been a great year for me," the understated Hurst admits. "I'm really proud of myself and what I've done."

———

With the top European and Asian juniors participating, the boys' Polo tournament sizes up as the toughest field of the year. Some standouts from the north struggle: Sean Brannan, the Pennsylvania-based semifinalist at the United States Junior Amateur, shoots an 80 on the second day of competition and finishes tied for sixty-seventh place. "He hasn't had much time to tune up his game," his grandfather, Scott Stultz, admits. As soon as Brannan walks off the course, he and his grandfather begin the long drive back home.

But the strong field also produces incredible scores. After the opening two rounds of play, the leader, Leadbetter Academy student Gregor Main, records the second-lowest stroke-play qualifying score ever, an astounding nine-under-par 135. Main cards eleven birdies and an eagle in two rounds. The cut falls at a severe one over par, and several standouts from Texas fail to make the grade: U.S. Junior Amateur runner-up Anthony Paolucci comes in at eight over par, and most surprising of all, Cody Gribble, shoots four over par.

Since the summer season, while academy students returned to Bradenton and Hilton Head and embarked on an almost full-time golf schedule, Gribble and the other Texans have returned to regular school and enjoyed downtime. Girls and grades have collided with golf. Gribble hasn't competed in a serious tournament since the end of July. "I need a break: I got caught up with social stuff," Gribble says. Instead of playing in some big tournaments in September and October, he opted instead to attend the Texas–Oklahoma college football game and go hunting with his dad. "I had my ups and downs this summer," he admits. "It just wasn't as consistent as I would have liked." He plans to keep his schedule slow during the winter, concentrate on school, and accelerate his training in March for the next year. "I don't want to burn out," he explains. For the future, Gribble still says he wants to become a golf professional, but admits to being intrigued by his neighbor, T. Boone Pickens's, career.

Corey Whitsett, the national junior champion from Texas, manages to survive the brutal cut. He finishes fifth in stroke play at five under par. His single-minded focus seems, once again, to explain his strong showing. "Corey isn't an outdoorsman like me—he just has golf," Gribble explains. "He is young; he hasn't watched the girls yet." Even so, an Oklahoman named Will Kropp whips Whitsett in the third round by 2&1. "Sometimes you slay the bear and sometimes the bear gets you," dazed dad Geoff Whitsett observes. "The bear got us today."

Mu Hu, playing on his home course, falls in the second round against Floridian Bud Cauley. Hu, one hole down on the eighteenth, looks in position to force overtime. He has an eight-foot birdie putt, while Cauley needs a forty-footer to save par. But Cauley sinks his putt, and Hu misses. "I thought Mu was going to make his putt and we were going to extra holes," the victorious Cauley says.

Player of the Year Peter Uihlein creates the biggest surprise. He coasts through the first two rounds, carding a confident two under par. His American peers watch with awe. "Peter is the best," says Cody Gribble. "Everyone is intimidated by him." In the first round of match play, Uihlein faces Norwegian Anders Kristiansen. The seventeen-

year-old, short, spiky-blond-haired Viking favors Gothic-style T-shirts
and shares none of the American players' fear of playing against the
Player of the Year. "Even though Peter is the number one seed and I
have to play him in the first round, I said to myself, I can't be afraid,"
he explains. The son of a greenkeeper, Kristiansen benefits from a
Swedish-style training program. The Norwegian Federation has paid
for his tournament travel since the age of thirteen. In Florida, his Norwegian Federation coach accompanies him. "I don't look at the scores
or my opponent," Kristiansen says. "I just concentrate on my own
game. You can't be afraid of Peter or anybody else."

Right from the first tee, Kristiansen applies pressure to his opponent. He birdies the first two holes, while Uihlein only pars. The American responds on the fourth hole with his own birdie to narrow the lead,
only to drop the next five holes to Norwegian birdies. As Kristiansen
takes the lead by six holes, Uihlein gasps. "I need a hug," he says to
himself. The Norwegian birdies both the twelfth and thirteenth holes
to close out the match. "I was just buzz sawed," a disappointed Uihlein says afterward.

Observers remain unsure about Peter Uihlein's future. Fellow academy students acknowledge that the Player of the Year is traversing a tu-
multuous period. He recently fired his coach, Tim Sheredy, replacing
him with Leadbetter Academy golf director David Wheelan. "Tim
couldn't take him any further," says his father, Wally Uihlein. For the
Player of the Year's fans, the Polo defeat is only a temporary setback.
"Everybody goes through a slump," his Leadbetter classmate Gregor
Main explains. But others believe the season-ending thud illustrates a
deeper problem. One college coach at the Polo wonders whether Uihlein will reach the top echelons of the game. "Peter just started earlier
than the others," the coach explains. "He was a rocket from 12 to 16
and he may now be leveling off." Tiger Woods has been a rocket that
has kept on climbing. Tiger bested all other twelve-year-olds. He beat
all other fourteen-year-olds, sixteen-year-olds, and eighteen-year-olds.

In contrast, most of the people who have followed the junior golf circuit believe Vicky Hurst will become a star professional. In part, girls mature earlier than boys. In part, the ranks of talented girl golfers remain much thinner than the deep pool of talented boy golfers. .After the top dozen junior girls, the next dozen's quality falls off. Hurst hits the ball farther and fairer than any other single junior female golfer. Dozens of boys strike the ball with similar authority as Peter Uihlen, making it difficult for a single player to dominate.

Among junior boys, any of the top players can beat anybody else, and the Polo proves this truism. Once Kristiansen slays Uihlein, he must play another eighteen-hole match in the afternoon against an Oklahoman named Will Kropp. The match seesaws. Kropp birdies the second hole to take an early lead. But Kristiansen responds with an eagle on the fifth hole to square. On the next hole Kropp birdies. Kristiansen again recovers, birdying the next two holes to square once again. The Norwegian birdies the eleventh and twelfth and stands two holes ahead, only to lose the two next holes. On the eighteenth the match is tied. Kristiansen pars. Kropp sinks a long birdie putt and triumphs.

A little-known Floridian, Sean Dale, knocks off Kropp in the next round and faces Wesley Graham in the semifinals. . In the U.S. Junior Amateur, Graham thumped Dale. This time, Dale takes the lead, finishing the match on the fifteenth hole. "Wesley beat me pretty hard at the Junior Am, so it was particularly nice to win this time," he says afterward. Dale wins his semifinal match and arrives in the finals.

His opponent is Swede Bjorn Akesson, a fresh-faced, medium-built, blond eighteen-year-old from Malmö who has signed with Arizona State University. Compared to the volatile Uihlein, Akesson projects a mature, adultlike poise, answering questions in measured words and a calm, assured voice. "I like going to a regular school and having non-golfers as friends," he says. "I like taking time off from the game. You shouldn't be too serious. I don't need a sports psychologist. I need to just have fun on the course."

Akesson beat fellow Swede Pontus Widegren 3&2 in the second round. During the quarterfinal match against David Chung, Akesson falls four holes down after twelve, only to sweep the next four holes to square the match and advance with a birdie on the final hole. Akesson needs no theatrics against Morgan Hoffmann in the semifinals. He takes early control and birdies the tenth to secure a three-hole lead. The rest of the match proves a formality.

Akesson wakes Friday morning, the day of the finals, with a slight cold and fever. It doesn't matter; he feels no nervousness. On the first hole, Akesson birdies. Although he continues hitting pinpoint iron shots at flags, his putts fail to drop. But at the fifteenth hole, he hits another solid iron to within four feet. This time, he birdies and builds a two-hole lead. Another birdie on the sixteenth hole secures the title. "It feels great," Akesson says. "I am really proud I was able to keep my focus all week long."

The Polo is the final junior golf event for Akesson, and represents the second time a Swede has captured the tournament. Countryman Niklas Lemke took the honors in 2002. The contrast between Akesson and his American opponent, Sean Dale, is striking. Akesson trains in the afternoons after school. During the long winter months, he often practices indoors or on the driving range, when his local courses are unplayable. The Swedish golf federation pays for travel to sunny Spain, but he goes without competition for a stretch of several months. When he competes in tournaments in Sweden he travels with his friends, and when he competes abroad he travels with the Swedish national team. "It's strange, the way the parents are always around here," he observes at the Polo.

American Sean Dale is a 365-day golfer. He attended the Leadbetter Academy in Bradenton for two years, but he was homesick and wanted more individual attention. He has returned to Jacksonville and is completing his degree through homeschooling. Dale is on the golf course every day by himself.

Both systems produce topflight professional golfers. Maybe one day Akesson will face off against Dale in the men's Ryder Cup. Or maybe they will end up running golf pro shops. As they leave Orlando, the victorious Swede and the defeated American pack up their trophies. Dale and his parents drive two hours home. Akesson faces a ten-hour overnight trip back to his cold, blustery hometown. Dale will be on the golf course the next morning. Before he departs, Akesson plans to take a day off to sightsee. "I'm going to Disney World," he says with a smile. "I need to recharge my batteries."

———

The long junior golf journey across the United States, and for some, across the Atlantic Ocean, has witnessed teenagers soar to victory and display impressive sportsmanship in one tournament, only to crumble in the subsequent event and descend into childish temper tantrums. Many parents have lived vicariously through their children's moments of triumph and failure; others have provided impressive and moving moments of selfless support to help their children ride out their rockiest moments. No single method of parenting or training has emerged as a magic ticket to ensuring future success. The boot camp academy approach has produced legions of standout players, but it is expensive and too young an institution to offer a conclusive track record. The method of homeschooling players to allow more dedicated golf time remains, at best, an experiment. The European socialist model, which relies on combing the countryside for the best players and enrolling them in rigorous training programs, is hard to imagine on American turf. The Korean method, which leans heavily on parents to play a steadfast role as coach and encourager, isn't easily replicable.

Perhaps more than ever before, today's society values youth. As families become smaller, parents who can afford to do so are investing more time, money, and energy in ensuring their children's success. From the recital hall to the art room, from the chessboard to the classroom, and of course from the tee to the green, parents are pushing and encouraging their children from an ever-younger age to be great in something. This better-than-ever-educated generation of parents aims to protect their children from the dangers of the world and often considers nurturing talented kids as another sign of their own success. Like the parents of young golfers, those of young gymnasts, ice-skaters, and musicians are more than ever willing to spend hundreds of thousands of dollars to cart their children around the nation, enrolling them in specialized schools and ensuring that they receive the best-possible training money can buy.

Nurtured in this environment of excellence, many children have turned their hobbies into anxiety-generating obsessions. They have little time to enjoy afternoons playing with neighborhood friends or lazy summer days. If teenagers want to succeed, in golf or any other athletic or artistic passion, they must practice and compete. Studies show that many stressed teenagers, under pressure to perform, risk tumbling into severe depression, while talented offspring of more laid-back, encouraging parents are more likely to be able to enjoy and excel at their passion.

Yet the same ambitious parents offer children the encouragement they require to excel. Without a strong helping hand, it is rare for a child to achieve true greatness. In junior golf, it's often difficult to discern whether parents or children take the lead. Many of the parents of young athletes were competitive or championship athletes in their youth. They understand the drive and desire required to win and have reorganized their lives to allow their children a similar opportunity. In turn, their kids have adopted golf passionately, infused it with new levels of athleticism and skill, and successfully made it their own.

Most of the protagonists in this season of junior golf have indulged in little in the way of reflection on their chosen paths. After all, they

are still kids. If, like Andrea Watts, they display a propensity toward re-
flecting on their game, it can serve to add to the level of stress. For the
most part, the junior golfers on the green are too young to ask tough
questions about their passion. They just go out and play. "I just love
golf," is the only answer Alexis Thompson offers when I ask her about
her choice to dedicate herself to this tough sport.

Genius is often tied to precocity, to the freshness and energy of youth.
Mozart composed his breakthrough pieces by the time he reached age
twenty. T. S. Eliot wrote *The Love Song of J. Alfred Prufrock* when he
was twenty-three. But many peak much later. Although Picasso was
recognized as a prodigy in his twenties, Cézanne thrived as an artist only
in his sixties. Architect Frank Gehry only designed his chef d'oeuvre as
a grandfather. Unlike artists, athletes dependent on speed and strength
most often retire before the age of thirty. Among sports, golf is a rare
exception, allowing talented players to compete at the highest levels
well into their forties and fifties. Many of today's top performers, such
as Professional Golf Association (PGA) and Ryder Cup standouts
Steve Stricker and Kenny Perry have achieved success only in their
fourth decade.

Picking future champions remains an inexact science. Hungarian
Laszlo Polzgar was convinced that he could cultivate exceptional talent through hard work and discipline. Chess, not golf, was his
medium for proving his theory. He hoped to have a son. Instead, he
found himself with three daughters, Judit, Zsuzsa, and Zsofi. When
Polzgar's daughters were born, no girl had established herself as a
champion chess player. All three Polzgar girls eventually became
champion chess players. Polzgar read biographies of famous intellec-
tuals and agreed with his wife Klara that ordinary schooling would
do nothing to achieve his plan. He quit his job to supervise his daughters' education. From age four, they practiced chess eight to ten hours
a day. Once a day, the girls would go outside to play soccer, run, or
play table tennis for variety.

The Hungarian government and the chess establishment resisted the Polzgar girls. Chess is a traditionally male game, and the Polzgars had difficulty entering male tournaments. (Police once arrived at the door of their home to save the children from potential abuse.) At fifteen years and four months, Judit Polzgar was the youngest grand master chess player ever. (Bobby Fischer became grand master at fifteen years and six months.) Judit's two older sisters are also grandmasters. Zsusa is the most talented of the three, but Judit was more determined, and she ended up highest on the grand master rankings.

Golf careers follow a similar, unpredictable trajectory. During the 1980s an American youngster named Bobby Clampett swept youth and college tournaments, winning a National Collegiate Athletic Association (NCAA) record twelve collegiate golf tournaments in three years. At age eighteen he became the youngest to ever finish in the top twenty-four finishers in the Masters, a record that stands to this day. He went pro and won his PGA card. Then he married, divorced, struggled with his swing, and watched his ambition vanish. He turned into a classic journeyman, spending more time commenting on golf for television than playing it.

Will Vicky Hurst turn into the next Michelle Wie, or will she keep rising? Will Peter Uihlein keep blasting off into the golf heavens like Tiger Woods, or will he burn out before he reaches the professional tour? Both Hurst and Woods have dominated their teenage peers and made huge strides in their final season of junior golf. Both have overcome a reputation for choking in crucial moments and have won their first AJGA Invitationals. Hurst faces better odds than Uihlein, because she has stood out more clearly from her peers, because girls mature faster than boys, and because competition among women is typically less fierce than that among men. She has already competed in numerous women's professional tournaments and will almost surely become a professional tour player. In contrast, Uihlein has participated in only one pro event, and it remains unclear whether he ever will become a regular on the PGA Tour. But since both are only seventeen-years-old, it is impossible to determine whether either Player of the Year possesses the special spark required to grow up into a champion. Neither managed to capture a national title, and it will take years to find a definitive answer to whether they will become stars, journeymen, or flameouts.

Today's global economic crisis accentuates the innate uncertainty of a player's potential. Hurst and Uihlein are coming of age at a time that is eerily similar to the Great Depression. The 1920s were golf's first golden age, marked by an increase in the number of new courses and the mastery of the remarkable Tiger Bobby Jones, who retired in 1930 after winning the Grand Slam. Today the 1990s and early 2000s look like golf's second golden age, with the construction of new courses, the rise of Tiger Woods, and the sport's resulting youthful revolution.

Rather than destroy the sport, the Great Depression effectively opened it up to newcomers. And although the professional tour experienced its fair share of financial difficulties, it nurtured a generation of popular figures led by Byron Nelson. President Franklin Roosevelt's public works program built more than 100 new courses, and the economic downturn destroyed many of the social barriers that had kept people from taking up the game.

If lucky, a similar scenario might play out on the green in the coming years. Lower green fees and improved access to teaching and training facilities could lure newcomers to the sport. At the same time, some of the present excesses may be tempered and the arms race in spending on junior golf may slow. Parents who shell out thousands of dollars annually on their children's golf careers may be forced to cut back. The explosive growth of new youth golf academies—Leadbetter protégé Gary Gilchrist opened a new one in 2008 near Orlando—may slow. Kids may travel less in the summer and take more weeks off to relax and have fun.

To date, however, the change seems far away. The number of rounds played in America declined a mere 1.4 percent on a yearly basis through September 2008. The AJGA reports steady membership, evidence of the game's centrality to the lives of most of the avid junior golfers and their parents. If these families must cut back their expenses, it's likely that they will look to make changes elsewhere before turning to their beloved sport. Although some sponsors have withdrawn support, others have filed in to replace them, according to AJGA chief of communications Rob Coleman. "Nothing has changed fundamentally for us so far because of the financial crisis," he insists.

Even if there is one Tiger or almost-Tiger for every generation, Woods has forever altered golf's landscape. He has proven that it is possible to achieve long-standing golf records as a twenty-something. With the higher bar that Woods has established, many others believe they have no choice but to accelerate their process. When Tiger was playing junior golf, golf academies were in their infancy. He never attended such an academy, though he had a decisive, determined father urging him along. When Tiger was competing on the AJGA, it was standard to wait until senior year to decide on a college, and virtually no one considered going pro straight out of high school. No teenage girls eyed jumping directly to the professional ranks. Tiger's success buried golf's old fogy image for good. In its place, a younger, more professionalized, and pressured pastime has emerged. There's less time to grow up and more expectation to outdo incredible records of athleticism.

Although the trend toward "professionalizing" childhood brings excess, it also brings benefits. Junior golf phenoms relish the excitement of participating in professionally run tournaments. The stiff competition gives them a kick of adrenalin that is far safer and more wholesome than any thrills they would find experimenting with drugs or alcohol. Fairways hone athletic skills, but also teach young players the life-long lessons of how to withstand pressure and manage emotion. Even at their lowest moments, none of the children in this story admitted to wanting to quit playing golf. Most have conflicts with their parents. But most also insist that they emerge with their family ties intact, or, in the best cases, strengthened. After a few days off the golf course, most cannot wait to return. Golf, these young players insist, doesn't ruin lives, it betters them. This is a game they love to play.

As they leave the Orlando fairways, most of the teenage participants at the Polo tournament have missed spending Thanksgiving at home. Some now will put down their clubs for the winter break and concentrate on school. Others will keep swinging. Year by year, the junior golf summer golf season is lengthening. By Christmas, many players are back in action at the annual Orange Bowl tournament.

My Son ... the Champion

Samuel Echikson, with his younger brother
Ben, also an aspiring golfer.

O N A SUNNY DECEMBER morning at the Biltmore Hotel, an in-
spiring Great Gatsby–era art deco castle in Coral Gables, Florida,
the world's best junior boys and girl golfers are competing at the Orange Bowl tournament. Built in 1926, the Biltmore's 276 rooms are lux-
uriously outfitted, and guests are welcomed to enjoy a spa, fitness
center, wine club, and the largest hotel swimming pool in the conti-
nental United States. By 9:00 a.m., white-shirted, bow-tied waiters can
be seen carrying refreshments to sunbathers.

At the hotel's eighteen-hole golf course, designed by the renowned
golf architect Donald Ross, the junior golfers gather at the practice tee.
By 9:06 a.m., the loudspeaker calls out the names of the last group, Germany's Sean Einhaus, Portugal's Pedro Figueiredo, and American
Peter Uihlein.

During the first two rounds, Einhaus shot 64 and 65, setting a record
in the forty-four-year history of the Orange Bowl. At the start of the

final day of play, the German is five shots ahead of his American rival. Peter Uihlein stages an impressive comeback and catches his German rival at the end of regulation. On the first hole of the sudden-death playoff, Uihlein misses the fairway off the tee and bogeys. Einhaus slams his drive straight in the middle of the fairway. His second shot lands just short of the green. After a solid chip he taps in an easy three-foot putt for the victory. Once again, a gifted European has slain an American Player of the Year.

Six months later Uihlein is playing adult tournaments and still struggling to control his emotions. He cracks another time at the United States Amateur Championship. Up two holes with only four to play, he bogeys the eleventh and sixteenth, allowing his opponent, Floridian Derek Fathauer, to catch him. On the twentieth hole Uihlein's four-footer fails to drop. "I hated to see him miss that," Fathauer says afterward. "I don't like seeing it go down like that."

Vicky Hurst, as promised, makes public her decision about her future at the end of 2007: she passes up college and turns professional. Since she is only seventeen, a year below the minimum age for a permanent place in the Ladies Professional Golf Association (LPGA), she must play on the so-called Futures Tour. Her mother Koko caddies for her. She becomes an immediate sensation, collects four victories and five other top ten finishes, and wins $93,107, surpassing the previous season record of $81,529 set by Beth Bauer in 2001. Throughout the season Hurst displays a flair for dramatic endings, finishing a combined twenty-two under in the four final rounds of the tournaments she won in Texas, Illinois, Indiana, and Connecticut. That includes an eight-under-par 64 in McAllen, Texas, her first professional victory. Despite her cool temperament, a sportswriter nicknames her Vicky "Tabasco" Hurst, for being the hottest player in terms of overall scoring average. Hurst's outstanding performance wins her an automatic spot on the LPGA starting in February 2009. Calloway has signed her to a multiyear contract to play and endorse its equipment. No financial details have been released.

Back on the junior fairways, the 2008 junior season is filled with surprises. Corey Whitsett begins as the odds-on favorite to capture Player of the Year. At the United States Junior Amateur, however, he fails in his attempt to match Tiger Woods in winning consecutive national titles. Seventeen-year-old Dominic Bozzelli from Rochester, New York, birdies the fourth hole and closes out Whitsett on the fifteenth hole. Cameron Peck of Olympia, Washington, the son of a Korean mother and American father, ranked only eighty-seven at the beginning of the season, captures the title. A week before winning the national championship, the seventeen-year-old Peck triumphed at the American Junior Golf Association's (AJGA) Hewlett Packard Boys Invitational. In November 2008 the AJGA names Peck as the 2008 Player of the Year, the first time anyone from the Pacific Northwest, boy or girl, has won the award. Among the male AJGA graduates, Sihwan "Big" Kim thrives at Stanford. During his freshman year, the Golf Coach's Association of America names him All-American, making him the second Stanford freshman after Tiger Woods (in 1995) to receive the honor. Although he plays a few pro tournaments during the summer, Kim says he plans to finish college before making any decisions about turning pro.

Devin Komline, the U.S. Junior Amateur qualifier from Vermont, signs a letter of intent to attend East Tennessee State University.

Chinese teenager Mu Hu shows sparks of brilliance, followed by letdowns. He is invited to play against the European Tour's top professionals in the Volvo China Open, the BMW Asian Open, and the Beijing Open. At the BWM Open, he enters the final round among the top dozen players, only to fall back to thirty-fifth place by the end. In August 2008 he enrolls at the University of Florida.

Among girls, Alexis Thompson, now a thirteen-year-old veteran, moves center stage. She captures the national junior amateur championship, defeating Karen Chung of Livingston, New Jersey, 5&4, in the thirty-six-hole championship match at Hartford Golf Club, and became the second-youngest winner in the event's sixty-year history.

At the U.S. Junior Girls championship Daniela, the youngest golf-playing Lendl daughter, cards a 69 and makes it to match play. Isabelle, who fails to keep pace, shot 81–78 and misses the cut. Marika is named to the East Canon Cup team, but otherwise fails to reach the top levels during the summer season, and heads off to college.

One of the most fearsome competitors, Jessica Korda, skips the national junior championship altogether. Earlier in the summer, fifteen-year-old Korda flashed her smile full of braces when shooting the lowest single round at the United States Women's Open, a four-under-par 69. With her dad Petr, the former tennis champion, caddying, Korda tied for nineteenth at the Open, finishing in front of Annika Sorenstam and Lorena Ochoa. After her impressive showing, she opts to spend the rest of the summer at home in the Czech Republic and playing tournaments in Europe.

Courtney Ellenbogen suffers through a disappointing season with no major wins, but still wins a full scholarship to attend Duke University—which boasts one of the best women's teams in the country. At Duke she will be joined by Mina Harigae, who considered turning pro early but has confided that she's not quite mature enough.

Andrea Watts follows her mother's advice. She plays only a few junior tournaments and enters the University of Florida, where she makes the varsity team in her freshman year.

None of the AJGA girl veterans capture the Player of the Year award. That distinction goes to a part-time Leadbetter Academy student and newcomer to the AJGA, fourteen-year old Victoria Tanco. From Buenos Aires, Argentina, Tanco finished in the top twenty of every tournament she entered and notched up victories in two AJGA Invitationals.

———

After spending the 2007 junior golf season in the United States, I promise my son Samuel, now fifteen, that he could play a full tournament season in Europe.

At Sam's age, I was passionate about tennis. But when I asked my parents if I could spend the summer competing in tournaments in California, they refused. They mistrusted the organizers who would have chaperoned me. My father had taken me to a tennis tournament in Mahwah, New Jersey. After I won the first set, my opponent's parents began screaming on the sidelines. My concentration evaporated. I choked and lost the match in the third set. During the ride home my dad, horrified by the courtside scene, vowed never to attend another tennis tournament. He kept his promise. That summer, instead of allowing me to play tennis, my parents sent me to France to learn French, a decision that ended after college graduation with me living for more than a decade in Paris. When I arrived for my freshman year at Yale, I asked to try out for the tennis team. The coach asked for my national ranking. I opted instead to join the *Yale Daily News*.

Samuel's request to play serious golf competitions this past summer reawakens these memories. I had spent a year watching parents holding their breath on the sidelines as their incredibly talented children played their hearts out, and I wonder whether this would be the correct path for a sensitive, shy teenager. But Samuel persisted. He worked hard over the winter and succeeded in bringing his handicap down to 4.6 by the middle of May— a score that offers him entry into the Skandia Invitational in Sweden.

Because I want him to miss as little school as possible, we arrive late at the event, and Sam had no time to play a practice round. The next day he tees off with national Danish junior champion Kasper Sörensen. Both boys par the first three holes. Samuel then picks the wrong club, a three-iron instead of the required fairway wood, and leaves his tee short of a long par three. He ends up double bogeying. As Kasper breezes through the course with meticulous efficiency, Samuel loses confidence. His shoulders slump. His normal pre-shot routine—a few practice swings, followed by a step back to visualize the shot and then a methodical movement to address and hit the ball—vanishes. He steps up to the ball and, almost in the same motion, swings. . As his rhythm accelerates, his mistakes multiply.

"I see a boy out there who's stopped trying," the Danish national coach, Thomas Larsson, comments. "He's not having fun."

Samuel finishes with an 85, and we have a long talk that evening. His poor score does not bother me, but I worry about his dejected attitude. "I was psyched out, Dad," he explains. "I felt I didn't belong out there with Kasper."

He promises to maintain a better self-image the next day. Through twelve holes, he keeps his promise and plays evenly with Kasper. But on the thirteenth hole, he makes a poor chip and loses confidence. I watch disheartened, as his shoulders slump. He ends with a score of 86 and fails to make the cut. For my part, I begin to harbor serious doubts about encouraging my child to take on the world's best junior golfers.

After the Swedish invitational, Samuel took a break from golf for his exams. When he finishes school he returns to the fairways with renewed vigor, and his scores improved. He ends third in the first Belgian national junior tournament of the summer. His confidence increases even though he continues to have difficulty concentrating through a full eighteen-hole round. Several times he plays even par through fifteen holes—only to blow up and end the round four or five over par.

In July Samuel participates in the elite French tournaments called Grand Prix—events that are open to all ages based on handicap. At a links style course south of Paris called Bondoufles, Samuel shoots a first round of 79. He is four over par heading into the fifteeth hole and loses four strokes in the final four holes. The next day, he reaches the ninth hole two under par. Despite double bogeying the tenth and seventeenth holes, he keeps his concentration and finishes with an excellent one-over-par 72 score, which lands him in tenth place out of 110 players.

The next week, at a course east of Paris called Ozoir, Samuel starts with a two-over-par 73. This puts him in the third-to-final group for the second day of the competition. He improves on the final day, shooting a one-over-par 72 and ties for fifth.

One week later at Coudray, a course near Fontainebleau, Samuel plays the first round in three-over-par 74. In the second round he starts with two bogeys in the first four holes and looks ready to lose his concentration. Instead, he refocuses and birdies five of the next six holes. On the tenth hole, a long par three, he hits his tee shot so close that it looks like a possible hole in one. As the pressure mounts, Samuel keeps improving and adding birdies. By the eighteenth hole, he is six under par. His hands tremble. His drive lands a little left under a tree, leaving him a hard punch shot to an elevated green. He finishes with a bogey for a five-under-par 66, matching the course record.

At the end of regulation play, Samuel ties for first place with Cedric Bourdy, the brother of a noted French touring pro. The two head to the first tee for a playoff, as dozens of spectators gather. Samuel smacks his three-iron drive straight down the middle of the fairway. Bourdy floats his tee shot off to the right and puts his second shot right of the green. Samuel smacks a five-iron dart right at the flag. Bourdy chips and misses his par effort. Samuel putts close, leaving himself a three-footer for the win.

"I just knew I was going to make it," Sam told me later. "I was already thinking of the celebration."

After his victory, Samuel's confidence soars. In a Belgian pro tournament, he finishes in the top fifteen, beating all other junior entrants.

At the end of the summer, Samuel is invited to the prestigious SAAB Junior International. In the practice round, he plays with two Dutch twenty-year-olds, who express confidence in their future as pro golfers. This time around, instead of being intimidated, Sam comes off the course with a smile and says, "I think I could give them a run for the money." His result in the tournament—three rounds in the 80s—is disappointing. Yet even as he struggles, Samuel doesn't give up. His shoulders do not slump, and he diligently sticks to his pre-shot routine.

Sam is surprised and pleased by his accomplishments. He speaks with more authority and confidence than before the summer, and he begins to realize his talents. By the end of 2008 he ranks twentieth among all male golfers in Belgium and number one among French-speaking players under sixteen. His handicap has dropped to a mere 1.3 and he now trains with the national Belgian team. In 2009 he plans to play in the most prestigious European and American junior tournaments. Already in December 2008 he will compete at the Dixie Amateur in Florida, where both Mu Hu and Peter Uihlein are entered.

Sam's ardor for the game and his will to improve are undiminished. He demands to be dropped off after school at the course and spends hours on the practice range. After the Grand Prix victory, several French golf federation officials told me that they thought Sam should consider a professional career. For now, this prospect seems overambitious to a teenager who is unsure whether he wants to spend his entire life playing golf. But Sam's successes have convinced him that he'll be good enough to compete at an acclaimed American university.

Off the green, in my hometown, I see a fair number of kids struggling with typical teenage insecurities. Some turn to alcohol. Others plunge into drugs. Most struggle with sex. All look for meaning in their lives and a tool for helping them move from childhood to adulthood. Sam, like most of the teenagers participating in the AJGA, seems to avoid these pitfalls. Golf has given a notable confidence to my son, on and off the course. Once timid and shy in front of adults and in the classroom, he has started to speak up and to express his feelings and his opinions.

As Samuel improves on the golf course, his grades have also begun to improve. He has learned that if he gives all his effort, he is capable of shooting for the stars. He has steadily become more extroverted and determined to succeed. He used to shy away from extra schoolwork. Not long ago, though, he signed up for a weekend course to study for the SATs and spent eight hours a day for two weekends immersed in preparation. In the past, he was disorganized and had trouble preparing his homework and managing his calendar. After learning to organize his golf bag and prepare his equipment for tournaments, he has deployed a similar technique to organize his books and agenda. Above all, golf has offered Sam untold hours of pleasure. He wants to spend his weekends playing golf tournaments, and comes off the course with a large smile.

I often wonder whether I have found the correct balance between pushing my son and encouraging him. My intentions are benevolent: I want to see Sam realize his potential, and above all, be happy. But I also know that his success gives me pleasure and pride. Many times I wonder what the best path for both of us is. Should I send Sam to sunny Florida and the Leadbetter Academy? Sam reassures me that he doesn't want to go, and we both agree that such dogged concentration on golf runs the risk of hurting his academic progress and turning a passion into an onerous obligation. Like all parents, I fear the moment Sam leaves the parental cocoon and steps out on his own, and at the same time recognize his need to for independence.

My son may have the talent to become a golf professional. He may end up choosing that path. More likely, after college he will move in another direction. For as Samuel often reminds me, there's only one Tiger.

ACKNOWLEDGMENTS

When my children ask me why I became a journalist, I respond with another question: In what other profession does one get paid for asking questions and having fun? Throughout my career I have been privileged to "work" on many intriguing topics. I covered the East European revolutions that brought down the Berlin Wall. I investigated the kitchen of a French three-star Michelin haute cuisine palace. I probed the conflict between traditional and modern winemakers in Bordeaux.

This book has proven the most fun of any that I have written to date. It involved watching and playing golf on some of the world's best layouts with my oldest son and having a chance to rediscover parts of America with my family in tow.

During the past fifteen years, I have worked at several media companies and book publishers. Throughout, Michael Carlisle has remained a faithful literary agent. Michael is a rare breed of partner who knows when a project will work and makes sure that it succeeds. I appreciate his encouragement and advice. Thanks also to Michael's sidekick, Ethan Bassoff, for adding judicious editing on the book proposal.

Morgen Van Vorst, my editor at Public Affairs, a self-professed non-golfer, has offered guidance and comments throughout that have allowed this book to become pertinent for a wide public. I hope that I can build a long-term professional relationship with her, as I have with Michael.

During my research, many people were generous with their time and thoughts. I am grateful to the American Junior Golf Association, its executive director Stephen Hamblin, and his assistants, Rob Janssen and Steve Ethun. They gave me free access to their events without any request to censor or even see a completed manuscript before publication. They asked for no commitments. Even when I proved a pest at some events, they never shut their welcoming door.

The United States Golf Association also proved helpful. Its headquarters contains one of the world's best libraries about golf, and librarian Patty Moran was generous with her time and photocopying. Press officer Pete Kowalski set up useful interviews.

Officials at golf clubs (too many to list) proved welcoming and helpful at all the venues described in this book.

Among journalistic colleagues, my main thanks go to Tim Carroll at the *Wall Street Journal*, who edited my golf stories for the newspaper and helped edit this manuscript. Tim shares my parental passion for the game. He also enjoys a sharp, constructively critical editorial passion.

With a few to-be-expected exceptions, most of the teenage golf phenoms and their parents proved open with their feelings. They allowed me to follow them through the entire season. Often I walked alongside parents during their children's rounds and listened as they poured out their emotions. This is their story, and I appreciate how they allowed me to hear their voices.

I want also to thank my new colleagues at Google, particularly David-John Collins and Jessica Powell, who gave me time to finish the manuscript before starting my new job.

We did most of the research for this book as a family. My wife, Anu, and my three children, Samuel, Julia (age ten), and Ben (age eight), accompanied me as we piled into our Chrysler minivan and traveled across the United States from tournament to tournament. While this book proved a great adventure for all of us, it failed to take into account many moments when a wife and children would have preferred either to play golf themselves or to be doing something other than watching other children compete on a golf course.

These days, I tee off with Julia and Benjamin. Both carry bright yellow bags of starter clubs that overwhelm their small frames. Julia recently started playing a short par-three course with proficiency. When Benjamin hit his first shot more than seventy-five yards, I applauded, content in the knowledge that I'll have two other co-conspirators to accompany me on the links once Samuel leaves for college.

January 2009

PublicAffairs is a publishing house founded in 1997. It is a tribute to the standards, values, and flair of three persons who have served as mentors to countless reporters, writers, editors, and book people of all kinds, including me.

I.F. STONE, proprietor of *I. F. Stone's Weekly*, combined a commitment to the First Amendment with entrepreneurial zeal and reporting skill and became one of the great independent journalists in American history. At the age of eighty, Izzy published *The Trial of Socrates*, which was a national bestseller. He wrote the book after he taught himself ancient Greek.

BENJAMIN C. BRADLEE was for nearly thirty years the charismatic editorial leader of *The Washington Post*. It was Ben who gave the *Post* the range and courage to pursue such historic issues as Watergate. He supported his reporters with a tenacity that made them fearless and it is no accident that so many became authors of influential, best-selling books.

ROBERT L. BERNSTEIN, the chief executive of Random House for more than a quarter century, guided one of the nation's premier publishing houses. Bob was personally responsible for many books of political dissent and argument that challenged tyranny around the globe. He is also the founder and longtime chair of Human Rights Watch, one of the most respected human rights organizations in the world.

.   .   .

For fifty years, the banner of Public Affairs Press was carried by its owner Morris B. Schnapper, who published Gandhi, Nasser, Toynbee, Truman, and about 1,500 other authors. In 1983, Schnapper was described by *The Washington Post* as "a redoubtable gadfly." His legacy will endure in the books to come.

Peter Osnos, *Founder and Editor-at-Large*